CRITICAL PRAISE FOR THE WORKS OF W. D. EHRHART

"IF YOU MISSED THE WAR, HERE'S THE WAY IT WAS."

The Virginia Quarterly Review

"Ehrhart's sense of timing, his imagery, his poetic sensitivity, and his passion make his book as enjoyable to read as it is troubling to endure."

Philadelphia Inquirer

"One of the greatest gifts any writer can have is the ability to convey in a few words the complex physical reality of experience. Ehrhart possesses that gift, in rare degree."

San Francisco Chronicle

"In wry observations on the Vietnam war brutalities, Ehrhart faces the horrors in which he has participated with unblinking courage."

Library Journal

Other Avon Books by
W. D. Ehrhart, (ed.)

CARRYING THE DARKNESS: AMERICAN INDOCHINA—
THE POETRY OF THE VIETNAM WAR

MARKING TIME

W. D. Ehrhart

AVON
PUBLISHERS OF BARD, CAMELOT, DISCUS AND FLARE BOOKS

Portions of this book first appeared in *The National Vietnam Veterans Review, Northwoods Journal*, and *Vietnam-Perkasie: A Combat Marine Memoir* (McFarland & Company, 1983).

"Hunting" first appeared in *Winning Hearts and Minds* (1st Casualty Press, 1972), and "A Relative Thing" in *A Generation of Peace* (New Voices, 1975). Both poems are reprinted from *To Those Who Have Gone Home Tired: New & Selected Poems* by W. D. Ehrhart (Thunder's Mouth Press, 1984).

MARKING TIME is an original publication of Avon Books. This work has never before appeared in book form.

AVON BOOKS
A division of
The Hearst Corporation
1790 Broadway
New York, New York 10019

First Avon Printing: July 1986

AVON TRADEMARK REG. U.S. PAT. OFF. AND IN OTHER COUNTRIES, MARCA REGISTRADA, HECHO EN U.S.A.

Printed in the U.S.A.

K-R 10 9 8 7 6 5 4 3 2 1

For Anne,
who was waiting on the beach,
and for all the people who kept me afloat
until I reached her.

Acknowledgments

This book is not a novel, though you are welcome to read it as such. Except for a few instances where liberties have been taken in order to speed the flow of the narrative or simplify complex events, whatever inaccuracies the book contains are errors of recollection or perception, not willful distortion of facts. Conversations have been reconstructed from memory, as accurately as I could manage after so many years. Most names have been changed in order to protect the privacy of the people I have written about—many of whom are still living—and their families.

My thanks to Jenny Beer, David Kalkstein, and Richard West, all of whom contributed in various ways to the completion of this book. Belated thanks to Robbie Franklin, who wouldn't permit me to thank him the last time around. I owe a special debt of gratitude to William D. Quesenbery, whose guidance and advice helped me to hammer the book into shape. Most of all, I must acknowledge the immeasurable patience and love provided by my wife Anne. This book would never have been written without her emotional and material support.

W. D. Ehrhart
Doylestown, PA.
August 1984

Chapter 1

"You bastard," Roger muttered as I picked up the ace of hearts, the two of spades, an eight, and a nine with my ten of diamonds.

"That's twenty-one, pal." I chuckled. "My game."

"I don't believe it!" he shouted. He bolted to his feet, stormed over to the open porthole, and tossed his cards into the Pacific Ocean. "How the hell do you *do* it?" he spluttered in frustration as he stared out at the dark water rolling away beyond the porthole. He had his back to me. He looked as though he were waiting for a message in a bottle to come floating by, the answer scrawled in blood on a piece of old canvas.

The two of us played a lot of casino, especially late at night after Roger got off the eight-to-twelve watch. "I can't sleep," he'd say, turning on the light in my cabin and shaking me, talking with a heavy Cape Cod accent. "Keep me company. Come on, wake up. Let's play some cards. You got any wine? Put on a tape. Where's your Rolling Stones tape?"

Defying all statistical odds, I won regularly. You could have charted the course of our ship through the high seas by the trail of playing cards Roger left floating in our wake.

Roger turned away abruptly from the porthole, walked resolutely back to the desk, sat down, opened a drawer, and pulled out a fresh deck. "Shut up and deal," he said.

Roger was the third engineer aboard the SS *Atlantic Endeavor*, an oil tanker out of Long Beach, California. He held a bachelor of science degree in nautical engineering from the Massachusetts Maritime Academy. He'd been sailing for seven or eight years. I was the engineroom wiper, a sort of seagoing janitor. I'd been sailing about five months.

Watching Roger work was an amazing experience. To me, the

engineroom was an incomprehensible Erector set of gargantuan proportions, a baffling collection of perpetual motion and deafening noise. To Roger, it was a living work of art, an animate entity that could be loved and fondled and cherished, a great beating heart. He handled machinery the way certain gifted and sensitive people work with thoroughbred horses or frightened children. He had a gentleness about him that inspired trust.

That's how I'd first gotten to know him. "What's that gizmo for?" I'd ask, and he'd explain that it was a centrifugal water purifier. "What are those wheels for?" And he'd explain that the steam throttles controlled the speed of the ship by regulating the amount of steam entering the turbines, which turned the mighty brass propeller. The other engineers limited themselves to irritated two-word answers, convinced that an engine wiper wouldn't be able to understand anyway. Roger always had time to explain—two or three times over again when it was necessary, as it often was—and he always grinned broadly whenever the light bulb finally flashed on in the murky depths of my brain.

The transition from mentor to friend happened as gradually and comfortably as the changing of the seasons, which made it especially remarkable. One doesn't have many friends on a ship. You pass time together, work side by side, shoot the breeze constantly. But you seldom really get to know anyone. At first, I'd found the shallow conversations about sports or the weather or how much longer to the next port confining and irritating. But I'd soon come to realize that in the close and closed world of a ship at sea, it didn't do to discover that your watchmate was a raving Klansman or a Born Again Fundamentalist or a New Left Democrat or anything else you happened passionately not to be. It was an unspoken law of the sea that you didn't get personal, and as time had passed, I'd accepted and then welcomed the necessity of the law. All that really mattered was the awesome majesty of open water.

But as the months went by, Roger and I seemed to be together more and more of the time, not just down in the engineroom any longer, but playing cards, doing sit-ups and push-ups out on the boat deck, leaning over the bow laughing at dolphins playing in the green phosphorescent bow wake like frisky squadrons of surfers.

"You know, Roger," I said one night, the two of us sitting up on the stack deck, our backs against the warm stack housing, our bodies rolling comfortably with the gentle rhythm of the ship, "a thousand years ago, men just like us sailed these oceans, watched the same stars, stared out over the same endless waves. I saw a whale today. Sometimes I half expect to see a Viking longship come sailing up over the horizon. Or a Phoenician merchantman. 'They that go down to the sea in ships, that do business in great waters; these see the works of the Lord, and His wonders in the deep.' ''

"What's that from?" asked Roger.

"The Bible, one of the Old Testament Psalms. Must have been written three thousand years ago. Imagine that, Roger; seamen just like us thousands and thousands of years ago—before people knew how to write, even."

"Probably got to see a lot more whales than we do."

"Yeah, I guess so," I laughed. "We're certainly managing to muck things up in a hurry. I wonder what they thought about."

"Who? The whales?"

"No, turkey, all those Polynesians and Arabs and Egyptians. They had wives, girlfriends, dreams."

"I saw a replica of the *Mayflower* once," said Roger. "They got it tied up at Plymouth. You ever seen it? Tiny little wooden keg, that's all it is. The Pilgrims musta been crazy to sail that thing across the North Atlantic. I wouldn't sail it in my bathtub."

"They believed in the New World, Roger. America. They were going to build the Kingdom of God on Earth."

We both sat quietly for a while, just watching the stars rotate through their perfect figure eights in the clear sky above the stack, feeling the deep vibrations of the engines far below us in the iron bowels of the ship.

"Why did you come to sea, Roger?"

"I don't know. Just something I always wanted to do. I grew up on the Cape. I used to watch the big ships come through the canal on their way in and out of Boston. Used to stand on the bank and wave. I don't remember ever wanting to do anything else."

"Don't you miss your family?"

" 'Course I do. My kid's growing up—six years old now, and he hardly even knows me. My wife's gotta do everything herself—look after the house, pay the bills, fix the car, all kinds of stuff a woman shouldn't have to do, at least not alone. Every time I'm home, I think maybe I oughta quit, get a job on the beach. But I never do."

" 'Keep true to the dreams of thy youth,' " I said.

"What?"

"That's you, Roger. That's why you sail. You've never abandoned your dreams."

"Yeah, maybe so. I've never thought about it like that. You really think about things, don't you?"

I shrugged my shoulders.

"I wish I could do that," he said.

"No, you don't," I replied. "It's a big pain in the ass."

"You know," Roger continued, ignoring my remark, "sometimes I feel things, and I don't even know how to say what I feel. I guess that's why I like machines—I can always figure 'em out if I work at it long enough."

"Well, I envy you your engines, so I guess we're even."

"I don't think so. What are you doing out here in the middle of nowhere, Ehrhart? I *belong* here. What could I do on the beach, run the boilerroom at the local high school? But you? An engine wiper with a college degree? Man, that's weird."

" 'From the hearts of infinite Pacifics, the thousand mermaids sing: Come hither, broken-hearted; here is another life without the guilt of intermediate death; here are wonders supernatural, without dying for them,' " I said, adopting a mock-heroic tone of voice and sweeping my arm in a grand gesture over the waves. " 'Come hither! Bury thyself in a life which is more oblivious than death. Come hither; put up thy gravestone within the churchyard and come hither, till we marry thee.' "

"That's an answer?"

"That's Herman Melville."

"Stop with the literary highbrow crap, Ehrhart. Just gimme a straight answer."

I'd first caught sea fever four years earlier in the summer of 1969, just after I'd gotten out of the Marine Corps. I'd gone to England with the intention of spending the summer hitchhiking around Europe, but I hadn't been in England two weeks when I met four young seamen one night in a pub in Liverpool. They were the deck crew of the Irish coastal freighter MV *Marizell*. We began drinking and shooting darts and talking, and sometime before the sun came up we all agreed that it would be a fine idea for me to spend the rest of the summer aboard the *Marizell*. Back at the ship, rousted from a deep sleep, the captain was considerably less enthusiastic. But the boys kept at him until he got too tired to argue anymore, and finally conferred upon me the rank of temporary ordinary seaman. Hot damn!

The next morning we sailed out through the locks at the entrance to our berth and headed up the Mersey River toward deep water. The *Marizell* was just a little slip of a boat really: 154 feet long, drawing 13 feet of water, and carrying an eight-man crew. But it was a ship, and the water beneath us was salty, and that was good enough for me. I had the fever already.

For six weeks we crisscrossed the Irish Sea between Liverpool and Dublin, occasionally putting in at Glasgow or Bristol, hauling cotton bales and chicken feed and steel girders and tractors. I chipped and scraped and painted and dreamed my way around the world a thousand times. Leaving port, I'd lean casually over the rail and wave to the people who hailed us from shore, their voices edged with wonder and envy. I wanted to shout, "Hey, look at me! I'm Joseph Conrad—and this here redheaded bloke is Starbuck, and the man at the wheel is Mr. Christian, and we're bound for Kingston or Calcutta or some damn place you'll never see if you live to be a hundred!" But I always restrained myself somehow, trying to give the impression that I'd been born to that deck. I'd lean casually over the rail and wave nonchalantly.

And then we'd clear the harbor, drop the pilot at the mouth of the Mersey, and head due west with the Welsh coastline off the port side and the gentle swells of summer rocking the ship as though it were a baby's cradle. The sea sparkled silver as the sun turned down toward the horizon over the bow, and then the stars would come up. After a few hours, we could pick out the beacon from the lighthouse on Holyhead far out on the port bow. And then it would be off the port beam. And then the thin finger of melancholy light would finally disappear down below the stern, and there would be nothing but the heavy drone of the engine, and the steady prop wash, and the waves lapping the steel hull.

We all took turns in the wheelhouse, two men to a four-hour watch, and in the dim light from the compass and the radar screen we'd talk quietly or just let the dark sea roll on forever beneath us. Ernie would nudge my arm and say, "Hold 'er steady, Billy boy; you're drifting off a wee north. See those lights off the starboard bow? Looks like a tanker; better give 'er plenty of room."

In the morning, I'd step out on deck with the coastline of Ireland rising out of the sea dead ahead. The green hills would be wild in the early sunlight, and I knew then in a blaze of glory why it's called the Emerald Isle. Then the ship would slow down, and the harbor pilot would come aboard from his waiting launch to guide us up the river Liffey and into our berth. The *Marizell* was so small and nimble that if the tides were right, we didn't even need the tugs to get the ship up to dockside. Just coast in and throw out the lines, clear the hatches for the stevedores, and off we'd go for a day in Dublin or out on the ancient Celtic hills beyond the city.

It was good to be free of America in that summer of 1969. Aside from a few cursory inquiries, my shipmates weren't even curious about Vietnam. In their own minds, they'd already settled the issue: "Well, you high-and-mighty Yanks have certainly gotten yourselves into a bloody mess *this* time; good luck to you." End of discussion. Their attention was focused on Northern Ireland, where fifty years of simmering hatred had boiled over into open fighting, and there were endless hours of proposals for solutions delivered with the fabled Irish temper that delighted and amused me because I didn't, for once, have to bear the burden of proof or the brunt of the anger.

But that lazy, gentle summer finally ended, and I went back to crazy America and started college. And America was indeed crazy: utterly stark raving mad—completely bonkers. Year after year, I kept thinking that it had to let up sometime, but it never did. Not once. It only got worse.

Four years later, on a warm afternoon in late August, I found myself standing on a dock in Long Beach, my old Marine Corps seabag slung over my shoulder, staring up at the SS *Atlantic Endeavor*. I'd spent the previous six months almost daily hounding the marine personnel director of Atlantic Richfield for a job. I'd finally driven *him* crazy, too, to the point that he became willing to do anything just to get me to stop calling him up. But I didn't want "anything." All I wanted was a job. I walked up the gangplank and reported aboard.

We sailed that evening just after sunset. The *Endeavor* was a lumbering monster compared to the *Marizell,* and it took two tugboats—their whistles shrieking and piping in the deepening twilight—to haul the ship from its berth, turn it around in the narrow channel of the San Pedro River, and guide it belching and steaming out into the basin of the harbor. Once clear of the harbor entrance, though, the tugs dropped off and the *Endeavor* slowly gathered speed under its own tremendous power.

The lights from the towns and cities all along the crowded southern California coastline shimmered and danced on the rim of the sea beneath a sky made pale by their brilliance. A new moon arched high over the mountains to the east, and the moonlight floated softly down until it broke into a hundred thousand shards of sparkling glass on the black surface of the water. Off the port side, in the darker night opposite the coast, stars outlined the low silhouette of Catalina Island.

For a long time, I stood on the fantail watching the lights along the coast. I imagined the whole American continent behind them, rolling away through the darkness over the mountains and deserts and prairies and rivers and fields and cities and towns toward the beaches of the Atlantic. And then the *Endeavor* turned west toward the Santa Barbara Channel and the vast Pacific beyond. I walked the length of the ship to the bow and looked out to sea. I thought of mermaids. And they were singing.

"Hey, spaceman," said Roger. "Hey. Bill."

"Oh. Yeah, what?"

"What the hell are you doing out here, anyway?"

"Just passin' time, Roger. Just passing time."

Chapter 2

In the fall of 1969, the student body of Swarthmore College was largely upper middle class, academically paranoid, politically aware, liberal tending strongly toward the radical-intellectual left, and socially freewheeling. The current popular folk hero was John Braxton, a senior facing a prison sentence for his open refusal to register for the draft. Vietcong flags regularly sprouted from the windows of the upper stories of Parrish Hall—which served as both the administration building and a women's dorm—and as often as not when you went to lunch, there'd be a troupe of guerrilla theater actors piled in a heap on the patio of Sharples Dining Hall, wrapped in black robes, draped with the entrails of pigs, and silently holding signs reading Stop the War. The last vestiges of parietal rules would be swept away by the end of the first semester that year, and by the next year there would be coed dorms. The native costume was faded blue jeans, heavily patched, and blue workshirts or used army greens. Marijuana was nearly as prevalent as tobacco.

Into the middle of all this, I arrived as a twenty-one-year-old freshman. The previous spring, while I was still overseas, the college had written to ask for a picture of me. The only picture I happened to have was one of me in a Marine dress uniform, so I'd sent that. Nobody told me what they wanted the picture for. I didn't find out until I showed up for college in September, and there's that picture of me in the freshman booklet for the whole college community to see. Wonderful. Fortunately, I didn't look like that anymore, so a lot of people hadn't yet figured out who this guy Ehrhart was.

Which was fine with me. In the fall of 1969, Vietnam veterans weren't exactly the most popular kids on the block. I'd enlisted in the Marines in the spring of 1966 with visions of brass bands, victory parades, free drinks in bars, and starry-eyed girls clinging to my neck like so many succulent grapes. But by the time I'd gotten back to the States from Vietnam, I considered myself lucky to get out of San Francisco Airport without being assaulted by bands of rabid hippies armed with snapdragons and daisies, and carrying placards reading Baby Killer.

And once I got to Swarthmore, I was damned glad I'd let my hair grow out over the previous summer and grown a beard. Anonymity. I washed my new blue jeans three times the first week I was there, and threw them in the dirt, and jumped up and down on them, trying to get the new blue to look like old blue. The older the better. Finding myself the only Vietnam veteran in the middle of an obviously antiwar environment, and having no idea what those guerrilla theater mimes might cook up for me if they once figured out who I was, I'd spent my first month at college trying to keep a low profile.

I got away with it, too. I kept to myself, and I kept my mouth shut, and I didn't bother anyone, and no one bothered me. It was kind of lonely, actually, and sometimes I'd sit out on the big green lawn in front of Parrish Hall, admiring the magnificent lush campus, and think about my buddies back in battalion scouts and how nice it would be for them to be here too, so I'd have someone to talk to that understood. Or maybe we wouldn't even talk because they'd all know what I was feeling because they'd be feeling it too, and we could just lie back on the green grass for a while and listen to the birds up in those elegant old trees.

But most of the time, I was too busy to think about even that.

I hadn't been to school in more than three years, and I had no idea before I got there that Swarthmore was supposed to be such a hotshot school. I'd never even seen the place. I'd met some middle-aged man trying to bodysurf one day in Ocean City, New Jersey, while I was home on leave in the early summer of 1968. He wasn't catching any waves, and I was catching all of them. He wanted to know how I did it, and our talked developed into a long and pleasant walk on the beach and a discussion about my future. He told me about this nice little school called Swarthmore, which he'd attended after getting out of the Navy in 1946. Later, I applied, and the college had offered me the biggest scholarship of the schools I had to choose from.

That's how I ended up sitting in the Quaker meetinghouse on the first night of school with all the other freshmen, listening to the president, Richard Cramer, talk about the cream of the crop of America's high school students and how brilliant this year's freshman class was, and I knew he wasn't talking about me. It dawned on me in a burst of abject terror that I'd made another wrong turn somewhere back up the pike. I just sat there thinking, "Jesus Christ, Ehrhart, what have you gotten yourself into *this* time?" I was so scared I spent the first month of school holed up in McCabe Library, trying desperately to keep from flunking out by midterm exams.

But the important thing is that during that first month or so, nobody attacked me with flowers or picketed my room in Pittenger Hall or covered me with pigs' entrails. The few people that did discover I'd been in the service seemed to take the knowledge comfortably enough. So by the middle of October, when the reporter for the campus newspaper *Phoenix* politely asked if he could interview me, and graciously volunteered that I didn't have to answer any questions that I considered inappropriate, I was feeling brave enough to say, "Well, what the hell, why not?" Everybody likes to read about himself in the newspapers.

It was a nice article, too. The guy that wrote it was real good about not trying to make me seem like a goon or a crazed maniac; if anything, he made me sound a whole lot more together than I really was. Here's the way the article began:

When most of his fellow freshmen were struggling through Algebra I, Bill Ehrhart was slogging through a Carolina swamp. When they were worried about getting a date for the junior prom, he was dodging shells at Con Thien and after that at Hue and at a dozen other places you never hear about.

Bill Ehrhart is now a Swarthmore freshman, but four months ago he was a Marine sergeant.

Bearded and quietly confident, he doesn't seem different from the rest of the freshmen. Like the others, he's busy wading through Chaucer and reading bulletin boards to see what meetings to attend. But the usual freshman problems don't seem as difficult to him. Most things don't. Because Bill Ehrhart spent thirteen months in Vietnam, and after that nothing seems quite as hard.

And it went on from there.

The article appeared under a three-column double headline—"Freshman Veteran Returns to School; From Battalion Intelligence to Chaucer"—and carried a picture of me complete with beard, long hair, and wire-rimmed glasses. Good-bye, anonymity. The effect was spectacular: instant celebrity. People began stopping me in the halls, after classes, on the lawn, in the library. They interrupted my meals in Sharples. They dropped by my room in Pittenger. I was *somebody;* I was the center of attention, and it felt good. I seemed to be meeting everybody in the whole school.

And the biggest surprise was that people weren't hostile at all. In fact, they were very friendly. They'd come up and introduce themselves and strike up a conversation. During those weeks after the article appeared, I can't recall anyone ever being rude or unkind—which was a great relief. I had truly been afraid of how people would receive me, and now I knew I didn't have to be afraid anymore. I would listen to their questions, and think about them, and try hard to answer them as honestly and accurately as I could. I often spent a long time answering a question because I wanted these people who were my peers and classmates to understand.

Soon, however, a pattern to the process began to emerge that made me begin to wonder if being a celebrity was such a good deal after all. Three or four or five or six times a day, seven days a week, some new stranger would approach me: "Hi! I'm Blah Blah Blah. You're Bill Ehrhart, aren't you? Do you mind if I ask you a few questions I've been wondering about? Why did you go to Vietnam? What was it like? Did you see much action? Did you ever kill anyone? No—I mean really see them die—know you were the one?"

I'm not exaggerating. It was those questions only, and in that order, nearly every time. It got to where I could spot strangers headed my way from a hundred yards off, and I knew what was coming, and I'd just grit my teeth and punch a button in my head and start spitting out answers. I didn't even have to wait for the questions. And my answers got shorter and shorter. And I began increasingly to feel a nebulous discomfort with the whole process because I couldn't help noticing something else, too.

Almost nobody ever asked me anything about anything but Vietnam. They didn't ask me what my favorite books were, or what I wanted to be when I finished school, or what I thought of the Mets winning the World Series, or what I was doing Saturday night. They asked me that handful of questions about the war, and then they thanked me and got up and left. And most of them never came back again. It was always somebody new: "Hi! I'm Blah Blah Blah. You're Bill Ehrhart, aren't you? Do you mind . . . ?"

Then one night toward the end of October, I had this girl in my room that I'd sort of gotten to know, and we were really getting down to the bare essentials. In fact, I was just about to make it happen, and it hadn't happened in a long time, and I was feeling particularly mellow about life in general when right in the middle of it all she asked me, "Did you *really* kill people?"

And it didn't happen.

Two days later, I was walking down the path between Parrish and Sharples when a girl approached from behind and stopped me.

"Are you Bill Ehrhart?" she asked.

"Uh, yes."

"Were you really in Vietnam?"

"Well, uh, actually, yes."

"Oh, wow, man. Far out. Incredible!"

And then she turned around and walked away. She wasn't nasty, or hostile, or anything but clearly amazed. And as I stood there alone in the middle of that broad green lawn beneath the shadow of Clothier Tower, surrounded by those elegant old trees and ivy-covered buildings, breathing in the crisp autumn air and watching other students all over campus as they went about their busy lives, I finally understood the intangible feeling that had been making me increasingly uneasy as the weeks of October had passed.

I was Swarthmore's real live Vietnam veteran. I was a specimen. A curiosity. I was a freak in a carnival sideshow.

Chapter 3

"Deal," Roger snapped. "You can't keep winning forever."

We were only a few hours from the ARCO refinery north of Bellingham, outbound, fully loaded, and rolling gently with the easy swells in the Strait of Juan de Fuca. Once we reached open water, we'd start plunging and bobbing like a sodden log, but that was still a few hours off.

"Jesus, Roger, it's nearly two. I gotta be down in the engine-room by eight."

"So do I, and we're not going to sleep till I win one."

"Yeah, well, I'm gonna sack out in the steering gear compartment during *your* watch this morning—and don't even come around bothering me."

"Fair enough. Now deal." I started dealing. "You were in Vietnam, weren't you?" he asked abruptly.

"How did you guess?"

"Well, there's that tattoo on your arm. And you're the right age. And there's all those scars on your chin and neck."

"I got the scars in a car accident when I was fifteen," I said. "Tried to eat a windshield for lunch."

"No kidding?"

"No kidding. What made you think of it now?"

"Nothing in particular," he replied. "I was just thinking that we've known each other for five months and you've never said a word about Vietnam."

"You never asked me about it."

"I don't really know what to ask, I guess. I mean, I don't want to pry or anything. And I really don't know much about it. I've been floating around out here since 1966. Never paid much attention to it. The whole thing kind of went right by me."

"It ain't over yet," I said.

Roger looked puzzled. "Didn't they sign some kind of treaty last year?"

"The Paris peace accords?" I snorted. "You've got to be kidding me." Roger laughed uncomfortably, fidgeting with embarrassment. "Yeah, they signed an agreement," I continued, "but it's not worth the paper it's written on, and everybody that signed it knew it. The war hasn't let up for a moment. Nixon and Kissinger never intended to let up. All they wanted was an excuse to get the troops out without making it look like we got kicked out. We're still sending—Christ, I don't know—billions and billions of dollars' worth of equipment and supplies to that piss-ass dictator in Saigon, Nguyen Van Thieu. And the place is still crawling with American military personnel, only now they're supposedly 'civilians' hired by Saigon and Dow Chemical Corporation as 'consultants.' Thieu couldn't stand on his own two assholes for half a day without U.S. muscle to prop him up. War by proxy. No more American boys coming home in Glad Bags to parents wanting to know what the fuck for. And the Vietnamese? Who the hell cares about a bunch of dead gooks, anyway? Nobody in this godforsaken country, that's for sure."

"My goodness, boy, but I do believe I detect a slight tone of bitterness in your voice," said Roger.

"Surely you're mistaken. And you can kiss the Big Ten goodbye, sucker." I grinned, sweeping up a seven and a three with the ten of diamonds.

"Damn! I don't believe it. Change the tape. I need some more wine. Were you drunk when you got that tattoo?"

"A lot of people *think* I was. Most folks, I just tell 'em I got it right before I left for Vietnam, when I was eighteen: 'Me and the boys—har, har—had a few too many, seemed like a good idea—har, har!' Like that. I've been telling people that for years. You wanna know the truth? I got it in 1970, and I was stone sober. Lyle Tuttle did it. Same guy that did Janis Joplin and Grace Slick. Imagine that: the hands that tattooed Grace Slick's tit were all over my arm."

"So why the big charade?" Roger asked.

"How the hell am I supposed to explain to people why somebody openly opposed to the Vietnam War would go out and get USMC tattooed on his arm nearly three years after he left Vietnam and eighteen months after he got discharged?"

"Well?"

"Well, what?"

"Why did you?"

"Hell, I don't know. Me and a buddy were knocking around the West Coast that Christmas and we drove up to San Francisco to visit another friend from college. We got there early and had a few hours to kill, and Daniel said he wanted to get a tattoo, and I thought what the hell, I'd wanted to get a tattoo when I was eighteen but I was scared I'd get hepatitis or whatever it is you get, and then there we were in Lyle Tuttle's studio. Daniel got a scorpion—and I got this." I pointed to the dark blue lettering on my left bicep. "Who knows why? Maybe there was some twisted, crippled place inside of me that still wanted somehow to be proud of it all. Guadalcanal, the Halls of Montezuma, Tell It to the Marines. Old myths die hard, Roger. I can't even explain the damned tattoo to myself. How was I supposed to explain it to anyone else? It was easier to lie. Amazing how easy it is to lie, Roger. I am not a crook. Peace with honor. One nation under God."

Roger had put down his cards and was looking at me intently. "You really *are* bitter, aren't you?"

"Bitter. Angry. A whole lot of things. I think too much, that's all. I told you, thinking's a big pain in the ass. Just gets you into trouble."

"Well, listen, I'm sorry. I didn't mean to go dragging it all up."

"You aren't dragging up anything that doesn't get dragged up every goddamned time I look at a newspaper. Anyway, I don't mind talking to you about it. You I trust."

"Was it really bad down there?"

"I'm glad you started with something simple," I laughed.

"Well, how the hell should I know?" said Roger, shrugging his shoulders sheepishly.

"Bad enough. One of these days when I'm not so tired, I'll tell you about it. Come on, let's finish the game."

The final score was 23–21, my game. When I left, Roger was staring out the porthole into the inky blackness, another deck of cards lost at sea.

Chapter 4

I was saved from rural society in Korea—or at least given a reprieve—by Daniel Kaufman. I'd been sitting in McCabe Library ever since supper, trying to plow through an unspeakably boring anthropology assignment, when Daniel and a guy I didn't know interrupted me.

"You got a few moments?" Daniel asked.

Ordinarily, I would have said no. I was tired of people's questions. My newfound celebrity had left me no less lonely than I'd been before, and carried with it new problems of its own, and more and more over the previous week, I had taken every opportunity to avoid any more questions than I had to put up with. Swarthmore was just too small to avoid most grillings, but the visible act of studying provided just such an opportunity: "Gee, I'd like to—but I've got this assignment here. Wow, the reading load they give you around here! Maybe another time." It wasn't entirely untrue.

But I was sorely weary of which corner of the ricefield Farmer Chung crapped in, and Daniel—whom I'd met earlier and who was one of the few people who *had* come back again—seemed like a nice guy.

"Yeah," I said. "What can I do for you?"

He introduced me to his friend, Mike Morris. "I can't stick around," he said, "but you guys ought to get to know each other." It seemed a little puzzling to me, and I was immediately sorry I'd agreed since Daniel wasn't even staying, but I was already committed. I got up and we went down into the basement stairwell. Mike seemed noticeably ill at ease.

"We can talk down here without getting interrupted," said Mike as we sat down on the floor beneath the last flight of stairs.

"I read that article in the *Phoenix* about you," he began. "Pretty interesting. We don't get many Vietnam veterans around here."

"So I've noticed." I laughed. Well, here we go again, I thought.

"This place must be pretty weird for you."

I laughed again. "Well, yeah, actually, it is."

"Why in hell did you come *here?*" he blurted out. Then he got flustered and turned red. "That didn't sound right, did it? I mean, this place isn't exactly a haven for ex-Marines, you know? It just seems like an odd choice."

"Well, yes, an odd choice," I said. Then I told him about the unsuccessful bodysurfer in Ocean City.

"That's all you knew about the place?" he asked incredulously.

"That's it. Name, location, and sixteen hundred dollars in scholarship."

"Didn't you read the catalog?"

"Sure, but it didn't say anything about guerrilla mimes or Vietcong flags. And I needed that scholarship. The GI Bill only gives me a hundred thirty-five dollars a month. You know how far that goes these days."

"Does it bother you, the antiwar stuff?"

"Well, yeah, I guess so. But it's hard to say why. I think maybe we made a big mistake getting involved in Vietnam. Most of the Vietnamese don't really seem to want us there, at least not many of them from what I could see. We're foreigners to them. It's not an ordinary war, you know, with front lines and soldiers in uniforms and stuff. Most of the time, we were fighting guerrillas—when the politicians let us fight at all; free-fire zones, no-fire zones, maybe-fire zones—anyway, you couldn't tell the VC from the rest of the population. Mostly we didn't make much of a distinction. Just treated them all the same: hostile."

"You really think the politicians won't let you fight?"

"Well, it felt like that sometimes," I said, lighting up a cigarette. "Like they put our asses out there, and then tied one hand behind our backs and blindfolded us. You're going to fight a war, you ought to fight it. You want to talk, send a platoon of diplomats in striped pants and top hats. I remember sitting up at Con Thien, up on the DMZ, and reading about trying to get the North Vietnamese to the negotiating table, and thinking why didn't they just give the damn table to us and let us deliver it to Hanoi. Fight or get out. A lot of guys felt like that. That's why a lot of us kind of liked Eugene McCarthy. If he wasn't going to fight, at least he was willing to get the hell out.''

I flicked the ash from my cigarette onto the leg of my jeans and brushed it in with the heel of my hand before continuing— every little bit helps, I figured.

''Anyway,'' I went on, ''I don't think there's much we can do about it now *except* get out. I'm not so sure it would matter if we tried to turn it into a more conventional war. I don't think the politicians *or* the generals really know what they're doing. I knew this guy there, an ARVN, South Vietnamese army staff sergeant assigned to my battalion as an interpreter. He'd been in the army six or seven years, and he'd been with my battalion since before I got there, like eighteen months or something. One day he just quit. Just like that. Walked right up to the battalion commander and said, 'I'm not going to fight your dirty little war for you anymore. Get lost.' Man, that was a real eye-opener. He said the longer we stayed, the more VC there were. 'Every year, the Vietcong grow stronger. You are their best recruiters. You Americans come with your tanks and your jets and your helicopters and your arrogance, and everywhere you go, the VC grow like new rice in the fields. You do not understand Vietnam. You have never understood us, and you will never bother because you think you have all the answers. You Americans are worse than the VC.' Something like that. And then he just flat quit. And he was one of the bravest men I ever knew. Saved *my* ass more than once.''

Mike let out a low whistle.

''Yeah,'' I said, rubbing another bit of ash into my jeans. ''Christ, there I am, eighteen years old, got my ass out on a wire, and here's Trinh telling me to go suck an egg. Well, not me really, but it was all the same. Anyway, by that time, I was perfectly willing to get the hell out. All I wanted to do was keep my ass alive long enough to get home and forget the whole thing.''

''Why did you go in the first place? You weren't drafted, were you?''

''Me?'' I snorted. ''Oh, no, I enlisted. Couldn't wait. Seventeen years old, right out of high school. I'd even been accepted to college. I don't know. I didn't know what I wanted to study. I figured I'd just get drafted when I got out of college anyway— right when I'm ready to start a career. I needed the GI money. And I guess I figured I owed it to my country. Maybe that sounds corny, but I still believe that. This place ain't perfect, but it's still worth something to be an American. If I were Russian, I'd be locked up for telling you stuff like this. That's worth something, isn't it?''

"It's not worth dying for a mistake, is it?"

"I don't know, Mike. People owe *something* to their country, don't they? How do you say it was all for nothing? It was all a mistake. Who's that flake up there in Parrish with the VC flag? Jesus, people carrying that flag killed a lot of my buddies. I'm not sure I blame them, really, but Jesus. And we still got half a million guys over there. I remember how I felt when I'd read about antiwar stuff going on back here. It made me angry; it hurt. I don't think those kids ever think about the guys over there very much. Not really. Not like they were real people.''

"Maybe not," said Mike. He paused, tugging at his shoelace as if he were studying it. Then he looked up and continued, "And maybe they do. Did you ever think that maybe they're trying to keep other guys like you from having to go?''

"Yeah, maybe. But you can't just walk away from it like it was a meal you just didn't feel like finishing, can you? I said we oughta get out, and I believe that. But you gotta give Nixon a chance. He's only been in office ten months—and he hasn't exactly gotten a hell of a lot of support on the home front.''

Mike cocked his head, lifting his chin slightly. "You really think he's trying to get us out?" he said.

"Well, he got the peace talks going. It takes time.''

"Peace talks?" he shot back. "It took them six months to figure out what kind of table they were going to use. Besides, Johnson started the peace talks, not Nixon.''

"Is that right?" I asked, feeling a slight flush of embarrassment.

"Yeah. That whole business started back in mid-sixty-eight, before Nixon ever got elected. For what it's worth.''

"Well, Johnson got us into it in the first place, so he *should* have gotten us out of it. Anyway, at least they're talking now. And at least Nixon's trying to get the ARVN to do something for once besides sit around on their duffs.''

"You think it'll work?"

"I don't know," I said, pausing for a long moment to think about it. I hadn't thought about it much. I really didn't want to deal with Vietnam anymore—though it was hard not to, since you couldn't pick up a newspaper or turn on a television or even go to lunch without being constantly reminded of it. I crushed the cigarette out on the bottom of my shoe, then ground the blackened tobacco into the cuff of my pants.

"Why do you keep doing that?" Mike asked.

"What?"

"Putting the ashes on your trousers."

"Oh, just ripening 'em on the vine," I replied. Mike looked puzzled. "Never mind." I laughed. "It's just a private joke. No, I don't suppose Vietnamization is likely to do much good. From what I saw, the ARVN were pretty bad. There was one unit, the First ARVN Regiment up around Quang Tri, they were pretty damned good. But they were all northern Catholic refugees. Most of the ARVN weren't worth a flying fuck. Armed to the teeth, and still couldn't—or wouldn't—fight their way out of a paper sack. That's one of the things that first got me thinking. The VC had nothing when I got there—just beat-up old rifles and bamboo stakes and whatever they could steal from us or buy from the ARVN. But they fought like hell. You really had to admire them. You'd bomb 'em and nape 'em and blow 'em up fifty different ways to Sunday, and the next day, there they'd be again, one or two guys, dingin' away at you, day after day, week after week."

"You said in that article that—how did you say it? If you had to weigh the positive effects of the whole thing with the negative effects, you'd still come out ahead."

"Something like that, yeah," I said, shaking my head. "That's what I get for talking to reporters."

"You didn't mean it?"

"I didn't say that," I replied.

"Well, that's what I wanna know," Mike said. "That's the part that struck me the most. If you had it to do again, would you still go?"

"Man, you like to stick to simple questions, don't you?" I laughed.

"Well, I'm just trying to understand," said Mike. It seemed like he really did want to understand. He seemed to be wrestling with my answers, trying to assimilate them. And he was willing to challenge me, to pose new questions from my answers. Most people just asked the usual questions, listened with glazed eyes, then got up and walked away. I liked him.

"Would I do it again?"

"Yeah, was it worth it?"

"How do you go through something like that and then say it wasn't worth it? I guess I learned a lot. Maybe I'm a better person for it. And maybe I could have come home in a body bag or minus a leg. A lot of guys I knew did. How do you tell them it was worth it, you're a better man now? How do you tell them it *wasn't* worth it? Sometimes it makes me want to cry. I want it to have been worth *something,* and I can't make myself believe that it was. It's a real bitch, I'll tell ya. No, I don't think I'd do it again." I glanced at my watch. It was getting late. "Listen, I hate to break this up, but I gotta get back to village life in Korea. I gotta finish this reading, and I read about as fast as you'd expect an ex-Marine sergeant to read!"

"Oh, yeah, sure," Mike said. "I didn't mean to take so much of your time."

"It's okay, I don't mind. Really. I enjoyed talking with you. Thanks for listening."

"Hey, thank *you,*" said Mike, extending his right hand and shaking mine. "Maybe you'd be interested in joining DU."

"What's that?"

"Delta Upsilon. The fraternity I belong to."

"Oh, yeah. Well, I haven't thought much about joining a frat."

"Listen, no matter what you hear around campus, DU's not so bad. And fraternities around here are a lot different from most schools."

"Well, maybe. Let me think about it. Next time, I'll pump *you* with a few questions."

"Fair enough." Mike smiled. "See ya later."

I was still reading when the library lights flickered: almost midnight, closing time. I gathered up my books, put on my coat, and stepped out into the chilly night air. It felt good after being cooped up in McCabe for nearly five hours. The moon was almost full, and the sky was clear, and the trees and buildings cast shadows on the dark earth. Funny, I thought, I'd never really noticed lunar illumination before I'd gone to Vietnam. Night was night, that's all. But in Vietnam I'd learned that the difference between full moon and no moon is like night and day. You could see forever under a full moon if you knew how to do it, looking askance at things instead of gazing directly, keeping your eyes constantly in motion, using peripheral vision to distinguish objects. No moon was the time the VC liked best. It made it harder for us to spot them.

I started across campus, then stopped and turned to look up at the facade of Parrish. With its two four-story wings sweeping out from a thick central section, it looked vaguely like some huge eagle cruising low over the crest of the hill, searching for prey. There was a light on in Pam's room. I'd met her in my Russian-language class and had been immediately attracted to her: small, not stunning but remarkably attractive, with large dark eyes and full sensual lips. I'd thought at first that there might be a few sparks growing in her, too, but nothing had come of it. She had a boyfriend at another college, and went to visit him nearly every weekend. Still, I took every opportunity I could get away with to study Russian with her—and I really did need the extra help. I thought about popping up to say hello, then thought better of it and turned away toward Pittenger.

Where was Jenny tonight, I wondered. Sweet Jenny, my high school sweetheart. Jenny of the golden hair and true-blue eyes. How proud she'd been of my uniform. She'd even asked me to wear it when we went to the high school Christmas dance in December 1966, just before I left for Vietnam—though it hadn't taken much persuasion. We were going to be married as soon as I got home. And then one day amid the heat and boredom and loneliness, the letters stopped arriving. Just like that. A letter a day for eight months, then nothing for six weeks, then the Dear John. Suckers like me in every war, I thought. At least we hadn't gotten married *before* I left. Calloway had gotten a Dear John from his wife— worse, actually, a divorce request from her lawyer—and had blown his brains out with a forty-five automatic. Put the barrel in his mouth and pulled the trigger and splattered his own head all over the tent right before our eyes before anybody realized what he was doing. My body shuddered involuntarily, and I pulled my collar tighter, adjusting the heavy load of books under my arm.

Sometimes on nights like this, it all seemed like a dream: the magnificent rolling campus, anthropology, early European history, a private room with a bed in a solid building, and no incoming mortars. Sometimes on nights like this, it was hard to remember which were the dreams and which reality. I'd be walking along across campus half expecting to wake up at any moment and discover Wally and Hoffy and Gravey in single file up ahead of me, Mogerty and Rolly and Kenny behind us, and all of us strung out at long intervals to minimize casualties in case we got ambushed or someone stepped on a mine. I felt naked and vulnerable at night without a rifle. I'd catch myself sweeping the bushes and trees with my eyes, looking for movement, for anything that didn't seem right. You never knew what you were looking for. Just something. Anything that might offer some split-second warning of impending violence. A shadow, a rustle of wind in trees, an odor suddenly familiar—and then it would be gone, leaving behind the awkward silence and a strange feeling that might have been relief but wasn't.

When I reached my room, I turned on the light, poured a shot of whiskey, and knocked it back. Then I sat down to finish my assignment. On the walls around me hung maps of the Philippines and Japan, a small photograph of the *Marizell,* a poster-drawing of Bob Dylan with psychedelic multicolored hair, and a half-dozen hand-lettered signs made with black magic marker on yellow lined paper saying things like "Are you going to quit now?" and "When the going gets tough . . ." On the desk was a small American flag with gold braid trim, the gift of someone in my father's congregation while I was still in the Marines.

I had several more shots of whiskey before I finished the reading. I usually stayed up until alcohol and exhaustion made it impossible to keep my eyes open any longer. When I shut them, the nightmares would be waiting: the old woman in the ricefield, the small boy with the grenade in the crowded marketplace at Hoi An, the old man on Barrier Island with his hands tied behind his back.

Chapter 5

"Water ballet?" I practically shouted. "You've got to be kidding me. I'm a goddamned ex-Marine sergeant, for Chrissake. You want me to get in the water and splash around to Mozart?"

"It won't be Mozart," Bart argued. "We're going to do a routine to 'The Stripper.' A comedy piece. Come on, Bill, lighten up a little. You're so damn serious all the time. It'll be fun. Think of it: the first men ever to be in the women's water ballet show. It's history in the making!"

"You're really serious, aren't you?"

"Sure. Let's do it. It'll be fun."

"Sounds wimpy, if you ask me," I said.

"Come on," Bart persisted. "Have some fun."

We were sitting in Bart's room in Wharton Dorm. It was a Friday night in mid-November. Somehow I'd managed to get through all my midterm exams, and Bart and I were celebrating. He was a premed student from Wisconsin, a senior, though we were both the same age.

I'd met him during the first week of classes. We were both taking Introduction to Anthropology, and one day after class he'd stopped me on the way out the door.

"You're a freshman, aren't you?" he'd asked.

"Yeah."

"My name's Bart Lewis," he'd said, sticking out his hand.

"I'm Bill Ehrhart."

"I was just wondering. I need a manager for the football team," he'd explained, "and I wondered if you'd be interested. You can cover your phys ed requirement that way, and it's really easy. Beats the hell out of gym class."

I'd wondered what the hell I must look like that somebody would ask me to be a *manager*. Back in high school, the managers were the nerds, the klutzes, the kids who couldn't make the team. I couldn't decide whether to laugh or knock this guy down. All I said was, "I don't have to take PE."

He'd looked puzzled, as though he were trying to figure out what deformity I suffered from that I was exempt from PE. "You don't?" he'd asked.

"No," I'd said. He seemed to be waiting for some kind of explanation. I wasn't much inclined to give him one, but he'd just stood there, so finally I'd continued: "They've got a rule around here that says veterans don't have to take PE."

"Oh, you're a veteran," he'd said, his voice flat.

"Why they've got a rule like that, I don't know. The place isn't exactly overflowing with vets. But they do. Anyway, I thought I'd go out for the swimming team this winter, so that would cover the PE requirement anyhow."

"Oh, you're a swimmer, too?" he'd said, his face brightening. "So am I." He hadn't said anything more about my being a veteran, and I'd been relieved to let the matter drop. Instead, he'd said, "Hey, that'll be fun. You'll like that. We've got a great coach—Jamie McAdams. One of a kind, he is. You'll see what I mean."

"Lewis," I said now, "you are a case. Do you insult me deliberately, or are you just too dumb to know any better? First you ask me to be a goddamned manager, and now you want me to put on a tutu and be a ballerina.''

''Well''—he grinned—''will you do it? Barney and I are going to do it with or without you.''

''Oh, what the hell,'' I said, amazed that I was actually agreeing to this.

''All right!'' Bart lit up, slapping me on the shoulder. ''Hey, you wanna get stoned?''

''Sure, why not?''

He got up and placed a rolled-up towel along the bottom of the door, then sat back down at his desk, rolled a joint, lighted it, and passed it to me. I took a deep drag of it and passed it back, trying to look as if I were an old hand.

''Why do you bother with that towel?'' I asked.

''Hangover from the old days, I guess. There's still some people around who might get excited. Did you ever smoke this stuff in Nam?''

''Oh, yeah,'' I said, nodding my head, ''Oh, yeah. Good stuff over there. Right off the vine. And cheap, too. It just grows there, like dandelions. Old mama-sans used to walk around all the time with big fat joints hanging out of their mouths. When they weren't getting high off betel nut. Stoned-out mama-sans,'' I laughed. ''I guess that's the only way they could cope with all the bullshit going down.''

I didn't tell Bart that I'd only smoked a half-dozen times or so in the previous two years. A few times up at Con Thien, that barren rain-swept lump of mud up on the demilitarized zone where we'd lived in holes with the rats for thirty-three days while the North Vietnamese gunners used us for target practice and there was nothing you could do about it but sit there and wait and hope they didn't put one right down your pipe like they'd done to Falcone and Stemkowski. Once in Boston in the summer of 1968 while I'd been home on leave before shipping overseas again, and I'd gone up there hoping to get laid by an old high school acquaintance and instead had spent three days roaring drunk on Black Russians and had nearly ended up in jail because a bartender had said I was underage and he didn't care how many stripes I had or how many wars I'd been in and I'd tried to take him out with a barstool. And once just the previous summer in Perkasie, sitting around with a couple of friends who'd seemed to have grown so distant from me that it was hard to believe we had ever known each other before, let alone grown up together, and we'd smoked from a pipe made out of a real rifle, the bowl in the breech, puffing through the barrel the same way Calloway had put his mouth over that forty-five, and then they'd left for peace and love in Woodstock and I'd left America for the third time in less than two and a half years, this time headed for England and the *Marizell*.

"You nervous about the lottery?" I asked, referring to Nixon's plan to convert the old draft system into a lottery.

"Hell, yes," Bart shot back. "I figured I could keep my student deferment all the way through medical school. The war would *have* to be over by then. Now I don't know. I'm going to try for a CO's deferment. I'd have tried it before, but it's such a hassle, and there just wasn't any need to go through it."

"*Are* you a conscientious objector?" I asked.

"Well, I can't imagine being in a war. I don't mean just Vietnam, either. I can't imagine being in *any* war. I don't think I could kill anybody."

"You'd be amazed at what you can do when your life's on the line," I said.

"No, I couldn't do it," Bart said, shaking his head. "I know it."

"How the hell do you *know* it?" I asked sharply. "You don't know squat till you been there."

"Well, I don't care to find out," he replied. "You want a beer?"

"Yeah."

"I'd go crazy," he continued.

"No, you wouldn't," I shot back, pointing my finger at him. "You'd try to survive. You'd do whatever was necessary to survive. It happens without you even trying to make it happen. Something deep inside. Thousands of years old—millions of years old. Survival instinct. The brain just kicks into gear. It's not even anything conscious."

But even as I spoke, I wondered. Sure, I'd killed in order to survive. That NVA soldier I'd almost bumped heads with in an abandoned building in Hue during the Tet offensive. The VC who'd ambushed Maloney, Roddenbery, and me in my first real firefight. And there'd been others. Even the kid with the grenade—Christ, he'd have blown my insides all over Hoi An if I hadn't fired.

But the old woman in the ricefield? The old man down on

Barrier Island? Taggart had ordered me to fire on the old man. And Hitler had ordered the extermination of the Jews. I didn't like this conversation. The marijuana had made me light-headed, and I couldn't think straight.

"That was a good workout we had today," I said, changing the subject. "Boy, I'll tell ya, I sure am rusty after all these years."

Bart let it drop, too. "Well, you're looking pretty quick," he replied.

"Not like the old days. I used to be good when I was a kid. Then I discovered cigarettes, booze, and girls." I laughed. "I sure never thought I'd find myself on a swimming team again. My old bones, wow."

"My old bones," Bart mimicked, making a face. "You're not any older than me."

"Well, I haven't been in a pool in nearly five years, man."

"Hey, you're a Marine!"

"An ex-Marine. Anyway, the only reason I'm doing it is to get a free coat. I need a new coat."

"Well"—Bart laughed—"you're practically guaranteed a letter jacket. You're the only guy on the team that can go two hundred yards of butterfly."

"I ain't guaranteed nothin'. At the moment, I can only go a hundred and seventy-five yards. That last twenty-five yards is gonna be a real ball-buster."

"Might be a lot easier if you got rid of those coffin nails," he said, pointing to my cigarette. I just shrugged. "Those things are gonna kill you someday."

"That's what my mom said," I laughed. "Listen, this is the God's honest truth. While I was up at Con Thien, my mom sent me a letter saying she hoped I wasn't smoking too much because it was bad for my health. Even sent me an article about the surgeon general's report. I read it in the middle of an artillery barrage. An artillery barrage! And I'm supposed to worry about getting lung cancer in thirty years? What the hell," I said, taking a puff and shrugging my shoulders again, "I'm living on borrowed time, anyway. Besides, if I didn't have the nicotine to calm my nerves, I'd be too scared even to *try* swimming two hundred yards of fly. You think we'll be ready for the first meet?"

"Oh, yeah," said Bart, "we'll be ready. Boy, I love beating PMC. All those military types with their short hair and ramrod spines. They just *hate* us! It's a real trip to kick their asses. We beat 'em twice last year.''

"They're just people," I said.

"Automatons. Robots. Can you imagine going to school at a military academy?"

"No. But I'm glad I got the training I did."

"You got brainwashed," Bart laughed.

"The hell I did. If you're going to send people off to fight a war, the least you can do is train 'em first. Christ, they send those poor doggies to summer camp for a few weeks—television sets in the barracks, beer privileges, weekend passes after two fucking weeks—and then they dump them in Vietnam. It's criminal. I'm glad I was in the Marines. At least they took the trouble to train us."

"You *liked* boot camp?" Bart asked incredulously.

"I didn't say that," I sighed. "But it was a real challenge. I did stuff I never even dreamed I could do. You should have seen some of the obstacle courses we had to run. They had one called the Confidence Course. Man, you get done with that, you know you've *done* something."

I really *had* felt like I'd done something. Graduation day, there on the parade deck at Parris Island, dress uniform with my new stripe signifying meritorious promotion to private first class, my parents and younger brother and Jenny in the reviewing stand: I was a *Marine*. It had been the proudest day of my life.

"You got brainwashed."

"I did *not,*" I barked, slamming my beer down against the arm of the chair. "What the hell, man, they didn't come looking for me. I came to them. I asked for it. I *wanted* to go to Vietnam. And they had eight weeks to take a seventeen-year-old high school kid and teach him how to survive in combat. What do you expect them to do, run a Sunday social? Listen, the Marine Corps didn't start the Vietnam War, you know."

"Hey, take it easy," said Bart. "I didn't mean anything."

"Yeah, well, I'll tell you, Bart, things got pretty weird down south—in Vietnam—it got pretty fucked up after a while. There were times I just didn't care anymore, especially after my girlfriend dumped me. And all I'd have had to do, any number of times, was just stand up and that would have been the end of my problems. I'd have been dead before I even got my knees locked, and I never would have felt a thing. And there were lots of times I thought about it, too. The kind of training I got in boot camp is all that kept me going. I kept functioning even when I didn't care about myself anymore. In boot camp, you learn that if *you* fuck up, a dozen other guys are going to pay for it. You just don't fuck up on other Marines—and they don't fuck up on you. You can call it brainwashing if you want. I call it esprit de corps. I owe my life to the Marine Corps. It's a fact.''

The needle on the record player stuck in the middle of a Moody Blues song. ''Shit!'' said Bart, getting up quickly and lifting the needle. He took the record off and inspected it. ''How did that happen? Anything you want to hear?''

''How about Crosby, Stills, and Nash?'' I suggested. I liked Bart's record collection—current stuff, but not too wild. I was slowly learning to live with the changes in music over the past few years, but it hadn't been easy. When I'd enlisted, Diana Ross and the Supremes were still wondering where our love had gone and the Beatles were still trying to hold your hand. The first ''acid rock'' I had encountered belonged to Randy Haller, a San Francisco hippie who'd shown up in Vietnam after burning his draft card and being confronted with the choice of prison or the Marines. I'd eventually become very fond of Randy, but I never could stomach his music—perhaps because it symbolized a change I wasn't part of. And the first record I'd heard upon returning to the States had been Frank Zappa and the Mothers of Invention. Mothers of Invention? God, they'd sounded like the Demons of Hell. America, where have you gone?

And the music was just for starters. There'd been a time only a few years ago when, if your hand reached bare thigh at the top of a girl's nylons, you knew you were home free. And I'd been on a date with some girl soon after I got back from Vietnam, and things were going pretty nicely, and my hand kept going higher and higher up those thighs, and God damn! Those nylons just wouldn't quit! They just kept on going up and up and up and they never did end, and I could neither understand it nor believe it, but afterwards, masturbating alone in my room, I became convinced that this new form of chastity belt called panty hose was the Invention of Mothers.

Later, in Japan, I'd bought $300 worth of tailor-made clothes for college the next year—which was a lot of clothes at $2.50 a shirt. But I'd come home in the summer of 1969 to discover that straight-cut trousers with cuffs and button-down shirts were out. You wore that kind of stuff, and you were a marked man: a square, a jerk, middle-aged at twenty, a Young Republican. Spiro

Agnew wore button-down shirts. The only things I owned that were fashionable—aside from my old green utility uniforms—were my wire-rimmed glasses. I didn't dare tell anybody they were actually Marine sharpshooter's glasses.

I was now working overtime trying to catch up to the rest of my generation. I'd even broken down and bought some bell-bottomed trousers—Marines don't wear bell-bottomed trousers, I'd grimaced, only sailors do—yet here I was, walking around in bells. I was even actually beginning to acquire a taste for Jimi Hendrix and Blind Faith and Jefferson Airplane. But it was definitely an acquired taste, and it was nice to sit in Bart's room and listen to something less frantic.

"Where's Marie tonight?" I asked.

"She went down to her sister's place in Baltimore." Bart frowned. "Her niece is getting christened this weekend. Speaking of which," he added, arching one eyebrow and leering suggestively, "I notice you've been spending a lot of time with Pam Casey lately."

I ducked my head slightly and broke into a broad grin.

"That's good," he smiled.

"You approve, do you?" I asked mockingly. "Yeah, it *is* good. Improves my outlook on life immensely. In fact, she went home this weekend to tell her boyfriend that he's now an ex-boyfriend."

"You, uh, been getting any?" Bart asked, pulling on the corner of his mustache.

"What the hell business is it of yours?" I snapped, feigning indignation.

"Idle speculation, that's all."

"Not yet," I said. "But it's just a matter of time."

For now, I was happy just to be sleeping with her. It was nice to be able to curl up next to a warm soft body. It made it easier to resign myself to sleep. The nightmares sometimes frightened Pam, but they didn't come quite so frequently now—and when they did, I didn't have to wake up to an empty room.

"I can't wait to meet her mother," I added, chuckling. "Pam called her last week from the phone booth in Pitt and told her about her new boyfriend. She had the door closed and I could *still* hear her mother at the other end. 'Marine sergeant? Twenty-one?' Wouldn't have batted an eyelash if Pam had said I was a twenty-one-year-old senior premed student. 'Vietnam veteran?' Godzilla? Like I'm some kind of animal or something."

Chapter 6

Back when I was a junior in high school, some student from Yale burned his draft card. He was the first one. He got his picture on the front page of the *New York Times*. I thought he was a Commie creep, or a coward, or both. I hope they throw the book at him, I'd thought.

And I wasn't the only one. Though Lyndon Johnson won reelection that year by a landslide, my hometown of Perkasie had gone heavily for Barry Goldwater. I'd even ridden around town on the back of a flatbed truck the night before the election wearing a Goldwater cowboy hat and singing Goldwater campaign songs. I'd gone to sleep that night, as I did every night, beneath a framed portrait of John F. Kennedy. Kennedy, who had said, "We will bear any burden, pay any price," and for whom I had traveled to Washington the year before and stood for eight dark, cold, uncomfortable hours just for a painful glimpse of the coffin lying in state beneath the Capital rotunda.

I didn't even know an antiwar movement existed—except for some insignificant radical fringe of Commie cowards like that creep at Yale—until I'd read about the October 1967 demonstration at the Pentagon in *Stars 'n' Stripes,* the military daily newspaper we got free in Vietnam. Suddenly, almost out of nowhere it had seemed, there were the photographs, thrust in my face like a raised middle finger: thousands and thousands of demonstrators, whole streets full of them.

Only a few weeks later, during a battalion-sized sweep up near the DMZ, we'd come upon hundreds of leaflets scattered all over the ground in our path. Each was a single sheet of white paper, folded in half to make four pages and containing still more photographs of the demonstration together with excerpts from some of the speeches. The last page said: "U.S. soldiers, join your brothers and sisters back home. Put down your weapons. Resist your officers and oppressors. Refuse to fight the criminal imperialist war. Demand peace now.'' Under the text on that page was a photo of demonstrators carrying a long banner reading "Liberate Vietnam— Stop the War.'' Beneath that, in small type, was printed "National Front for the Liberation of South Vietnam,'' the formal name for the political wing of the Vietcong.

My brothers and sisters back home? Less than three weeks after the demonstration! That *proved* it. Jane Fonda and Dr. Spock worked for the VC. Fucking traitors.

Not that I was all that gung ho about the war by then. I'd been in Vietnam for nine months. I had eyes—and I still had most of a brain. And Sergeant Trinh's words had been eating away at me for two months. But what could you do out in the boondocks with four months still to go on the calendar, one interminably slow day after another lined up in a long row like bottles of beer on a wall stretching away to the horizon and beyond?

I'd almost deserted the month before during R and R in Hong Kong, had told the bellboy to tell the bus to go on to the airport without me and climbed back into bed beside the beautiful Danish faerie queene who'd come from heaven to deliver me from the evil. But she had said no, you can't run away, and I had believed her, and then the door to deliverance had closed forever and I'd found myself back in the boondocks staring at a leaflet of organized mass treason in the streets of the city that would be burning with rage and fire six months later as I drove around the Capital Beltway one sad night in April.

Later that summer of 1968, after King had been shot dead, after Robert Kennedy had been shot dead, Chicago had exploded. Sitting alone on the margins of the world, I'd stared at the color photos in *Time* of Combat America: the Stars and Stripes flying upside down from a statue in Grant Park, the demonstrators looking like so many circus clowns, the ranks and ranks of riot police advancing through clouds of tear gas, long black nightsticks flailing. "Pigs,'' the Yippies had called the cops. The Yippies, who hadn't bathed or even bothered to comb their hair in years.

After the Democratic National Convention, Lieutenant Abrams had asked me who I'd vote for: "*if* you were old enough to vote''—a standing joke between us that fall, that a Marine sergeant with three rows of ribbons still wasn't old enough to vote. And I'd told him, "Nixon, sir.'' Richard Milhous Nixon. Vietnam was Lyndon Johnson's war. And Hubert Humphrey was Lyndon Johnson's man. "Nixon."

Yet more than a year after the election in which the people of the United States had voted for an end to Vietnam, the war still raged. The first Moratorium had taken place a month earlier on October 15, 1969, two days before the article about me appeared in the *Phoenix*. No one had asked me to go to Washington to join the demonstration, and I had not gone. Now another Moratorium—this one promising to be even bigger and better—was scheduled to take place in just a few days.

Pam and I were sitting in her room watching the two guppies she'd just bought exploring their new home. Laura Nyro was singing on the phonograph: "Bill, I love you so. I always will." There was a knock at the door, and a girl stuck her head in.

"Hi! Can I come in?" she asked. I recognized her from my history class.

"Hi. Sure," said Pam. "Come look at the fish!" The fish delighted Pam, as though she had just discovered fish for the first time in her life. I loved the little girl in her.

"What's her name?" I whispered to Pam.

"Pat," Pam replied out loud. I could feel my face flush. Pat looked at me and laughed.

"I'm sorry," I said. "I should have remembered."

"That's okay." She laughed again. "Listen, the reason I stopped by, we've chartered a couple of buses to go down to Washington on the fifteenth. I'm signing people up to go. Are you two interested?"

"Sure!" Pam responded immediately, squeezing my hand at the same time. "Let's go, Bill. It'll be fun."

I tried not to wince as my stomach tightened into a knot. "Gee, I don't know," I said slowly. "I, uh, I really don't think I can make it. I've got a *lot* of work to do."

"Oh, come on," Pam urged. "You just finished midterms. What have you got to do this week?"

"It's important, Bill," added Pat. "Every voice counts. We've *got* to make them listen."

"I *know* it's important," I replied, trying not to sound too impatient. "It's not that. It's just, you don't understand, I'm really swamped. I've got two hundred pages of *The Making of Europe* to read for Smith—"

"So do I," Pat interrupted, "and *I'm* going."

"Well, yeah, but you don't read like I do," I argued. I felt extremely uncomfortable. I wanted Pat to go away, and I knew she wasn't going to. "I read *slow,* man; I mean *really* slow. You remember that first assignment Smith gave us? You remember what he did to me? I read *all night,* and the first question he asks me, I don't know the answer. 'Well, Mr. Ehrhart, the least you could have done was read the assignment.' Geez, I felt like a worm, a stupid ignorant worm. I don't *ever* want that to happen again."

"But you can read on the bus," Pat replied. She made no effort to hide her impatience. "You'll have six hours to read."

"I can't read in cars—or a bus; I get motion sickness." It wasn't true.

"But this is important!" Pat practically shouted, her face contorting, her arms rising from her sides, palms up, beseeching.

What the hell did these kids know about what was important? These children of the rich and the powerful and the privileged. Pam's father was a lawyer, Mike's father was a lawyer, Bart's father was a doctor, Daniel's father was a chemical engineer, the father of the kid down the hall from me in Pitt was a Harvard professor. What had these children ever done that gave them the knowledge to determine what was important and what was not? To pass judgment on the children of millhands and farmers and steelworkers? What had they ever earned that hadn't been handed to them on a silver platter? Who needs an education? Let's go to Washington and play while the children of the uneducated die for our right to say school's not important, we'd rather play grown-up. What did any of them know about right and wrong?

"Look, Pat," I said abruptly, "I'm sorry, but school's important too. I've waited three years for the chance to be here. Whether I go to Washington or not isn't going to change the outcome of the war. But it *will* affect how well I do for Bernard Smith. I honestly don't have time right now." I felt sick. I wanted to punch her face. She made me feel like a worm.

"Oh. Well, okay, if that's the way you feel," said Pat, her voice cold and distant. "Pam?"

Pam looked at me, whether in disapproval of my response or by way of looking for my approval for her, I couldn't tell.

"It's up to you," I said to her.

"We won't be gone overnight, will we?" Pam asked.

"No," said Pat. "It's just a day trip."

"Okay, sign me up."

"Good," said Pat, looking only at Pam. "Thanks a lot."

Pam and I didn't say anything for a long time after Pat left. I felt terrible inside, as though an intense heat were pressing in on me from all sides. "Well, say something, will you please?" I finally blurted out.

"Do you really feel that way?" she asked.

"What way?"

"That it doesn't matter whether or not you go?"

"Come on, Pam, you know how long it takes me to get things done around here. You *know* how hard I've been working."

"Yes," she said. "Too hard. I thought it would be good for you to get away for a day."

"I can't," I replied, pausing to take a deep breath that was almost a sigh. "I don't know how I ended up at this pressure cooker of a school, but now that I'm here, I'm going to finish what I started."

"You're so serious, Bill," she chided gently, stroking the side of my neck with the palm of her hand. "You don't mind if I go, do you?"

"No, I guess not," I said—then smiled—"but I'll miss you." She leaned over and kissed me on the lips. I pulled her down into my arms and laid us both back gently across the bed. "Besides," I added, "what would I do down there? Burn my draft card?"

Chapter 7

Mr. and Mrs. Casey sat across the room from Pam and me. Neither of them spoke. They seemed to be waiting for me to begin. I felt intensely ill at ease. The dark wood wall paneling of the room was elegantly hand-carved and clearly expensive— like the stone house itself, and everything else in it. But that wasn't the problem.

Pam had begun to talk about marriage within a month after we'd started dating. She would put on Laura Nyro—"Am I ever gonna see my wedding day?"—and we'd make love, and then she'd gaze into my eyes and say, "Bill, let's get married. Faye and Steve got engaged at Thanksgiving. Why don't we?"

"But we're only freshmen, Pam; we've still got three and a half years before we even graduate."

"There's no law that says you have to graduate before you get married, is there?" she'd cajole.

"Well, no," I'd have to concede.

"Then why not? You love me, don't you?"

"Of course I love you—more than anything."

"We could get married at the end of next year and get a place off campus."

"But we hardly even know each other yet. Why the big rush?"

"We love each other," she'd protest. "What else do we need to know?"

"Pam, there's a *lot* you don't know about me yet."

"Mom and Dad only knew each other for three weeks, Bill."

"That was different," I'd argue. "It was wartime. Heck, he was going off to invade Japan, for all they knew. People did stuff like that then. You had to. But we've got all the time in the world. Hey, I've fought my war already. I'm home free. What's the big hurry?"

And then Pam would look at me with that soft, pouting, little-girl look in her eyes, as if to say: "If you really loved me . . ." and I would forget about Jenny and the promises she had made that had come to nothing, and remember only the long loneliness, and the lying down night after night in an empty bed in an empty room, like lowering oneself into a coffin.

Now it was Christmas vacation, and I was sitting in the Casey den.

"Well," I said, trying to figure out how to begin. I crossed my legs, then uncrossed them. I took a deep breath, and fixed my eyes on Mr. and Mrs. Casey, trying to look confident. "Pam and I want to get married," I said.

There was a long silence. I tried to think of something else to say, but nothing came. Finally, Mr. Casey cleared his throat and said, "Isn't this a little premature?"

"Oh, I don't mean immediately," I replied. "Not till next year. At the end of next school year."

"Do you think you know each other well enough to make that kind of decision yet?" asked Mrs. Casey.

The first time I'd met her, she'd reminded me of a hawk: watching, watching, always waiting for an opening, a slip, a flaw, some weakness, some confirmation that I was unfit for her precious daughter, a chance to extend her talons and strike. But in our several weekend trips to the Casey home, she'd seemed to warm considerably. Perhaps my initial perception had only been a reaction to my first impression of her, formed that night when Pam had called her and I could hear her shrieking, "A Marine sergeant?" Though I still didn't feel as though she really trusted me, which bothered me, I sort of liked her—and him too, for that matter.

"You and Daddy only knew each other for three weeks before you got married," Pam quickly interjected. "You should talk."

"That was different," Mrs. Casey replied without hesitation.

"Why?" asked Pam.

Her parents looked at each other. Mr. Casey seemed to be suppressing a grin.

"Well, Alice?" said Mr. Casey. "Was it really so different for us? Remember what your mother said when we told her?"

Mrs. Casey seemed to be having a war in her head between the staid suburban Connecticut mother she was and the brash starry-eyed Brooklyn teenager she'd been. "I remember," she finally said, smiling at her husband and taking his hand. Then she looked at me. "But you know, Bill," she said slowly, "Pam's, well, she's used to—certain things. . . ."

"Mother!" Pam protested, clearly embarrassed.

"Well, you have to think about that," said Mrs. Casey.

I didn't understand at first. Then what she was trying to say dawned on me. And it made me angry. "When you two got married," I said, trying to keep the indignation I felt out of my voice, "could Mr. Casey guarantee that he was going to be able to provide for you so well?" I raised both hands in a gesture encompassing the room and everything in it. "I know I don't have much now, and maybe I never will have very much. But I guarantee you this: If all we ever have is one overcoat between us, Pam will be wearing it, not me. That's all I can promise, but I can promise you that absolutely."

"You were wonderful, Bill!" Pam practically shouted when we were finally alone. She put her arms around my neck and kissed me deeply. "I'd really like to . . . you know what."

"That's all we'd need." I laughed. "Your mom doesn't trust me as it is."

"It's not you," she replied, rolling her eyes in a gesture of eternal daughterhood. "She doesn't trust *any* boy with me."

"Not me?" I said, only half teasing. "Whaddaya mean, not

me? 'A Vietnam veteran?' Besides, I'm hardly a boy''—I grinned broadly—''I think that's what scares her!''

''Well, you were wonderful,'' she said again, kissing me on the cheek this time.

''Wow, kid, that was really intense,'' I said, shaking my head. ''I'm glad that's over with.''

''I wish we could sleep together tonight,'' said Pam.

''So do I. Geez, the next couple of days are gonna be rough.''

''We'll have a good time, anyway,'' said Pam. Then she giggled. ''Maybe we can do it on the ski slope,'' she added. ''Wouldn't that be fun?''

The next morning, the four of us, along with Pam's sister Eilene and Eilene's boyfriend Paul, piled into the family car and headed for Vermont. The Caseys were avid skiers, but this was my first time. I'd borrowed equipment from a family friend in Perkasie. Mr. Casey had taken one look at the skis and said, ''They're going to be way too long for you, Bill; maybe you'd better rent some shorter ones when we get there.''

''Oh, I'll manage okay,'' I'd said, not wanting to add that I didn't have enough money to rent equipment.

By the time we finally arrived, it was too late to do anything more than check in at the hotel and eat dinner. Pam and Eilene shared a room, Paul and I were in a room down the hall from them, and Mr. and Mrs. Casey had a room on the floor below us. We were toying with the idea of trying to rearrange the younger couples when Mrs. Casey knocked on the door of the room we'd congregated in.

''Now, don't stay up too late,'' she said. ''We want to get an early start tomorrow morning.''

''Like a hawk,'' I said after she'd left. ''She'll probably be back again. We'd better not try it.''

It made me angry that I had to be scheming and plotting like some high school kid—and even angrier that no plot seemed to be feasible. After the girls had gone and Paul went off to the bathroom, I took out the bottle of ginger brandy I had in my suitcase and took a long swig straight from the bottle. Then I took another, and then another, stashing the bottle just before Paul returned. With the kid here, I thought with dismay, I won't even be able to jerk off.

The next day, I strapped on my borrowed skis and immediately entered another dimension. It was as though I had suddenly turned into a spastic. "Okay, legs, do this," I'd say, but my legs would do something else instead. Then I'd say, "Okay, legs, do that," but once more my legs would do something else. They did whatever they felt like doing. Sometimes they did nothing at all. At other times, they invented startlingly new and remarkable things to do. Occasionally, they did everything all at the same time. And I hadn't even left the dressing area yet.

"You ought to learn how to snowplow," Pam gently suggested. But I could look around and see that the only people using the snowplow technique to turn and stop were the beginners.

"No," I barked, "I'll figure out how to parallel. It can't be that hard. Let's go."

I hobble-shuffled over to the chair lift and managed to get on beside Pam without killing myself. We rode up the mountain in silence. I didn't like dangling in space. The mountain hadn't looked so high, or so steep, from the lodge. When we reached the top, I fell down trying to get off the lift. One ski popped off and I hit myself on the head with one of the poles. Hundreds of people were watching me. I could feel my face getting red with fire. I got up, managed to replace the ski, then turned to look down the mountain. God almighty, I thought.

"How do I do this, Pam?" I asked, trying not to sound too frightened. She explained a bunch of things that I didn't understand, and then I pointed myself down the hill and pushed off with my poles. I got about fifty feet, then I fell over. I went another fifty feet and fell over again. Then I went thirty feet and fell over. Then the trail curved and I crashed into a bush. Pam stayed right with me. She tried to coach me. "Do this," she'd say, "try that." And I'd say, "Okay, okay," but my body had abandoned me utterly. It belonged to somebody else who had gone on holiday, leaving no forwarding address.

At first, I was laughing, trying to make it seem like a joke. But it wasn't funny. It was humiliating. Soon I was swearing, and I wasn't kidding. By the time I was a third of the way down the slope, people must have been able to hear me bellowing all over the mountainside. Pam was on the verge of tears. She had never seen me like this. She'd been so excited about this trip, so eager to share with me one of her greatest loves, and here I was screaming bloody murder and accusing her and the mountain of trying to make me the laughingstock of New England. Something inside of me spoke up once or twice, trying to say, "Stop it, Bill, for Chrissake, you're acting like a child"—but the rest of me simply refused to listen. I couldn't help myself. I stumbled on down the slope, the fury mounting with each fall.

The capper was the little kid no more than eight years old who came flying down the mountain like Speed Racer, bounding over moguls and executing a ninety-degree turn in midair before stopping on a dime five feet away from the wreckage of arms and legs and skis and poles that I had become.

"What are you lying down for, mister?" he said with a perfectly straight face. "That's not the way you're supposed to do it. Don't you know how to ski, mister?"

I grabbed a pole and tried to skewer the kid through the face. I'd have run him through if he hadn't been quick enough to get out of reach, but he took off down the slope, easily outrunning the pole and the barrage of epithets I hurled after him.

That did it. I took off my skis. "Go on," I said to Pam angrily. "Go ski. Enjoy yourself! That's what you came here for, isn't it?" Pam started to take off her skis, too. "What the fuck are you doing?" I snapped.

"I'll walk down with you," she said in a subdued voice.

"Like fucking hell you will. Go on, get the fuck out of here!" I shouted, cocking a fist at her. "Get lost! Leave me the hell alone!" She backed up quickly, staring at me for a moment before bursting into tears. Then she turned and skied off, leaving me alone in a heap on the mountain.

By the time I got down off the mountain, it was nearly noon. I was still angry, but had cooled off enough to realize that I had really blown it. I spent the rest of the afternoon sitting alone in the lodge, dreading the moment when I would have to face Pam and her parents. I wanted to pack up and leave before they returned, but that was impossible. Christ, I thought, I seemed to be spending my entire life stuck in places and situations I didn't want to be in and couldn't get out of.

That night at dinner, Pam was very quiet and the whole family seemed uneasy. I could hardly eat. One part of me wanted to shout, "All right, come on, get it over with, tell me what kind of asshole I am!" Another part of me wanted to shout, "What right do any of you have to judge me—after all I've been through? None of *you* have ever been in combat. They dropped the bomb and saved *your* ass, Mr. Casey. What the hell do you know?" Still another part of me kept saying, "What's that got to do with anything, dildo brain?" It was confusing, and it hurt, and I didn't know what to think, much less what to say.

"Gee, that was fun today," I finally said, trying to smile. "But I'm sure not very good at it. In fact, I'm really a klutz—I guess Pam told you. Boy, you people make it look so easy." My stomach seemed filled with a sour bile.

"It just takes a little practice," said Mr. Casey. "That's all. Don't be discouraged." He didn't look at me.

After dinner, I finally managed to get Pam alone in my room. "Look, Pam, I'm really sorry," I said. "I don't know what happened to me today." She didn't say anything. "Come on, Pam, I'm *really* sorry. Please forgive me. You've been skiing all your life. You can't expect me to be an Olympic champion, can you?"

"I didn't mind that," she said. "I'd have been happy to spend all day with you. I don't care if you can't ski." Her eyes filled with tears. "Bill, you said some *awful* things to me. You were going to hit me—"

"Oh, heck, Pam," I protested, "I wasn't going to hit you. Honest. I was just mad. I wouldn't hurt you."

"Well, you looked like you meant it," she sniffed. "And you *did* hurt me. The things you said, Bill. You've got a real mean streak in you."

It suddenly felt as though she'd jammed an ice pick into my chest: the running figure in black, the halfhearted warning to halt, the single shot punching a hole in the boredom of the hot afternoon, the spinning twisted body, nudging the corpse faceup with my boot—an old woman, unarmed—and not a shadow of remorse anywhere under that scorching Asian sun.

Jesus Christ, I thought, catching my breath sharply. "Pam, *please*, I'm sorry. I didn't mean it. I don't know what got into me." I reached out and took her hand. She didn't remove it. "Please forgive me. It won't happen again."

"You really frightened me today," she said. "Please don't ever be like that again."

"I won't," I said, lifting her hand to my lips and kissing it, "I promise. Not ever again." Her body shifted slightly toward mine. I reached one arm around her back, and with the other hand slowly began to massage one of her breasts. She leaned into me and began licking the inside of my ear with her tongue. "You think we've got time?" I asked.

"We can't," she purred into my ear. "Unh, that feels good."

I felt another flush of anger. I'm a grown man, I thought, and here I am playing cat and mouse with a grown woman's parents like I was a kid in high school or something. My groin ached.

"The hawk!" I snapped, crooking the fingers of one hand into a set of talons.

Pam pulled away laughing and stood up. "We'll be back at school soon," she said, tracing the curve of her hips with both hands.

Chapter 8

"Hey, Mike, this is Bill," I spoke into the telephone.

"Bill? Bill! Where are you?"

"At the ARCO dock over in Oakland. Can you come pick me up?"

"Sure, buddy! I'll be there in half an hour," said Mike.

I hung up the phone and went back aboard the *Endeavor* to sign out. Then I went down to the engineroom to find Roger.

"You sure you can't come along?" I shouted in Roger's ear, trying to be heard over the tremendous whine of turbines and generators.

"Yeah," he shouted back. "I'm taking the First's four-to-eight for him tomorrow morning so I can get off in Portland. Have a good time."

I nodded and smiled, then bounded up the long series of narrow metal stairs from the maneuvering platform to the main exit of the engineroom. I was excited about seeing Mike Morris again; I hadn't seen him since the first time we'd put in to San Francisco Bay months ago.

San Francisco Bay is unmatched in beauty on the West Coast run—except perhaps by Puget Sound on the trip down to Seattle— and towering over the mouth of the bay, like a vast highway of dreams gracefully soaring through thin air, is the Golden Gate Bridge. At night, from the sea, the bridge's lights appear like a string of elegant pearls dangling from the bare throat of the continent. And then the bridge looms high overhead, dwarfing the ship, and slips away astern. Sausalito and Tiberon appear on the north shore of the bay, Alcatraz lies dead ahead, and beyond that, Treasure Island and the Oakland Bay Bridge. And all along the south shore is the City of Saint Francis, scattered over the hills like Solomon's jewels.

Strange, I'd thought as we'd sailed in that evening, how many indelible memories had been collected here in the six years since I'd first seen San Francisco. Actually, the first time, I hadn't really seen it at all. Just back from Vietnam, I'd taken a taxi from Treasure Island navy base early one morning on my way to San Francisco Airport and the East. Thirteen months of imagining my first sight of America—and all I'd encountered had been the solid iron fog of the bay, and a cabbie who'd told me about Purple Hearts and U.S. Navy destroyers and Japs and who couldn't understand why "you kids" couldn't make a bunch of rice-propelled zipperheads say Uncle Sam, and I'd sat alone in my uniform in the airport in a pool of my own sweat, sickeningly aware that I was more afraid in my own country than I'd ever been in Vietnam.

I'd returned less than four months later, on my way to gamble my life against a few thousand dollars—or so I'd thought at the time—and had motored around the bay in a tourist boat with a newly divorced woman from Nebraska just to pass the few remaining hours before I had to report for the long flight back to Asia, gazing up in silence at the great bridge and the broken dreams it represented, and later passing Alcatraz and seeing the Native Americans who had made headlines by occupying the island, reclaiming it from the U.S. government that had taken it from them a century earlier. "Red Power!" shouted across the bay from the ten-foot-high letters splashed on the prison walls, and the tour boat guide had chuckled into the microphone, "Wild Indians, folks! Look out for flaming arrows!"

Two and a half years later, Daniel Kaufman and I had blown into town in my red VW, staying just long enough to get tattooed and relieve Jack Gold's parents' refrigerator of the greater portion of its contents before roaring off again in search of the road to Sacramento. High on loaded brownies, we'd circled the bay two and a half times ("Hey, this is the Oakland Bridge again! We're headed back into San Francisco again!") before stumbling onto the right road, arriving just in time to crash the Air Force officers' Christmas party, nearly scuttling my brother's budding career ("Your brother? He's your brother?").

And six months later when Gold, Bart Lewis, and I went salmon fishing on a charter boat full of middle-aged men from Des Moines who'd saved all year for a trip like this and who didn't catch six fish between the twenty-three of them while the three beer-drinking long-haired freaks from Sleazetown U.S.A. roared and hollered and laughed all day long, hauling in so many big fat salmon that we caught the limit and then some, and we'd ended up at the end of the day giving the extras away to the middle-aged men from Des Moines, and you could hear their teeth grinding like steel girders in high wind behind their tight-lipped thank-yous.

And finally only the previous June when I'd graduated from college and headed west to live with Mike while waiting and hoping for a chance to return to the sea, and I'd spent the summer watching Mitchell and Haldeman and Ehrlichman and Colson and company raising the bushy eyebrows of Senator Sam Ervin as they spun out an intricate tale of lies and corruption and filth that had long since ceased to amaze me. I'd finally run out of money, and had had to take a job in downtown San Francisco with the Bechtel Corporation, riding the streetcar to work in a coat and tie on the fifteenth floor for three days until they'd offered to make me the project safety analysis coordinator for a nuclear power plant project in Massachusetts and all I had to do was sign a little paper that promised I'd work for them for at least three years, and I'd bolted from the building at lunchtime and had headed straight for the nearest pay phone, calling the ARCO marine personnel director for the umpteen-millionth time, begging and pleading to be saved from a horrible end in Massachusetts, and I wasn't kidding, and he'd called me back the next morning at seven to tell me that if I could make it to Long Beach by one that afternoon I had a ship, and I was gone before he'd hung up the phone.

I was thinking about the divorcée from Nebraska—wondering if she'd ever managed to put her life back together again after twenty-three years of marriage and a husband who'd called one day from a hotel room in Montreal to tell her he wouldn't be home for supper anymore—when Mike pulled up to the dock. I jumped in and we took off.

"Where to?" he asked.

"Where are we going, Walt Whitman?" I roared in as sonorous a voice as I could manage. "The doors close in an hour. Which way does your beard point tonight?"

"How about my place?" Mike suggested, ignoring me.

"You got any beer there?"

"Yeah."

"Home, James, and don't spare the horses!"

"You drunk already?" Mike asked.

"Just in a good mood," I replied. "Happy to see *you*, I guess— don't ask me why, I certainly can't imagine why, there's no logical explanation for it."

Mike laughed. We were on the Oakland Bridge now, headed into San Francisco. It was a clear night, and the lights of the city sparkled.

"Pretty, isn't it?" I said. "No fog."

"When do you have to be back?" Mike asked.

"Ten tomorrow morning. You working tomorrow?"

"Not till tomorrow night," he said. "We gotta play the Pizza Hut in Richmond tomorrow night." He paused and groaned. "It's Okie night again. I quit that job in the law office; couldn't deal with working all day and playing music three or four nights a week."

"You making enough money?"

"For now," he said. Then he shook his head slowly. "I don't know, though. I don't think I'll be doing that much longer, either. Gettin' harder and harder to deal with the rest of the band. We've got *nothin'* in common but bluegrass."

"Yeah, well, I noticed that last summer," I said.

"It just gets worse all the time," he continued. "They're just such a bunch of ignorant redneck shitkickers. It wouldn't even be so bad if they just kept their mouths shut, but they go on and on about the Commie hippie pinkos and bleeding hearts that are ruining America. They think Nixon ought to be made king of America and all the fairies persecuting the poor man ought to be castrated. What do you say to people like that? You can't even *begin* to reason with 'em."

"America, America, God shed his grace on thee. That's what you get for being a Dobro player," I laughed. "You couldn't settle for trumpet or clarinet. What are you gonna do?"

"I've been thinking about going to graduate school in Seattle."

"For what?"

"Marine biology," he replied.

"What do you do, learn to dissect Marines?"

"Up yours. Anyway," said Mike, "it won't happen before next fall."

We drove along the waterfront for a while, then turned south into the heart of the city.

"So how the hell have you been?" asked Mike.

"Fine," I said. "I tried to call you last month when we were in—it was a weekend, Saturday I think—tried a couple of times, but you weren't in."

"That was probably the weekend I went skiing up at Tahoe," he replied.

"Skiing?" I snorted. "I didn't know you were a skier."

"Well, I'm not much of one, but I fake it every now and then."

"You can have it," I said, lighting a cigarette. "I tried it once. It was a disaster."

Mike pulled open the ashtray on the dashboard. "You wanna use this?" he asked. "Or are you still using your pants?" We both laughed. "So, you're doing okay out there? You still like it?"

"Oh, yeah, a lot," I said. "I'm doing just fine. All I do is float around all day playing with my own private Erector set and getting paid good money for it. Suits me just fine. Actually, I'm learning a heck of a lot about engines and stuff. I've gotten to be pretty good friends with one of the engineers and he's been teaching me a lot. I was going to bring him along tonight, but he couldn't get off."

"You're about due for vacation, aren't you?" he asked. "You've been out there, what, five months already?"

"Vacation?" I replied. "What the hell do I need vacation for? I'm *on* vacation, man. It's been the most peaceful five months of my life. No pigs trying to bash your brains out; no headlines screaming in your face; no fuckin' women trying to play head games with you. Hell, Mike, there's no traffic lights, no grocery bills, no electric company, no rent payments, no politicians, no generals, no potholes, no assholes, no—"

"Okay, okay," Mike laughed. "I get the idea."

"No fuckin' hassles, man. It's beautiful. I'm in hog heaven."

"For now, maybe," said Mike thoughtfully.

"Forever, man," I shot back instantly. "I'm home. Free at last, free at last, thank God almighty, I'm free at last."

Mike started to reply, then shook his head slowly and let pass whatever he'd been about to say. We pulled up in front of the apartment on Rivoli Street where I'd lived the previous summer.

"Don't worry about it, Mike," I said as we started up the steps. "I really am doing okay. It's been a long time since I've been able to say that and really mean it. I don't think I want to mess with it."

Mike put his arm around my shoulder for a moment, gently

squeezing my upper arm with his hand. "It's good to see you, Bill," he said. Then he unlocked the door and we went in. "Beer's in the fridge," he said. "Get one for me, too."

"You seen Archie Davison at all lately?" I asked, opening two bottles and putting them down on the kitchen table.

"No," he said quietly. "Not since that time last summer before you got out here. I told you about that."

"Yeah."

"I don't know, Bill, he just went right off the deep end."

"Yeah, well," I said, "I can remember back at Swarthmore trying to tell him how screwed up America is. I guess it finally sank in."

"But those Labor Committee people are crazy, man," Mike said adamantly, referring to the National Caucus of Labor Committees, a radical leftist group Davison had joined after graduating from Swarthmore. "They even have to listen to ideologically correct music—which is whatever Lynn Marcus tells them is okay to listen to. They're a bunch of totalitarian fanatics. Trade one form of oppression for another. Geez, Archie sounded like a broken record, for Chrissake, like a zombie or something. Whatever the great leader says, Archie says, and he's got nothing else to say."

"It really hurt, didn't it?" I said.

"Yeah, it did. You'd think after all those years, friendship would count for something."

"Well, I'm glad I didn't try to see him last summer."

"You'd have gone right through the roof, Bill."

"I know. That's why I didn't try," I said. "But you know, I can sort of understand how you can get like that. How do you change a system like this? Money, power, property—and all of it so deeply entrenched that even the people getting screwed every day think it's the greatest system in the universe. Christ, look at that shithead Nixon; if anybody in America had half a brain, they'd have hung that fucker from the yardarm years ago. Look at the goddamned war, for Chrissake. It's *still* going on. After all these years. There's no way they can win. There's no way they could *ever* have won. But they're going to keep on killing until they've turned all of Southeast Asia into a parking lot for Disneyland. All those wasted lives, Mike—and nobody in America cares. Just so long as it isn't their kids coming home in Baggies anymore."

"Some of us care," said Mike quietly.

"Not nearly enough of us, Mike, not enough to even begin to make a dent in it. I think Archie cared too, once—no, he probably still does care, in his own twisted way. You see it all going down, and you want to be able to change it so badly—somehow change it before it's just too late—and there's nothing you can do no matter how hard you try because it's already too late, it just keeps happening the way it's always happened, and after a while it just makes you crazy.''

"I don't think he's crazy," said Mike. "He's turned into a fanatic, that's all."

"What's the difference?" I shrugged. "You've got to be a fanatic to think you can ever change the way it is in the land of the free and the home of the brave."

"Well, what scares me," said Mike—then he laughed—"Well, a lot of things scare me, but one of them is, just suppose the system really does come unglued one of these days. Like the Russian revolution—who ever imagined that the Romanov dynasty could crumble so quickly and completely? And if it ever does, it'll be a small group of disciplined fanatics who come rushing into the vacuum. Nobody took the Bolshies seriously until it was too late—and now look what they're stuck with over there."

"Maybe." I nodded, taking a swig of beer. "Most of the time I'm inclined to think that anything would be better than what we've got now anything at all, just to shake up the system—but I don't suppose I really believe that. I don't know what I believe. I certainly don't believe in what we've got. Anyway, for better or worse, I don't think we're in any danger of having the system collapse. I used to think it might be possible, but not anymore. I expect we'll just keep stumbling along until we all go up in a forest of mushroom clouds."

"Nice thought," Mike groaned. "How the hell do we always end up talking about this stuff? You want another beer?"

"Yeah, gimme another. We've been talking about this stuff since the first damned night I met you," I laughed. "We were meant for each other. Sooner or later, we're going to figure it all out. Marx and Engels. Gilbert and Sullivan. Sears and Roebuck. Hey, you wanna hear another nice thought? Remember Didi Barnesly?"

"Remember?" said Mike, turning away from the refrigerator to face me. "One doesn't forget the Didi Barneslys of the world."

"Well, she's a junkie."

"Heroin? Are you kidding me?"

"I wish I was," I said.

"How do you know? Have you heard from her?"

"No, not directly," I replied. "I stayed at her parents' house in Laguna Beach a couple of days ago. We get twenty-four-hour relief crews in Long Beach, you know, because it's home port, so I had a full day off. Just for the hell of it, I rented a car and drove down to Laguna. I don't know why; I haven't seen or heard from her since she dropped out of school. But anyway, her mother told me she's in some hospital in Hawaii; she got hepatitis from a dirty needle."

"Jesus, what a waste," said Mike. He put the two fresh beers he was holding down on the table and sat down.

"Yeah," I said, picking up one of the bottles. "She was a beautiful person. Strange—but really a classic. Only woman I knew at Swarthmore that had sense enough not to tangle with me."

Mike peered across the table at me. "I thought you two, uh . . ." His voice trailed off.

"Nope."

"Really?"

"Yep. Not even once."

"Well, I'll be damned," he snorted. "You sure had a lot of people fooled."

"I never tried to fool anybody," I said. "Other people's imaginations always seem to run wild in the streets without any help from me."

"Well, you never denied anything!"

"Denied what? What was I supposed to do? Put on a hair shirt and run around campus screaming, 'Didi Barnesly is not screwing me!'?" I took a long swallow of beer. "Anyway, it doesn't matter now."

"No, I guess not," said Mike. "Geez, what a waste." He reached across the table and picked up the pack of cigarettes. "You allowed to smoke on the ship?"

"Oh, yeah. Anywhere inside the ship, and anywhere outside behind the red line. They've got a red stripe painted on deck about two-thirds of the way forward on the stern housing—right across the poop deck, the boat deck, the stack deck, and back down the other side. Behind that, you're okay."

"That would make me nervous," Mike laughed. "Floating around on top of all that oil."

"Nah," I said. "Actually, you're okay when its fully loaded. It's only when you're unloading or running only partly filled that you've gotta be careful—when the tanks have a lot of fumes in them. It's the fumes that blow; the oil itself is pretty stable."

"I'll take your word for it," said Mike. "Where you headed from here?"

"Portland," I answered.

Mike finished his beer and got up to get another.

"Me, too," I said, chugging the rest of mine down.

"I've got some Jack Daniel's. You want some of that?"

"No," I replied. "Well, hell, why not? One for old times' sake. Join me?"

"Sure," said Mike. He got two glasses and poured a half inch of sour mash whiskey into each.

"Here's to Archie Davison," I said, lifting one of the glasses.

"Here's to Didi Barnesly," said Mike, lifting the other glass.

"To a generation of peace," I added. We clinked the glasses together, and took the whiskey down in one swallow.

Chapter 9

"Ehrhart, you stick with me," said Sergeant Wilson, the chief scout. It was still dark, but I could see armed men milling around, and the outlines of thatch-roofed hooches in the near distance. Two platoons from Alpha Company had already moved into position along the far side of the village to serve as a blocking force should any Vietcong try to run. The third platoon, together with the scouts, would sweep through the village, searching every house in every hamlet, rounding up man, woman, and child in the process.

We waited now only for first light. It was late February 1967. I'd been in Vietnam only a few weeks, and this was my first County Fair. The County Fair was a special counterinsurgency operation. It was supposed to build goodwill among the civilian population by distributing food and medical aid while rooting out VC guerrillas and political cadre and gathering intelligence.

As the gray false dawn gave way to a glowing pink fringe on

the edge of a cloudless sky, we fanned out in a single line abreast along a front of several hundred meters and started forward through the ricefields. "Keep your interval and watch your step," Wilson cautioned me. "Especially crossing dikes and hedgerows."

Chickens squawked and flapped on the hard-packed ground between hooches as we approached the first hamlet. Most of the villagers came out of their hooches before we even got there, as though they knew we were coming, but one hooch nearby remained closed and shuttered. A couple of Marines approached and banged on the door with their rifle butts. Without waiting for a response, one of them kicked the door in, jumping back quickly as though expecting it to explode. An old man and a very young girl emerged. Both were immediately knocked to the ground by the two Marines.

"Whaddaya doin' in there, hiding?" one of the men screamed as he kicked the old man heavily in the ribs. "You goddamned gook motherfucker!" He began to kick the old man toward the other villagers who were rapidly being formed into a large herd behind the sweep force, prodded along by a few guards.

"A little rough, aren't they?" I said to Sergeant Wilson, trying to keep my voice on an even keel.

"Look at these people, Ehrhart," he replied. I looked at the ragtag band. Some of them looked sleepy, others bored, still others frightened, but most of them were expressionless. "See any young men about your age? Where do you think they are? Some of them are ARVN—but a lot of them are Vietcong guerrillas. And these people are their mothers and fathers and sisters and wives and children."

Just about then, someone hollered, "Fire in the hole!" and a loud explosion erupted 150 meters to the left of us, leaving splintered trees and white smoke in the middle of a hedgerow. It was obviously a mine someone had managed to discover without stepping on it first.

Without interruption, Sergeant Wilson went right on talking. "That mine they found—maybe the next one will take somebody's leg off. Maybe yours. Ever wonder why none of these villagers step on mines? You haven't been here very long. A lot of these guys have been dealing with this shit day in and day out for a long time. You do what you have to. With any luck at all, you might get to go home in one piece. Come on; I'll teach you how to check out a hooch." And he entered the one nearest to us.

I followed him. There was no one inside, but we found two

large bags of rice in an underground hole large enough to hold five or six people. Wilson shouldered one of the bags, gesturing for me to take the other one. "Let's dump this stuff on the tractors," he said. As we passed Calloway, Wilson pointed to the hooch we'd just left. "There's a bunker in there," said Wilson. "Blow it." A few minutes later, the bunker, along with the house on top of it, disappeared in a smoky roar, debris shooting a hundred meters into the air like a fountain, raining down again slowly in a tinkle of tiny pieces.

The whole process was repeated over and over again for several hours, hooches periodically disappearing in great fireballs, occasional gunfire, the herd of Vietnamese swelling to many hundreds of souls as we moved slowly from one hamlet to the next. The temperature must have been up somewhere around ninety-five. Finally, the blocking force came into view, standing like a line of sentries at the edge of a ricefield, and I could see a large barbed-wire enclosure set up on a sandy patch of dry ground off to the right. Three large tents, two with their sides rolled up, had been erected inside the wire. As we approached the enclosure, Marines herded the Vietnamese into it. There was no place to sit but the ground, and there was no shade except for the tents.

Under one of the open tents, cooks had begun heating up half a dozen huge tubs of rice which would be fed to the Vietnamese. Under the second open tent, several medical corpsmen soon began treating people for cuts and bruises, giving shots of penicillin and other simple medications. The three Vietnamese national policemen who had accompanied us immediately began picking through the throng of people, shouting at some, slapping others, now and then hauling one out by the scruff of the neck and dragging him or her off to the one tent with its sides still down.

That's where I found Staff Sergeant Taggart and Staff Sergeant Trinh. Taggart was standing over an old man who was squatting down on his haunches so that his rear end almost touched the ground. Taggart held an M-16 rifle, barrel down, so that the sharp three-pronged flash suppressor pressed against the flesh on the top of the old man's foot just behind the toes. He kept twisting the rifle in a rotating fashion, causing the flash suppressor to cut deeply into the old man's foot. The foot was bleeding. Trinh stood off to one side translating for Taggart.

"Who dug the bunker?" Taggart was shouting as I walked in. The old man mumbled something. He was crying.

"He says he dug it," said Trinh. "At night the artillery explodes in his village. He says he dug it for his family to hide in when the artillery comes."

"You're lying!" Taggart shouted into the old man's face, twisting the rifle harder. The man shook his head frantically, not understanding the words, but clearly comprehending the gesture and tone of voice. One of the national policemen punched the old man on the side of the face.

"Do the VC hide in the bunker?" Taggart shouted. "How many VC are in this village? Were the VC here last night? Where is your son?" As Taggart continued the interrogation, Trinh glanced over at me for a moment. His face was expressionless, but his dark piercing eyes burned like glowing coals. It made me uncomfortable. I turned and walked out into the bright sunlight.

The cooks were serving rice now, dolloping out gluey dipperfuls into tin pans. Sergeant Wilson called to me from a small barbed-wire enclosure set in one corner of the larger one. It contained about fifteen or twenty Vietnamese, some of them bleeding from their feet and noses, and all of them bound hand and foot. "These are the ones the national police want to keep," he said. "There'll be a few more before we leave. Make sure you get them on the tractors before we go in."

"Any of 'em confirmed VC?" I asked.

"Nope," said Sergeant Wilson.

"We didn't get any weapons either, did we?"

"Nope."

As we were standing there the civil affairs assistant, an enlisted man who spoke almost no Vietnamese, approached us. "Sergeant Wilson, that gook over there's yammering about some chickens or something," he said, pointing to an old woman with black teeth who was talking excitedly and waving her arms in the face of the civil affairs officer, who was responsible for the battalion's dealings with the civilian population and who spoke no Vietnamese at all.

"What's the trouble, sir?" asked Wilson, who was one of the very few Americans in Vietnam who could speak Vietnamese.

"I don't know, Wilson," said the lieutenant. "Can you understand her?"

"She says we killed three of her chickens this morning," said Sergeant Wilson, after a brief dialogue with the woman. "A guy shot 'em. She doesn't know why. She wants to be paid."

"I can't pay her!" the lieutenant said with a pained expression. "If I pay *her*, I'll have to pay the whole village! Tell her

I'm sorry, there's nothing I can do. Tell her she's lucky she still has her house."

Chapter 10

"Hey, wait a minute. Slow down!" I snapped.

"Don't shout at me," said Pam.

"I'm not shouting. I'm sorry," I replied, taking her hand. "Let's just take things a little more slowly, okay? You wanted me to tell your parents, so I did that. But why do we need a formal engagement announcement? What difference does it make?" Pam didn't say anything; she just looked hurt. "Come on, sweetheart," I continued after a pause. "We've got eighteen months to worry about engagement announcements. Besides, where am I going to get the money to buy a ring? You know I don't have that kind of money lying around."

Just then, Pam's friend Faye Mills knocked on the door. "Hi!" she bubbled. "How was vacation? How was Vermont?" She broke into a wide knowing grin. "Did you tell your parents?"

"Yes!" Pam responded quickly, her face lighting up.

"Yeh, we told 'em," I laughed. "I felt like Humphrey Bogart on the wrong end of the third degree."

"Bill!" said Pam.

"Well, it was pretty intense. They weren't exactly captivated by the idea."

"Bill was wonderful," Pam said to Faye. "He had them wrapped around his little finger."

I looked down at my little finger, shaking my head slowly and turning my hand this way and that, the way a painter might study an object before beginning to paint. Pam made an irritated face at me.

"What about your parents, Bill?" asked Faye.

"I'm free, male, and twenty-one," I laughed. "I don't need

to ask my parents' blessing for things anymore. I just tell 'em what I'm going to do.'' I didn't tell Faye—and hadn't told Pam—that I hadn't mentioned the marriage to my parents yet.

"Did you have a good time in Vermont?" Faye asked.

I shifted nervously on the bed and didn't reply. Pam nodded her head and said, "It was okay."

I put my arm around Pam's shoulders and rocked her gently. "You're all right, kid," I said quietly.

We talked for a while about Faye's Christmas vacation. Then, somehow, we got around to the impending trial of William Calley, the Army lieutenant accused of murdering anywhere from 22 to 108 unarmed civilians—perhaps more; no one seemed to know for sure—in the Vietnamese hamlet of My Lai nearly two years earlier. I could see the conversation turning in that direction, but I couldn't think of a way to divert it. Lately, the My Lai massacre had been added to the list of stock questions strangers and acquaintances still persisted in asking me.

"I think it's just horrible," Faye said in disgust. "They ought to put him in prison and throw away the key. They ought to give him the electric chair."

"It's not as simple as that, Faye," I said, reluctant to get into it. "The guy's just a scapegoat. Don't get me wrong," I added quickly as Faye's face darkened with disapproval. "I'm not saying I condone what he did, because I don't. But that's the way we dealt over there. Kick ass and take names—and always in that order. It was just routine procedure."

"Cold-blooded murder was routine?" Faye asked sarcastically.

"Well, not on that scale," I replied slowly, trying to choose my words carefully, "but the same kind of thing happened to a lesser degree every day. You go through a ville, people get in your way, you waste 'em." Faye and Pam both stared at me, clearly repulsed and fascinated at the same time. "Look, you don't understand what it's like. You got people trying to kill you every minute of every day and every night. And you can't even see them. You can't find them. They're like ghosts. Hey, it's not like World War Two—like we're on this side and you're on that side and here's the line between us. They don't walk around with neon signs flashing, 'Hey! I'm a VC!' They're guerrillas. They look like everybody else, dress the same way, work in the fields; anybody you see could be VC—and everybody you *don't* see probably is. Women, children—anybody. Hell, Faye, the first eight months I was in Vietnam, I saw maybe a dozen armed guerrillas, that's all. But we took casualties

every day, day after day. You're out on patrol just strolling along
and—*kerbloom!* And there's your buddy lyin' on the ground without
any legs, just lyin' there like a hunk of raw meat, and there's
nobody to fight back at. Nobody around except Farmer Jones over
in the ricefield behind his water buffalo—he's so close to the mine
that it probably ruptured his eardrums—and he don't even look up.
He doesn't step on the mine. Hey, you *know* that guy's gotta know
it was there. Does he try to warn us? Hell, no. Hell, he probably
planted the damned thing—him or his wife or his daughter. And
you go through this Mickey Mouse routine every day, day after day
after day—same patrols, same villages, same staring blank-faced
people. The only thing that changes is the name of the guy who
packs it all in that day. And every day you wake up wondering if
today's the day *you* pack it in. You can't even begin to imagine
what that does to your head after a while. It makes you crazy. And
then one day you realize that you can blow away civilians and you
don't get into trouble for it. Christ, you get promotions and medals
for it. And when you realize that, there's nothing left to stop you.
Next time some Marine steps on a mine, Farmer Jones gets turned
into a piece of Swiss cheese: one Vietcong guerrilla killed in action.
Maybe he was and maybe he wasn't, but once he's dead, he sure
as hell is—and no questions asked.''

The two girls didn't say anything at first. Then Pam asked,
''Did you ever do anything like that?''

''Yes.''

''That's awful,'' she said.

''Hey, you try feeling bad about it when your buddy's lying
there with his belly ripped open like a pig in a butcher shop.''
Pam looked like she was about to throw up. ''Look, I'm not
proud of it. It's certainly not what I expected to be doing. But
that's the thing about Calley. Nobody back in the World has any
idea what it's like. They send their kids off to fight an impossible
war, and then they expect you to act like GI Joe—go around
handing out candy to kids''—my stomach wrenched as I thought
about Tranh, to whom I'd often given candy, and about the kid
in Hoi An who'd tried to give me a grenade—'' 'Hey, Joe, hey,
Joe, you got gum?' That isn't what gripes me about Calley,
though. The kicker is that the military brass knows goddamned
good and well what's going on. Hell, Calley's company commander ordered him into that ville to produce a body count. *His*
boss ordered *him* to get a body count. And *that* guy's boss . . .
right on up the line all the way to the Pentagon. The only thing

that went wrong with My Lai is that the press got hold of the story. Now all the generals and politicians are backpedaling like all getout—'Shocking! Appalling!'—and they're gonna hang Calley's ass out to take the heat off their own. You watch, everybody but Calley's gonna walk away scot free.''

"Well, they shouldn't just let him go," Faye insisted.

"Maybe not," I said. "I just keep thinking, 'There but for the grace of God . . .'"

"Would you have done what he did?" asked Pam.

"I don't know. I'd like to think that I wouldn't," I said, pausing. "But I don't know. Given the right circumstances, there were times. There were times. I know where the guy's head must have been that morning. I don't know."

"What's the worst thing you ever did?" Faye asked.

Good God! How could I answer a question like that? I got up from the bed and walked over to the window of Pam's room, gazing out over the broad rolling campus—so beautiful, so peaceful, so far removed from anything real. What did these people know about anything? The lawyer's daughter. The doctor's daughter.

"One night up in Hue City," I said without turning around, "during the Tet offensive, a bunch of the scouts gang-banged some refugee." There in the rain in the dark in the bottom of a sixty-millimeter mortar pit, one after another of us climbing down into the pit, the rest of us sitting around the edge smoking, and then her body beneath mine: cold, motionless, driven by fear and hatred and hunger. Surely it had been a kind of death for her, a giving up of the soul. "We paid her with C rations. She wasn't a prostitute, I don't think—she was just starving, probably had a couple of kids to feed—"

"Oh, God," Faye interrupted. "That's sick."

"Well, you asked me!" I snapped, suddenly wheeling around to face them, my voice angry, my face hot with shame. "What did you ask me for? Haven't you been listening? What do you think I was, some kind of knight in shining armor?" Pam's eyes were full of tears. "Christ," I said less violently, "you don't wanna know, don't ask." Neither of them said anything. "Look, it's not like we raped her. She got what she came for. She needed food, she got it. Worse things can happen to a person."

But we *had* raped her—or might as well have: homeless, devastated, perhaps the rest of her family dead, God only knew, the city aflame and in ruins. My stomach churned furiously. I hated Pam and Faye. I felt like a caged animal.

"Just forget it, will you?" I said, almost pleading. "Forget I ever said anything. I made it all up. I thought that's what you wanted to hear. I thought you wanted to hear war stories, so I made one up."

"You didn't make that up," Pam said accusingly.

"I did, I did, I mean it," I replied quickly. "Honest. I thought you two just wanted a little thrill. Really. How could I do something like that?" I walked over to Pam and rested both hands lightly on her shoulders, leaning down and whispering in her ear. "You've felt these hands in action, kid." I stuck out my tongue and gently licked the inside of her ear. "Are these the hands of a man who could do something like that?"

Pam's face softened. She reached up and hugged me to her, putting her face next to mine. I could feel the dampness from her tears. "Come on," I said, "blow your nose and wipe your eyes. I was just kidding. You two want some ice cream? Let's go get some ice cream. My treat."

Chapter 11

I remember the moment precisely. The temperature was a comfortable eighty-two degrees, and the sky sparkled cloudless and blue, reflecting the blue tropical waters off central Luzon that lapped the white beach where I sat sipping beer with Fat Pat, TR, and Smitty, awaiting my turn up behind the ski boat.

I'd been going to the beach at lunchtime nearly every day. It was only a five-minute walk from the hangar where my office was located. The combat intelligence chief of an air squadron not engaged in combat doesn't really have all that much to do, and my boss, the squadron intelligence officer, had the grace and sensibility never to require busywork of me. I did what little there was to do—the lieutenant never had to worry about getting caught flatfooted—and in return, he let me come and go pretty much as I pleased. Lunches at the beach usually lasted two to three hours.

The squadron had been in the Philippines less than two weeks, but already my tan was deepening to a golden brown. And already I'd met a pretty young Filipino girl from Alongapo, the liberty town just outside the gates of Subic Bay Naval Base. Jackie was only sixteen or seventeen—but then, I was only twenty. She was a prostitute, but Filipino hookers are apparently like no others in the world, or at least that I'd encountered. They could make a fortune just working the bars in town, hustling drinks off the Fleet sailors who'd been off the coast of Vietnam for 90 to 120 days, and who hit port loaded with money, starved for a night's worth of alcohol and female companionship, and bereft of all sense. The girls got a percentage of every drink the sailors bought, and those swabbies bought a lot of drinks. The girls didn't need to turn tricks if they didn't want to. And if they liked you, they'd do it for love or fun. Jackie liked me. She took the sailors' money and spent it on me. I thought it was a great arrangement.

On this particular day, I'd gotten back to base from a night with Jackie, put in an appearance at work, and then toddled off to the beach to catch up on the sleep I'd missed the night before. The sun was seductively bright, and the high whine of the ski boat and the cold beer combined to leave me drowsing in a world of private dreams as intoxicating as Jackie, who waited for me to return again that night.

Suddenly, in the middle of my reveries, I found myself confronted by a question I hadn't seriously contemplated in more than eight months: "Now why the hell do you want to go back to Vietnam?" I couldn't have been more startled if I'd heard the Voice of God. The words lit up the inside of my head like lightning, the following thunder rolling over the plain of my mind with a deep resonance that came back in echoes from the walls of my skull before falling away into silence—profound silence, deep and vaguely threatening.

I'd already spent one full tour of duty in Vietnam—thirteen months' worth, February 1967 to March 1968. But when I'd gotten back to the States, I discovered that in my absence America had become an alien place in which and to which I no longer seemed to belong. Assigned to Cherry Point Marine Air Station, North Carolina, I was depressed and unhappy, drinking heavily and thinking suicidally when I was sober enough to think at all. Somewhere in the dim fog, I knew I had to get out of there, and there was only one place in those days to which you could readily be transferred, no questions asked. And so, within a few months of returning stateside, I'd requested orders back to Vietnam, where at least it made sense to be lonely.

And I got my request too, or thought I had: Fleet Marine Forces, Western Pacific—which is exactly what my orders had said the first time I'd gone overseas. So when I left America in June 1968, I just assumed I was headed for Vietnam. But FMFWesPac included not only the Marine units in Vietnam, but also all other Marine units in the entire western Pacific, including those stationed in Japan, Okinawa, and the Philippines. And when I got to the processing center on Okinawa, I found myself assigned to Marine Air Group 15 stationed at Iwakuni, Japan.

I was furious. I'd requested orders specifically for Vietnam. It had never even occurred to me that I'd get sent anywhere but Vietnam. *Everybody* was getting sent to Vietnam in those days, for crying out loud. The whole point of my requesting a transfer in the first place—aside from simply removing myself from America—was to gamble my life against the money I could make. You got sixty-five dollars a month extra combat pay in Vietnam, in addition to your regular pay, and you could save almost everything you made because there was seldom opportunity to spend money out in the boondocks.

In Japan, I couldn't get killed and I couldn't get the extra combat pay, and there were a million ways to spend the money I did make. Besides, my request for a transfer out of the air wing and back into the infantry, where I'd earned all my rank and knew my job and felt at ease, had also been ignored. So the very first thing I did upon reporting for duty with MAG-15 was to collar the group first sergeant and explain about wanting out of the air wing and back into Vietnam.

He said there was nothing he could do about getting me out of the air wing. Way back when I was a private first class just out of boot camp, I'd spent two months in a helicopter squadron at New River, North Carolina, and I had more or less arbitrarily received a little number after my name designating me as air intelligence rather than ground intelligence. At the rank of PFC, it doesn't make much difference if you're an 0221 or an 0231 since you don't know anything anyway, so when I volunteered for Vietnam a few months later, I found myself in an infantry battalion. But during my whole thirteen months, nobody had bothered to change my military occupational specialty number from air to ground intelligence. So lo and behold, when I left Vietnam, I suddenly found myself back in the air wing because the people who make assignments for sergeants and above don't read anything in the service record book but those little four-digit MOS numbers. "There it is, Ehrhart," said the first sergeant.

But, he added, he *could* get me transferred to one of the group's squadrons stationed back on Okinawa, VMGR-152, a squadron of C-130 Hercules transport and aerial refueler planes. The squadron had a substation in Danang, he explained, since its main job was to ferry supplies between Okinawa and Vietnam. Perhaps I could get myself assigned to the substation. Within a week, I flew back to Okinawa and joined VMGR-152.

But when I reported in to the squadron at Futema, Okinawa, and told them what I had in mind, they said it would be impossible. The squadron already had one intelligence man, and he was already down at the substation, and he wasn't due to rotate back to the States for another nine months. And not only that, but the squadron didn't need two intelligence men, so I would be assigned to the administrative section.

I developed an immediate and severe case of apoplexy. A combat infantry sergeant typing correspondence and supervising clerks? And Okinawa one of the worst duty stations in the world to boot: nothing but a U.S. fortress in the middle of the ocean, covered from end to end with U.S. military installations and U.S. servicemen, bars, military police, and prostitutes who *never* did it for love or fun.

I immediately requested a transfer out of VMGR-152. The squadron first sergeant said I had to submit a written request to the administrative officer, who happened to be my boss. So I typed up the request and gave it to Lieutenant Lane. And that's as far as it got; it sat in the lieutenant's hold basket for three weeks without going anywhere else or being seen by anyone else. Lane had gotten his hands on an admin assistant with a few brains, and he knew it, and he wasn't about to let me go.

Finally I could stand it no longer. One night after work, I was alone in the office with no one around but me and the squadron executive officer, Lieutenant Colonel Sims. I picked up my transfer request from Lane's desk, knocked on the colonel's door, and asked if I could speak with him. I handed him the letter and asked him to read it.

"You know," he said when he'd finished reading, "you could

get into a lot of trouble going outside the chain of command like this.'' He meant coming to see him directly.

"I know I can, sir," I replied. "Maybe that gives you some idea just how badly I want this transfer. Besides, I did try to go through channels. Look at the date on that letter, sir. It's been sitting on Lieutenant Lane's desk since the day I got here, and it'll go on sitting there until the day I die if I stick to procedure."

The colonel didn't say anything. He got up and left the office and came back with my service record book and two cups of coffee. He studied my SRB for a while, and then he looked up and said, "Pretty impressive record you've got here. Purple Heart, Presidential Unit Citation, Combat Action Ribbon. Got your sergeant's stripes in twenty-one months. Son, you've done your duty. No one can ask any more of you. You only have ten months left to go. Why don't you just serve out your time and go home? You've got your whole life ahead of you."

I didn't try to explain to the colonel what it had been like to come home and find your childhood friends grown suddenly distant and your girlfriend gone and the streets filled with angry people and the bars filled with people who didn't care. What it had felt like to drive around the Washington Beltway on a Friday night in early April with Martin Luther King, Jr., lying dead and the Capitol dome silhouetted by the flames of the burning city and Simon and Garfunkel on the radio singing, "Where have you gone, Joe DiMaggio?" I didn't try to explain that my whole life didn't really lie in front of me, but rather lay behind me broken and scattered like the bodies of the Vietnamese I had left broken and scattered among the green rice shoots. That I could think of no good reason for any of it, that I no longer had a home to go back to, and that if I got killed in Vietnam, it would be all right, and might even be a kind of poetic justice.

Instead, I told him about feeling out of place in the air wing, especially doing administrative work, and about needing the extra money for college. I told him I couldn't explain it any better than that, but I just had to go back—it was important. And I told him that if I had to stay here and type correspondence for the next ten months, I'd go bananas and get myself into real trouble sooner or later, and he said he could appreciate that, and I believe he could. Then we talked about the schools I'd applied to for the following year, and about what I wanted to study, and about my family. We talked for nearly an hour.

"Here's what I'll do, Sergeant," he finally said with obvious reluctance. "I can't get you transferred to the infantry, and I can't get you sent directly to Vietnam. But there's a squadron of F-4s up at Iwakuni right now, and they've got orders to Vietnam for mid-November. We've got an Inspector General's review coming up at the end of October, and if you'll stick around and help the squadron get through that inspection, I'll do my best to get you transferred to VMFA-122." That sounded fair enough.

For the next two months, I busted my chops typing orders and correspondence and supervising clerks. I hated every minute of it, but I got that administrative section squared away. And we passed the inspection. And the colonel awarded me a Meritorious Mast. And he kept his word: On October 30, I left Okinawa and flew to Japan to join VMFA-122.

I reported for duty on October 31, 1968. The next day, Lyndon Johnson declared yet another one of his bombing halts over North Vietnam. Because VMFA-122 was supposed to be going to Vietnam with the primary mission of bombing the north, the squadron's orders were canceled.

God-fucking-damnit! I couldn't believe it. Warm bodies were going to Vietnam as fast as Uncle Sam could get them there—whether they wanted to go or not. And here I was, fully trained and combat-experienced, begging to go, and they wouldn't send me. The whole world was conspiring against me! *God in heaven* was on the side of bureaucrats and fools.

The day after I officially reported for duty with Marine Fighter Attack Squadron 122, I officially requested a transfer. I found the squadron first sergeant and one more time went through my whole song-and-dance routine, which by this time was getting very long indeed. The first sergeant said he'd do what he could.

In the meantime, the squadron got transferred to Cubi Point Naval Air Station in the Philippines for six weeks of live weapons training. And once we got there, I quickly slipped into a remarkably comfortable routine: come in to work about nine in the morning, lunch from eleven to one or two, off by three or three-thirty. Every bar in town had its own live band, and the girls loved to dance and so did I. The San Miguel beer wasn't bad, and it was cheap. The nights were long and the days were warm, and the tropical sun and the tropical water and the tropical palm trees and the tropical birds and the tropical women made one begin to believe that there might be a paradise after all. I had every weekend off, and Manila and the hill country villages were within easy reach.

So when the Voice of God came to me out of my beer can that day as I drowsed on the beach like a fat snake sunning itself after a good meal, and asked me why the hell I wanted to go back to Vietnam, I couldn't think of a single thing to say. Not one thing. I tried and tried, but nothing came.

And then the Voice of God suddenly broke the deep silence into which I had fallen. "Listen, chump," said the Voice, "if you can't recognize a good thing when it's tossed right into your lap, I really am going to send you back to Vietnam. And I'm going to see to it that you get popped right on the snoot with one of those big-ass hundred-thirty-millimeter Russian rockets. And what's left of you is going to be shipped back to the States in a matchbox. So you better wise up fast, because I'm getting fuckin' tired of arguing with you."

I tipped up the Voice of God and took a long pull on it. And then I studied the clear blue water for a while, watching another Marine take a spill off the skis and come up laughing. And then I turned to Fat Pat and TR and Smitty. "You know something, guys," I said, "Vietnam was the pits."

Chapter 12

Spring break was a total disaster.

I'd looked forward to the trip to Florida for nearly three months. Perry Paulson, one of the guys on the swimming team, had suggested it. He lived in Sarasota and was going home over vacation anyway. Why didn't Pam and I come along? We could all camp out on one of the keys: a week of sun, surf, and easy living. I'd never been to Florida, and it sounded like fun. Even Pam's parents had agreed.

"I expect you and Pam to behave yourselves," Mrs. Casey had said, peering at us, and I'd solemnly sworn that we would, wondering how she could possibly delude herself into believing that we weren't sleeping together at Swarthmore.

"You'd better get your hair cut," Mr. Casey had warned. "You don't want to take any chances with southern justice. They'll shave your head with a rusty razor blade, and there won't be a thing you can do about it. Why go looking for trouble?" So I'd reluctantly cut my hair and shaved my beard, angry at having to toady to a bunch of nameless rednecks—hadn't I earned the right to wear my hair any way I pleased?—but not willing to gamble on being able to explain that to some southern sheriff's deputy.

Things went wrong from the start. As we were loading up Paulson's car, he mentioned that we had to drive by the University of Pennsylvania to pick up his sister and a friend of hers. So we rode all the way to Florida with five people and all of our luggage crammed into a Volvo. It was impossible to move, let alone sleep. We arrived tired and irritable.

No sooner had we set up camp on the tip of a beautiful key off Sarasota than Paulson disappeared to find his hometown sweetheart. He didn't come back until well after dark, and when he did, it was only to tell us that his girlfriend didn't feel like camping, so he wouldn't be staying with us either. Then he got into his car and drove away, leaving us stranded.

When we woke up the next morning, it was raining hard. The tent leaked. So did the tarp over the extra gear and food. We put as much of the extra things in the tent as we could get inside, then we sat there waiting for Perry to come and get us out of the rain. Hour after hour went by. It was too wet outside to start a fire. We ate a cold lunch out of cans. We played cards for a while, but how much gin rummy can two people play? We tried to go for a walk, but it was just too wet and chilly and miserable out. We ate a cold supper out of cans. We got on each other's nerves. We argued. We tried to make love, but Pam had developed a vaginal infection. We argued some more. Pam kept asking me to explain Paulson's behavior, as though I were somehow responsible for it. What was I supposed to say? I hardly even knew the guy. He'd seemed nice enough during swimming season. How was I supposed to know he'd stiff us?

The rain didn't let up for three days. Paulson never came back either, and we had no car and no way to contact him. On the fourth day, the sun came out. We were finally able to put on our bathing suits and lie out on the beach and do a little swimming, but late in the morning a group of kids took up residence just down the beach from us and spent the rest of the day partying loudly and leaving us no privacy.

That night, it began raining again. In the middle of the night, I woke up to the sound of water gurgling loudly. I grabbed the flashlight and went outside to investigate. Christ! The whole tip of the key was gone—washed away by the storm—and seawater a foot deep sloshed through the thin stand of trees not five yards from the tent. The island was sinking into the ocean!

"Pam we've got to move the campsite!" I shouted excitedly as I rushed back into the tent. "Come on, get up, we've got to get out of here."

Pam just grunted and rolled over.

"Get up!" I shouted, grabbing a corner of the cot and tipping the whole cot over, dumping Pam onto the ground.

"Ouch!" Pam cried. "What's the matter with you?" She was still three-quarters asleep.

"Don't argue with me!" I shouted. "Get the hell up and help."

"You're crazy," she said angrily.

"You wanna get washed out to sea? Go on out and look for yourself. We gotta move. Come on, help me! I'll break your fucking neck."

We packed up in the dark and the rain and moved everything two hundred yards up the beach. Pam didn't say a word the whole time. An hour later, when the task was completed, she crawled into her sleeping bag and turned her face away from me.

"Come on, Pam," I said. "I'm sorry. We *had* to move. It was dangerous to stay there. This storm must have taken forty yards of beach just since we went to bed."

"Why do you treat me like that?" Pam almost whimpered.

"Like what?"

"Threatening to break my neck. Dumping me on the ground. You treat me like—like you don't even care about me."

"Oh, come on, Pam, don't be so dramatic. You know I care about you. I just get mad sometimes."

"Sometimes I think you really are mad."

"What the hell's that supposed to mean?" I snapped.

"Listen to yourself, Bill," she said. "That's exactly what I mean. Your voice sounds so *ugly*. I just try to talk to you, and you get ugly and mean. Why?"

"What is this, the third degree?"

"I mean it, Bill. I don't understand how you can be so gentle and loving sometimes—and so mean and ugly a minute later. The stupidest little thing goes wrong, and you fly off the handle.''

"You think it's stupid that I don't want us to get washed out to sea in the middle of the night?"

"You didn't have to throw me out of the cot. Why do you have to threaten me? Does it give you a thrill? Big tough Marine. How can you treat someone you're supposed to love like that?"

"Oh, sure, now you're going to tell me I don't love you. Christ, I should have left you there.''

Pam burst into tears. "Oh, God!" she sobbed. "Who are you? What kind of a person are you?"

"Hey, goddamn it," I shouted, "you're the one that put the moves on me, remember? You're the one wanted to get married! It wasn't my idea. I told you to slow down, but *no*, you've got it all worked out just like the storybooks. You can't just screw somebody for the fun of it—your mother's got you so guilt-ridden that you gotta be in love forever and ever before you can fuck. Christ, Pam, that old boyfriend of yours—you suck him off, you let him eat you out, you even ass-fuck the guy! And then you tell me you're still a virgin! And you really believe it! How sick is that? And you're asking me who *I* am?"

"I hate you," Pam hissed. And then she screamed: "I hate you! I hate you! Leave me alone!"

"Suit yourself!" I shouted.

I spent the rest of the night sitting in the rain on the beach, smoking cigarette after cigarette and listening to Pam crying. Jesus, what a mess, I thought; if only it hadn't rained so much; if only Paulson hadn't stiffed us. I felt angry and ashamed and cheated. I didn't want to think about the things Pam had said. What kind of person could gang-fuck some poor starving refugee in the middle of a war? What kind of person could shoot down old men and women for—for what? What for? What the hell had happened to me over there? I didn't want to be here alone with nothing but my own thoughts on a beach in Florida at night in the rain, and I had no way out. Christ, I thought, is my whole fucking life going to be like this? When do I get my rotation date? This is the world? This is what I used to dream about? When do I wake up?

Hours later, in the wet gray light of early morning, I crawled back into the tent and knelt over Pam. I could tell she was awake, but she wouldn't look at me. I suddenly started to cry. I couldn't stop myself. I started blubbering like some kind of fool, begging her to forgive me, hating myself for not being able to act like a man, refusing to accept anything but reconciliation. "I can't live without you," I sobbed. I hated her for making me stoop to this. "Please, please, baby, I'm sorry."

And she forgave me one more time.

But when Paulson finally did show up later that day, she insisted on packing up and leaving immediately. "But we don't have to be back for four more days," said Paulson, looking at me imploringly.

What does he want from me, I thought. Was I supposed to help him talk her out of it? "Hey, man," I said, "I spent enough time sleeping out in the rain and eating cold canned food just because I didn't have any choice about it. I can't see doing it when I don't have to."

"Well, okay," said Paulson, "but I'll have to make a few adjustments. I hadn't planned on leaving today. I'll come back and get you later."

"No way," I said. "We pack up now, and we load the car now, and we go with you—now. It's not up to you. Understand?"

Chapter 13

"Annunciate radio check," the radio crackled softly.

Roddenbery keyed the mike and replied, "Annunciate, Annunciate; this is Lima Papa One. All secure. We're coming in. Over." He lifted the radio pack to his back, the headset still crackling as the other listening posts checked in.

Listening posts were supposed to be a kind of advance warning system in case the VC tried to hit the battalion compound. I didn't like the idea very much: three guys sitting out there in the darkness four or five hundred meters beyond the wire; sometimes, like tonight, a whole ville between you and safety; if the VC ever did try to attack the compound, you'd probably have just about enough time to radio in a warning before the VC canceled your ticket. Back in high school, it had been easy to imagine myself a hero. But over here—well, most of the heroes seemed to be dead, or likely to be dead soon. My fantasies had never included me among the dead.

So I was relieved that the night's LP was finally over and that it had passed without incident. It was 0200. I stood up stiffly, my seat wet from the damp ground, and moved out behind Roddenbery and Maloney, passing along the back of the hamlet toward the road. You could hear the Vietnamese turning in their sleep. There was a baby crying somewhere.

And then the night erupted.

Roddenbery lit up in a quick flash of light like a silhouette, leaping off the ground helter-skelter and crumpling into darkness. If he screamed, it was lost in the blast of the explosion. My heart stopped dead, then took off full throttle, and my stomach filled with acid. I hit the deck and came up ready to fire, but the silence that followed the explosion was deeper than ever, and all I could hear through the ringing in my ears was someone crying, "I'm hit, I'm hit."

I crawled over to Maloney. "Jesus, I'm hit, I'm hit, oh, God, it hurts!" he cried.

"You're okay, you're okay," I kept whispering. "You'll be okay. Hang loose; I'll be right back." I crawled over to Roddenbery. One leg was gone from the knee down; the other was gone from the ankle. His crotch was split open. The radio, miraculously, was still working. There was frantic chatter coming from the headset. I broke in:

"Annunciate, Annunciate; this is Lima Papa One. We're in trouble; get somebody out here quick. We got casualties, over."

"Lima Papa One, Annunciate. What's happening? Repeat. What's happening?"

"Hit a mine, I think. I don't know. We're not taking any fire. I got one Kilo India Alpha, one Whiskey India Alpha. Hurry the hell up, will you? And put up some illumination."

"That's a roger on the illum, One. Sit tight. Where are you now?"

"Along the first paddy dike on the north edge of the ville, about one hundred and fifty meters east of the highway."

"Roger, One, we're on our way. Look for a red pencil. Fire your red pop-up when you see it. Over."

"Roger, Annunciate, red pencil, red pop-up, over."

I crawled back over to Maloney, who was groaning loudly. "It's okay, buddy," I whispered. "Lemme see." He was clutching the top of his right thigh. I ripped away the cloth. A chunk of his thigh had been torn out, and he was bleeding heavily. I took out my bandage and wrapped it around his leg as tightly as I could. "It's okay, buddy, it's just the muscle, it doesn't look too bad."

"Oh, Jesus, it hurts!" he kept saying over and over again.

"You're gonna be okay, Maloney. Got help coming right now; they'll bring a corpsman. They'll be here soon. Here, bite on this," and I took the wrapper from the bandage and stuck it between his teeth. I could hear mortars firing in the compound, and shortly a half-dozen parachute flares burst overhead, lighting up the whole area.

Jesus fucking Christ! There were three Vietcong running down the road toward me, maybe two hundred meters away, trying to make the cover of the paddy dike. Jesus, shit! I threw myself down prone and opened fire. One of the running figures snapped up straight and dropped over backwards. The other two dove headlong into an irrigation ditch on my side of the road. I kept firing as I crawled back over to the radio. The VC started firing back. I could hear the sharp thwack of bullets striking the dirt around me.

"What is it? What's going on?" Maloney shouted.

"Shut up! Can you reach your rifle? There's VC along the highway. Annunciate, Annunciate; this is Papa One. I'm taking fire. Repeat. I'm taking fire! Three Victor Charlie at least, right along the highway north of me."

"Gimme coordinates, One; I'll get cover fire."

"Coordinates, fuck! I don't even know where the map is, for Chrissake! Roddenbery had it. Where the hell's the relief?"

"This is Annunciate Zulu, Papa One," someone broke in. It sounded like the scouts' radioman. "We're on the highway right in front of the ville. We got muzzle flashes up ahead on the east side of the road."

"That's Charlie, Zulu. I can't see you yet. I'm behind the hooches. I don't think they see you yet either; they're still firing at me. Hurry it up, will you?"

"That's a roger." Small-arms fire opened up on my left, and I could see tracers following the highway toward the VC. The VC fire shifted toward the approaching patrol, then stopped altogether.

"I can see you now, Zulu. Hold your flare, and get off the road— you're an easy target." Illumination rounds were still popping overhead, the burning magnesium hissing loudly, the flares drifting slowly toward earth beneath their tiny parachutes, casting an eerie patchwork of moving light and shadows. Figures moved through the shadows of the hooches. I held my finger on the trigger.

"Hold your fire, Ehrhart; it's us," someone whispered hoarsely. It sounded like Sergeant Wilson.

"Over there," I said to the corpsman, pointing toward Maloney, who was quiet now. "Roddenbery's dead. Jesus Christ, am I glad to see you."

"Welcome to the war, Ehrhart," said Sergeant Wilson. "Calloway, take your fireteam over and find out if we got anyone."

"I think I hit one of 'em," I added.

"You did," said Calloway later during debriefing in the command bunker. "We found a lot of blood on the road, and heavy drag marks. The other two must have taken the body with 'em. Damn! How the hell do they do it? The whole goddamned road was lit up like Broadway. Just once, I'd like to find a dead goddamned gook with a goddamned weapon in his hands."

Just then the corpsman who'd come out with the scouts entered the bunker. "The other guy—Maloney—he just died," he said. "Had a lump of steel in his belly the size of a golf ball."

"Oh, Jesus! I didn't see it," I said. "I didn't see it. I wrapped the leg; he had a big chunk out of his leg. I don't know, I was taking fire, and trying to operate the radio; I didn't have time—"

"You did okay, Ehrhart," said Lieutenant Roberts, the intelligence officer, cutting me off. "It happens. It's not your fault. You got one of them, at least. Don't worry about it. Go get some sleep."

I walked out of the bunker, leaned over with my weight against the sandbag wall, and threw up.

Chapter 14

"All you have to do is answer a few questions," Bart smiled, his exasperation clearly growing. "It's really no big deal. It's just a tradition, that's all."

"Well, I ain't gonna do it, and that's that," I replied. "I've got enough to deal with as it is. I don't need people going out of their way to aggravate me."

"Come on, Bill! Nobody's trying to aggravate you."

"Just forget it," I said. "I'm sorry; I'm not gonna do it."

Bart scratched his head and sank back heavily into his chair. "What's with you, Bill?" he asked. "I don't get it."

"What's with me?" I said. I wasn't sure myself where this iron feeling of revulsion—a combination of distaste, fear, indignation, and anger—had come from. All I knew was that I wasn't going to prostrate myself before some national examiner, or anybody else.

I'd pledged Delta Upsilon fraternity four months earlier at the beginning of spring semester in January, largely at Bart's urging. Aside from Mike Morris, the Kaufman brothers, and several others—none of whom I knew very well—I didn't really know any of the members any better than I knew most other people at Swarthmore.

My decision, in fact, had been motivated by perversity as much as anything. When I'd first suggested to Pam that I might join DU, she'd gotten a stricken look on her face. Faye Mills's reaction had been even stronger. "You want to join DU?" she'd blurted out in total disbelief. "Oh, Bill, they're nothing but a bunch of dumb jocks!"

"Bart's a DU," I'd pointed out. "What's wrong with him? How many DUs do you really know, anyway?"

"Well, I just never thought *you'd* join DU," she'd replied, ignoring my questions, her face contorting as though she'd encountered a bad smell.

"Why not?"

"I just thought you were a little more together," she'd responded. "They're so"—she'd paused, searching for a word—"immature."

"Oh, and my whole personality suddenly changes because I join DU?" I'd snapped. "Is that how much credit you give me? Certainly think a lot of me, don't you?"

"Faye's not saying that, Bill," Pam had said.

"Well, what are you saying, then?"

"You know the kind of reputation DU has," Faye had replied. "I just hate to see you associated with it, that's all."

"Reputation? Oh, yeah, I know a thing or two about reputations. Anybody ever call you a baby-killer? People who don't know me from Adam think they got it all figured out. How do you like it when people write you off as a Jewish American Princess, Faye?''

''That's different!'' Faye had practically shouted, instantly turning red-faced.

''What's different about it? Oh, he's an ex-Marine, he's a DU, she's a JAP. Judgment by stereotype—it's only different when you're the victim. I don't want to hear any more about reputations, ladies; they don't mean jack squat.''

And so I'd pledged DU. And all through the winter and into the spring, I'd gone to the meetings every Tuesday night, sitting there in a corner of the meeting room in my green field jacket drinking Boone's Farm wine from a brown paper bag while the brothers sang, ''Wherever you find two rivers converging to the sea,/You'll find the Delta written there as plainly as can be. . . .'' It had all seemed a little beneath me, and I had never felt comfortable.

Worst of all were the pledge classes. All the prospective new members—the pledges, eighteen-year-olds except for myself— would meet once a week to learn about the history and tradition of the fraternity. Before you could become a member, you had to pass an oral exam administered by the national examiner for DU. It was this test that was the final stumbling block for me, and about which Bart and I were arguing. ''Listen, Bart,'' I tried to explain, ''I don't need any interrogations, that's all. I'm not going to be treated like some kind of prisoner of war. You guys want me in your fraternity, fine. But I'm not going to kiss anybody's ass for it—least of all some national examiner who hasn't got a thing to do with Swarthmore, whom I've never seen before and will never see again.''

''You won't be kissing anybody's ass, Bill,'' Bart insisted.

''You're damn right I won't.''

''Jesus,'' he sighed.

''Look, Bart, I don't think I belong in a fraternity, anyway.''

''You had a good time with water ballet, didn't you?''

''Well, yeah, I guess so.''

''You had a good time with the swimming team, didn't you?''

''Well, yeah.''

''And you got your letter jacket—just like I said you would! So when are you going to start trusting me? The guys like you a lot. They *want* you.''

"Hell, I don't even know most of them, Bart—and they sure as hell don't know me."

"You haven't *tried* to get to know them, Bill."

"Yeah, well, if I did, I probably wouldn't like them anyway. Look what that jerk Paulson turned out to be. Anyway, that's all irrelevant. The point is, I'm not going through with this national examiner crap." I could see it in my mind: like escape and evasion training at Camp Pendleton—only for what? Just to join a lousy fraternity?

Bart massaged his chin slowly. "Ehrhart," he said, "I'll tell you a little secret—but so help me God, if you ever let the cat out of the bag, I'll murder you."

"What?"

"There *is* no national examiner."

"What?"

"The national examiner is a hoax," Bart grinned. "We made it all up. Every year a guy named Oscar Bennett pretends to be the national examiner. He's a DU from the fifties. We go through this whole put-on, and he asks a bunch of stupid questions that don't have anything to do with the stuff in the pledge book. It's a practical joke, that's all. It's just a way to get the guys to learn a little bit about the fraternity and have some fun too."

"Fun? You mean you've made all those pledges sweat it out for the last three months just for laughs?"

"That's right," said Bart, by now grinning from ear to ear.

"That sucks, man!"

"Oh, get off your high horse, Bill. It doesn't hurt anybody. Next year, when you're in on it, you'll think it's the funniest thing you ever did."

"Like hell I will."

"Hey, think about it," Bart said more seriously. "We don't do any hazing here. We don't have a Hell Week. We don't make pledges run around blindfolded in traffic in the middle of the night. This is the only dues you have to pay. That's really pretty tame, if you'd stop to think about it."

"Yeah, well—maybe. Just seems pretty childish to me."

"Geez, how come I always have to *make* you have fun? Lighten up, will you?"

"You really want me to join, don't you?"

"Yes."

"Shit."

"You gonna do it?"

"Yeah, okay," I said slowly, "I guess so."

"That's more like it," Bart smiled. "Now listen, I'm not kidding about the national examiner—you don't breathe a word to anyone. Nobody. If anybody ever found out I told you, I'd be crucified. It's the *only* pledge prank we have, so don't blow it."

"Don't worry," I said, "I won't."

"You're probably the first pledge in DU history to know about it."

"Don't worry, don't worry, I won't say a word to anyone."

"Okay," said Bart. "Be here tomorrow night at seven. The pledges are supposed to go to the house with their Big Brothers. You think you can manage a coat and tie for one evening?"

"Yeah, I suppose so," I said. "But I don't see why."

"Oh, no," Bart laughed. "Don't start again. Just get out of here and come back tomorrow night."

"Slow down," I said. "I gotta ask you something."

"What now?"

"Don't worry, this isn't about DU. I'm applying for dorm proctor next year, and I need a junior or senior to vouch for me with the selection committee."

"But you'll only be a sophomore."

"So what?" I replied. "I'll be twenty-two years old. Hell, man, I had three stripes before most people around here got out of freshman biology. I used to run a fifty-man barracks. I oughta be able to keep the lid on a college dormitory. Anyway, I asked Dean Bradley and he said I could apply. If I get picked, it means I won't have to pay for my room. How about it?"

"Sure," said Bart.

"Thanks! See you tomorrow night."

"I've got a little surprise for the national examiner," I grinned as Bart and I walked down to the DU house the next night.

"Yeah, what?" asked Bart.

"This," I said, pulling a plastic squirt gun out of my pocket. "It's filled with Burgundy wine."

"You can't do that, Bill," said Bart, suddenly alarmed.

"Why not?"

"Come on, if you use that, people will know you were tipped off."

"So what? They won't know who told me."

"Come on, Bill. Can't you just play it straight for one night?

I really stuck my neck out telling you. You owe me one. Give it to me. Please.''

"How come you guys are the only ones that get to have any fun?" I complained, but I handed him the squirt gun. When we reached the house, Bart deposited me in the game room with the other pledges, then went upstairs to the meeting room. The other pledges were sitting around frantically reading through their pledge books, trying to cram in that one last tidbit of knowledge that might make the difference between passing and failing. I sat in a corner by myself, amused by their visible concern.

One by one the pledges were called out. Tension, already running high, increased markedly as each pledge returned and the next one was taken out. The other pledges would gather around the latest returnee, pumping him with questions: "Was it hard?" "What did he ask you?" "Did you pass?" And the center of attention would reply: "Geez, it was brutal! I don't think I passed. They told me to come back down here and wait." In spite of myself, I found my anger rising again. I didn't like the idea of a bunch of near-strangers making sport of me. I was grappling with the idea of leaving when my name was called.

As I stepped into the meeting room it was completely dark except for two candles burning on a table at the other end of the room. The brothers were seated in coats and ties all around the walls, leaving a large empty space in the center of the room. Behind the heavy wooden table, dressed in a black robe, sat the national examiner, his face lit by the two candles.

"Pledge Ehrhart," said the examiner in an ominous tone of voice, "step forward."

I didn't like the atmosphere. I didn't like being some kind of laboratory rat. I walked stiffly to the table and stood rigidly at military attention.

"Pledge Ehrhart," said the examiner in the same tone of voice, "you want to be admitted to the solemn and noble order of Delta Upsilon fraternity. Is this so?"

"Yes, sir," I said, my anger barely under control. No, I didn't like this at all. Assholes. I wished I hadn't relinquished the squirt gun. At least that would have been something. What the hell right did they have to try to make me the butt end of their childish jokes? I'd been playing for keeps while these guys had taken their student deferments and gone off to play for pennies on Easy Street.

"Do you fully understand the seriousness of the responsibilities and obligations you desire to assume?" asked the examiner.

Seriousness, I thought; you bloody fucking bastard! How dare you try to tell me about responsibilities and obligations? I'll tell you about serious, you dumb fuck. Roddenbery blown to shreds like a paper doll. Basinski shot dead on his last day in Vietnam. Rowe drowning in his own blood. Amagasu's arm sheared off above the elbow. I didn't want to be here, and there was no way out. My mind thrashed around inside my head, grasping for something—anything—to shut these people down. I felt like I was going to explode at any moment.

"Under the rules of the Geneva Convention on prisoners of war," I blurted out, "I am required to tell you only my name, rank, branch of service, date of birth, and service number." The minute I spoke, I regretted it, but I couldn't get the words back.

"What is the significance of the three-cornered beaver?" asked the examiner.

And I couldn't shut myself up: "My name is Ehrhart, W. D., Sergeant, U.S. Marine Corps, September 30, 1948, 2279361." I couldn't think of anything else to say. I could feel my face getting hot with embarrassment, the sweat forming in beads along my hairline.

"What is the significance of the bearded clam?" asked the examiner.

"My name is Ehrhart, W. D., Sergeant, U.S. Marine Corps, 9 30-48, 2279361," I said woodenly. God, oh, God, you're making a *fool* of yourself! What am I doing here? I don't want to be a DU. Take your stupid fraternity and shove it! Don't you understand? Leave me alone, you goddamned bastards! Leave me alone!

"What is the first rule of—"

"Ehrhart, W. D.," I shouted, "Sergeant, U.S. Marine—"

Suddenly my face was dripping wet, the examiner was holding my squirt gun, pointing it at me, pumping stream after stream of Burgundy wine into my eyes—Bart! You double-crossing—the lights went on, the brothers cheering and laughing and clapping, Oscar Bennett shaking my hand, the brothers all around me, jostling me, slapping my back, congratulating me, shaking my hand, I hated them all, I hated the fool I'd made of myself, I tried to laugh, I tried to make them all think it had all been a grand joke all around, I could hardly breathe, I was suffocating, suffocating.

Somehow I managed to stand my ground without breaking until the hoopla finally died down and I was able to leave the meeting room without appearing to run. I walked stiffly down the stairs, brushing quickly past the other pledges without speaking, and disappeared into the cool night air.

Chapter 15

The marketplace is very crowded, people and their goods spilling out onto the main street through the center of Hoi An. Saunders barely manages to inch the jeep forward through the sea of alien faces chattering and clucking loudly in their strange tongue not a word of which either of us can understand. It makes me nervous to be so closed in. Hemmed in. Pinned in. I check my rifle to make sure I've chambered a round, then check the safety to make sure it's off. The throng is so close I could reach out and touch the conical straw hats, or crack the side of a head with my rifle butt. They seem oblivious to us. Only with great effort do we manage to force people aside and make any headway at all. Is it paranoia, or are they deliberately trying to impede us? You never know what these people are thinking. Old men with long thin scraggly gray beards. Old women with black teeth and ancient wrinkles. Children with flies buzzing around their ears. All of them inscrutable. And never any young men. Never. Where are these people's sons and brothers? I want to shout at Saunders, "Step on it! Let's go! Run the fuckers over if they won't move!" Is that what I came here for? Why am I here? I used to have a reason—right here in my pocket—but I've lost it, it's gone, it's out there somewhere in the marketplace, lost among the sea of alien faces, and I can't find it, and it hurts. That kid—hey! That kid's got a grenade! "Jimmy! Jimmy! The kid's got a grenade! Step on it!" With the touch of a finger, barely a flicker of effort, a dozen rounds of unforgiving 5.56-millimeter steel send the kid sprawling over backwards into the crowd, arms and legs akimbo like a rag doll, the grenade rolling out of his hand like an egg about to shatter. And then we're beyond it, ducking and flinching and waiting, and then the explosion and the air filled with the screams of the wounded and the dying—

"Hey! Hey, Bill! Wake up!"

"What? What is it?" I was suddenly sitting bolt upright in bed. Mike had a hold of me, a hand on either arm just above the elbows, pinning them to my sides. I was breathing heavily and soaked with sweat; my heart was pounding.

"You were having a nightmare," said Mike gently.

"Oh, Jesus," I said, letting my head fall limply against Mike's chest. He put both arms around me, stroking the back of my head with one hand.

"Are you all right?" Mike asked.

"Yeah, I guess so. Wow. Where am I?"

"San Francisco. My place," said Mike.

My head began to clear. We were docked in Oakland. Mike had met me at the ship last night. "Yeah, okay. I'm okay now."

"What was it this time?" asked Mike.

"Remember that kid I told you about? The one with the grenade?"

"Yeah."

"Him," I said as Mike released his grip on me. "It's funny, you know. All these years, and I don't think I've ever once dreamed about killing armed soldiers in a firefight. It's always the ones they never showed me at the Saturday matinee."

"Well, it would hardly do to have John Wayne killing women and babies, now would it?" Mike laughed.

"John Wayne doesn't surprise me," I said. "The only war he ever fought in was in Hollywood. I wonder about Audie Murphy, though. Did you know that he was the most decorated soldier in World War Two? Man, he musta seen some trash. And then he comes back and spends the rest of his life making hell-for-glory it-was-the-greatest-experience-of-my-life you-oughta-try-it-sometime-kids war movies. What makes a man sell out the truth like that?"

"Money, I suppose," said Mike, shaking his head. "I don't know. Maybe it *was* the greatest experience of his life."

"Yeah, maybe," I replied. "I knew a guy—one of the scouts, guy named Thurston from Kentucky—one time he said to me, 'Hey, shucks, this ain't nothin' but a little ol' squirrel shoot, only the squirrels are cagier.' He got killed up in Hue City. Never could bring myself to feel too bad about it. I mean, it wasn't like I wanted him to get killed or anything, you know? I just think he really didn't notice any difference at all between squirrels and human beings. Scares me to think how many people there are like that just running around loose.''

"Yeah,'' Mike laughed. "Half the people in Washington.''

"Only half?'' I said. "I don't think there's a one of them that feels a blessed thing for anyone but them and theirs. Truth, justice, and the American way means fat dividend checks, lucrative government contracts, private schools for the kids, and fuck anybody and everybody foreign and domestic that's not included in the cocktail circuit. You know, it's really no wonder Archie Davison flipped out. Imagine what guys like Thomas Paine would do if they could see what's happened to their revolution. What is it that keeps *us* from flippin' out, Mike? Is it good sense or simply cowardice?''

"I don't know,'' said Mike. "But I know Lynn Marcus and the National Caucus of Labor Committees certainly aren't the answer. Come on, get up, we gotta get moving.''

But I was thinking. "You know,'' I said, "I've always tried to tell myself that that kid didn't really know what he was doing. Hell, he was just a little kid. I always tell myself some guy down the block gave the kid the grenade and said, 'Here, give this to GI Joe; he'll give you some candy.' But I really wonder. Maybe even at that age, the kid already knew how to hate Americans. That was one of the worst things about it all—I never really hated those people. I tried to, but it never felt very convincing. Even after I'd been there awhile—especially after I'd been there awhile. You just had this creepy feeling that the Vietnamese weren't the enemy at all. None of them. Not even the VC or the NVA. And it turned out to be true, too. But I was *their* enemy. Oh, man, if I had my life to do again.''

"Well, it's not over yet, buddy,'' said Mike. "And if you want to keep your job, you better get moving. It's almost nine.''

I swung my feet over the edge of the bed and stood up unsteadily. "Did we drink that whole bottle last night?''

"We did,'' Mike grinned.

"Ouch. You'd think I'da learned by now. That bacon I smell?''

"Yeah. Coffee's ready, too. You want some eggs?''

"We got time?''

"Yeah,'' said Mike, "but we don't have time to waste. Come on.'' Thirty minutes later, we were headed toward the docks in Oakland. "You ever hear from Denise Sawyer?'' Mike asked.

"No. Move over,'' I said. "There's the exit for the bridge. How we doing on time?''

"Close," said Mike, looking at his watch, "but we'll make it."

"No, I haven't heard from Sawyer, and I don't suppose I'm going to. You know, man, this'll probably sound crazy, but sometimes I think the stuff I did in Vietnam has left me—well, like something inside got broken and isn't ever going to get better. Like I've fallen from grace or something, and I'm never going to be able to climb back again."

"That's nuts," Mike snorted.

"I know it is," I said. "But I just can't figure out any other explanation for it."

"For what?"

"Well, for never being able to find a woman who really loves me, you know, who's willing to deal with the real me, warts and all."

"You've had your share, pal."

"But that's what I mean," I replied. "I've never had all that much trouble attracting women. But where are they now? The minute they start getting a glimpse of what's going on beneath the surface, presto! Gone. Just like that. Just when I'm thinking, 'Maybe this time.' If I believed in God, I'd think it was some kind of divine retribution for all the murder and mayhem."

"Don't talk like that."

"Can't I even talk to *you* about it?" I said. "I've been carrying this stuff around inside me for years, and there's never been anyone I can talk to."

"Hey, knock it off," said Mike, throwing his right arm across the seat and shaking me. "Of course you can talk to me. You know better than that. I just don't like to see you so down, that's all."

"I wish I knew some other way to be," I replied. "It just hurts all the time. All the time. Been seven years now. I went to Vietnam and came back to Mars. 'Ehrhart to Earth, Ehrhart to Earth, come in, please.' But nobody answers. Nothing but static."

"I know," said Mike. "I know it isn't the same, but sometimes I feel like that, too. You didn't have to go to Vietnam to get burned."

"No, I guess not."

"You'll get it together. You just gotta keep hangin' in there."

"Think that's all there is to it, huh?"

"Yep. Basically. Here we are," said Mike, turning in at the entrance to the ARCO dock.

"Holy mackerel!" I shouted. "Hurry up! They're throwing off the lines." We wheeled right up next to the ship as I stuck my head out the window shouting, "Hey, John! Jake! Wait a minute! Leave the gangplank!"

I leaped out of the car as Mike braked to a halt, running around to the driver's side and sticking my head in the window. "Thanks, Mike," I said, leaning in and kissing him on the neck.

"Let me know when you're coming back, okay?" said Mike.

"Yeah, sure, see you soon."

"Take care."

"You, too, Mike."

And then I was up the gangplank and onto the deck.

"Cut that pretty close, didn't you, Ehrhart?" said the first mate.

"I'm here, ain't I?" I laughed. I walked down the deck and leaned over the railing directly above Mike. He was standing beside his car now, looking the ship over from bow to stern.

"You really live on this thing, don't you?" he shouted up.

"Yeah," I called down. "Pretty neat, huh?"

Two tugboats hooted and piped as they jockeyed into position, preparing to haul the great ship away from the dock. Deckhands moved back and forth quickly, coiling heavy ropes and checking lines between the tugs and the *Endeavor*. The ship's steam whistle let out a deafening blast, then another. The tugs answered. I waved one more time to Mike, then walked back to the stern and went below.

Roger was standing down on the maneuvering platform when I entered the engineroom. Because of the noise, I got all the way down and was standing beside him before he realized I was there. He gave a little start when I tapped him on the shoulder.

"Goddamn it, man, don't do that," he shouted in my ear. "Gimme a heart attack. Where did you come from?"

"I just got back," I shouted back.

"Have a good time?"

"Yes."

"Get laid?"

"Hell, no," I said, making a face. "We just went to Mike's place and talked all night. I wish you could meet him."

"What?" Roger hollered. It was next to impossible to carry on a conversation in the engineroom.

"No, I didn't get laid," I shouted, leaning into Roger's ear.

"Maybe next time," he shrugged. "You wanna take it out?" He gestured toward the steam throttles and control panel.

"You serious?"

"Sure! You've watched me do it enough, haven't you?"

"Well, yeah, I guess so."

"Go on, give it a try."

"What do I do?" I asked nervously.

"Just do what I showed you," he shouted. "Watch the telegraph, and give the bridge what they ask for, that's all there is to it."

I stepped up to the throttles, two small wheels like the wheel of an old-time sailing vessel with the spokes protruding beyond the rim, but made of brass and only about eighteen inches across. One controlled the huge forward turbine, the other the smaller stern or reverse turbine. Between them was the telegraph connecting the engineroom with the ship's bridge, where the deck officers were. The telegraph was a large dial with a handle on it, just like you see in the movies. On the face of the dial were marked various speeds from full ahead through dead stop to full reverse. The bridge had a similar device. When the bridge wanted a particular speed, someone up there would move the handle on their telegraph to that position. Simultaneously, down in the engineroom, a small red needle on the dial would move to the speed indicated by the bridge, a bell would ring, and if you were changing not just speed but direction of thrust—forward to reverse or vice versa—a red light would go on. Once the engineroom got a command from the bridge, you would have to move your handle over to match the position of the red needle. At the same time, a red needle on the bridge telegraph would move to the same position, telling the bridge that the engineroom had received and understood the command and would proceed to execute it. Surrounding the throttles and telegraph was a bewildering array of hundreds of dials and gauges recording everything from boiler pressure to turbine revolutions per minute.

You didn't steer from the engineroom, of course. The people on the bridge did that. Deep in the belly of the ship, there were no windows or portholes. You had no idea where you were going or why you were executing a command. All you could do was provide the power—forward or backward—and hope the guys on the bridge knew what they were doing. And what power those engines generated: enough to drive through water at speeds up to twenty miles an hour a fully loaded oil tanker more than two football fields long. It was a real rush. Like riding a steel elephant pell-mell through the jungle.

When the maneuvering bell rang, I almost jumped out of my skin. I gripped the forward throttle with both hands and looked back over my shoulder at Roger. He was sitting on the step at the back of the platform between the two turbines. I started to open the throttle, but he waved me off and pointed to the telegraph. Oh, yeah, acknowledge the bridge; I'd forgotten already. I reached up and pulled the handle over to slow ahead, where the red needle was. Roger gestured with both hands, as though he were turning the throttle himself—ease it open slowly, he seemed to be indicating.

I gave the throttle a quarter turn, watching the RPM gauge begin to climb as the turbine started turning. I nudged the throttle open a little more. The needle on the RPM gauge climbed higher, the turbine whining, the reduction gears grinding into motion, the long fat propeller shaft beginning to turn. The ship began to move under its own power. It was scary, and exhilarating. Ahoy, there, Captain Bligh! Shiver me timbers! This enormous roaring beautiful floating power plant—and I controlled it. Avast, mateys!

I jumped six inches when the bell rang again: half ahead. More power! More power! Pour on the coal, lads! I rang the telegraph over to half ahead, then opened the throttle farther. I was sweating profusely and gripping the wheel as though I would fall forever into the abyss if I lost my grip. Roger made it look so easy, I thought as I tried to watch the boiler pressure, boiler water level, turbine RPMs, and ship's speed all at once—not to mention a hundred other dials that didn't mean a thing to me.

We must be free of the tugs by now, I thought, somewhere out in the bay, cutting through the water on our way out to sea. Passing Alcatraz, perhaps.

The harsh clang of the maneuvering bell brought me around with a start. The red light was on, too! I looked at the telegraph: the red needle indicated dead stop. Dead stop? Jesus H. Christ, we're going to collide with another ship! We're going to run aground! How do you stop this thing?

I gave a mighty heave on the forward throttle, spinning the wheel and shutting down the forward turbine instantly. Then I reached over and threw the stern turbine throttle wide open. Two more lights flashed on in front of me and a siren went off. A siren? Hell's bells! What the hell's going on here? Roger was up beside me, throwing the telegraph handle over to stop. "Shut down the stern turbine!'' he shouted. The telephone from the bridge was ringing. Roger answered it. I couldn't hear what he said. He shrugged his shoulders and hung up. The siren stopped. ''Open the stern throttle again,'' he shouted into my ear. ''Do it slowly. Ease it open. Watch your knot indicator. Shut down again just before it reaches zero.''

He sat back down on the steps. I was twitching like a punch-drunk boxer. Christ, what the hell had happened? There was a muffled banging coming from somewhere. What now? I looked around nervously. Then I looked up. High above us, the chief engineer was banging on the railing with a huge pipe wrench. I thought he was going to throw it at me. He looked angry. He must have been making a heck of a racket, but you could hardly hear the banging down where we were and his voice was lost completely. It was clear, however, that he wanted to know what the devil the wiper was doing at the throttles. Still sitting, Roger grinned nonchalantly and went through a series of gestures that loosely translated into: Don't worry, Chief, everything's under control. The chief threw up his hands, the pipe wrench still in one of them, shook his head, and disappeared out the hatchway. I gestured for Roger to come over.

''Here,'' I said, still shaking. ''Take this thing, will you?''

''What for? You're doing fine,'' he shouted. ''Just remember to answer the telegraph first, and *ease* the throttles open and closed *slowly*. Keep up the good work.'' And he sat back down on the step again.

An hour later, with the ship well beyond the Golden Gate and running north along the California coast toward Oregon, Roger and I sat in his cabin.

''Geez, I thought we'd had it down there,'' I said, letting out a deep breath. ''Half ahead to dead stop. I had visions of us plowing right over top of one of those little harbor tour boats.''

''We were just changing pilots,'' Roger laughed. ''We always change pilots just off Alcatraz. I should have warned you.''

''What was that siren?'' I asked. ''What did I do? It sounded like all hell was breaking loose for a while there.''

''When you threw open the throttle to the stern turbine, you sucked all the steam out of the boilers,'' he explained. ''That's what set the siren off, and that's why I had you shut it down again. You can't do a thing without steam. We hadda let it build up a head again. You gotta remember to handle the throttles gently. When the bridge gives you a command like that, a big change in speed, they don't expect you to stop on a dime. Just take your time and go through the motions slowly. You did pretty good today."

"You really think so?"

"Sure," he said. "First time, what the heck. Once you settled down, you were fine. If I thought you were in any trouble, I would have relieved you. Next time, you'll be an old hand."

"No kidding? I thought I'd blown it royally."

"Nah. You're already better than half the oilers I've sailed with."

"What was that phone call from the bridge?" I asked. "They wanna know what was going on?"

"Yeah."

"What did you tell 'em?"

"I said everything was fine." Roger grinned. "Well, everything *was* fine. I was having a swell time watching you shit bricks."

"You bastard," I said. Roger laughed. "Thanks for letting me do that, Roger. It was fun. Are you gonna get in any trouble?"

"What for? We didn't hit anything or blow up, did we?"

"I don't know," I said. "The chief looked pissed as hell." We looked at each other and cracked up laughing.

"He'll get over it," Roger finally said, wiping the tears from his eyes. "Hey, you wanna hear something interesting?"

"What?" I asked.

"Last night, I was talking to the chief, and I don't know how we got onto it, but I ended up asking him if he'd gone to Vietnam. He's an old Navy man, you know. And you know what he said?"

"If I knew what he said, you wouldn't have to tell me, would you?"

"Well, he said he had orders to go, but he refused them. Retired instead. After twenty-three years. Just walked right out rather than go to Vietnam. Pretty amazing, huh?"

"No kidding?" I said, shaking my head slowly. "Did he say why?"

"He said it was chickenshit," Roger replied. "I was just about to ask him what he meant when we got interrupted by that new second engineer."

"Huh. Twenty-three years and he quits just like that. I wonder why."

"You oughta ask him about it sometime," said Roger.

"Maybe I will. You know the military really went to hell in a basket over there."

"What do you mean?"

"By sixty-nine, they had whole units refusing to take the field," I explained. "And I don't mean just like squads and platoons. I mean companies and battalions refusing to make contact. Damn near the whole army smoking dope or shooting up heroin or both, walking around with peace signs on their flak jackets, refusing to salute their officers. Junior enlisted guys would actually blow up officers and senior NCOs that got too gung ho—it's called fragging because they used fragmentation grenades. Real hard to figure out who did it when the evidence is blown to smithereens."

"Really?" asked Roger in disbelief.

"Oh, yeah," I said. "I'm not kidding. One of the reasons King Richard finally got the troops out was that the generals told him he *had* to get 'em out while they still had anything left that resembled an army at all. I know guys who were over there in the later years, and it was bad. What the hell, man, everybody knew the war was bullshit from 1968 on. Nobody wanted to be the last man to die for Peace with Honor. Can ya blame 'em? There's fuckin' Nixon on the Great Wall of China—"

Just then, there was a knock on the door.

"Come in," Roger shouted. It was the new second engineer.

"Ehrhart," he said, "Winston told me I'd probably find you here. I need your help in the engineroom. We've got some oil you've got to clean up."

"Yeah, okay, I'll be right down. This guy's gonna bust my chops," I said to Roger after the second engineer had left. "I don't think I like him very much. Treats me a bit too much like the hired help, you know?"

"Hang in there," Roger laughed. "I don't think he'll last very long. He doesn't know what he's doing."

"Well, I hope they get him off before he gets me killed. I'll see you later."

Chapter 16

"Please excuse me for interrupting the concert," said a student I didn't know, "but I have an important announcement to make. Tonight American soldiers have invaded neutral Cambodia." A loud murmur arose from the audience, punctuated by boos and hisses. "For anyone who's interested, there will be a meeting convening immediately in Tarbles to organize resistance activities."

Oh, bloody hell, I thought, why tonight? Couldn't I spend even one evening without the war? I'd paid good money to see this band, and they were putting on one hell of a good show, and I didn't want it to end—not yet at least, and certainly not because of a goddamned war ten thousand miles away. I wanted to stand up and shout, "God damn you all! Can't you leave me alone?"

There just seemed to be no getting away from Vietnam. You opened a newspaper, and there was J. Edgar Hoover tracking down ruthless Communist agitators. You turned on the television, and there was John Chancellor giving the weekly casualty figures like baseball box scores—Vietcong: one run, three hits, no errors; Yankees: three runs, 519 wounded, 127 dead. You turned on the radio, and there was the WDAS disc jockey asking, "Hey, is the war over yet?" And after eight months at Swarthmore, still there was the steady succession of strangers and their questions: "Hi! I'm Blah Blah Blah. . . ."

All right! All right! It had been a mistake. There weren't going to be any victory parades or heroes' welcomes or free drinks in bars. I'd cast the dice for glory, and I had lost. I concede, I yield, I surrender. But resistance activities? What on God's green earth did these people know about war and resistance? People younger than they were had fought me to the death with sticks and stones and homemade bombs. What are you going to do, kids, send flowers to the Pentagon?

Besides, hadn't Lyndon Johnson been driven from office for persisting in the war? Hadn't Richard Nixon promised to get the United States unstuck from the tar baby? I didn't want to believe that Spiro Agnew—with his rabid attacks on the nattering nabobs of negativism—was the real voice of Richard Nixon. I didn't want to believe that John Stennis—with his fist-pounding vow never to allow the American flag to be dragged home through the mud of dishonor and defeat—was the real voice of American policy in Asia. I wanted to believe that the war was winding down, that it would soon go away and leave me alone, that beneath the awful nightmare there still existed a nation and a government fundamentally good, still honorable, still worth believing in.

And most of all, I didn't want to deal with it. I'd done my time in the ricefields and mangrove swamps and sand barrens. For what it was worth, I'd survived. It was somebody else's problem now. Hadn't I earned the right to get on with my life?

God almighty, I'd only tried to do my duty as my duty had been taught to me by parents, teachers, and elders of every stripe. I had done what my nation had asked of me. How much longer would I have to go on paying for it? There were times in the dead of night, alone with my thoughts and nightmares, when I almost wished that nameless faceless NVA rocketeer who'd splattered me with steel slivers in Hue City had been a better shot. He couldn't have missed my head by more than a foot, perhaps less, we'd calculated later. How many times already had those few inches come back to taunt me?

Not that anyone at Swarthmore ever realized the turmoil that was tearing at me. The great myth of war holds that combat is the ultimate test of manhood, and that once a man has been to war, he has been initiated into the realm of greater wisdom. He has been to the mountain and stared into the great abyss beyond, and having done so, the ordinary concerns of mortal beings can never again hold real importance or significance, dwarfed as they are by the brilliant clarity of the struggle between life and death. All Quiet on the Western Front. The Red Badge of Courage.

And in spite of my classmates' passionate opposition to the war in Vietnam, most if not all of them had bought into the myth as readily as any blue-collar kid from South Boston. As early as October, when no one at Swarthmore knew me from Adam, the

Phoenix reporter had written: "But the usual freshman problems don't seem so difficult to him. Most things don't. Because Bill Ehrhart spent thirteen months in Vietnam, and after that nothing seems quite as hard." The proctor selection committee had chosen me to be the first sophomore dorm proctor in the history of the school, citing my maturity, perspective, and experience as reasons for the precedent-setting decision. The brothers of DU, it turned out, had found my performance before the "national examiner" a remarkably clever practical joke, full of poise, wit, and good humor.

I was unflappable, down to earth, together. A bit strange, perhaps, a bit aloof—but wasn't that to be expected from a man who had lived on the knife-edge of eternity and survived? The silence of the wounded beast was mistaken for the silence of wisdom. The degree of respect accorded to me by my peers—even the ones who must have been utterly repulsed by everything they thought I stood for—astounded me. Christ, they didn't even *know* me. They had only their misconceptions, and their preconceived notions derived from the same Audie Murphy movies and biographies of John Paul Jones that had led me to Vietnam.

Well, what was I supposed to do? Wear a sandwich board? Take out an ad in the school newspaper? "Hey, really, gang, I'm all messed up; I'm a walking time bomb." Hell, I was perfectly happy to have them think I was Joe Cool. Even Pam, who had long since begun to feel the heat from the fire raging inside, had no idea where the fuel was coming from—and I was incapable of explaining it to her. As for the others, let 'em think what they liked. It was no business of mine. I had enough to deal with without spilling my guts all over campus. I didn't care what they thought or did so long as they left me alone.

But they wouldn't. And now here they were again, bringing their stupid war into Clothier Hall and ruining my concert. I wanted to strangle somebody.

One of the musicians stepped to the microphone. "I realize there are more important things than music," he began. I bit my lip with anger. "We won't be offended if anyone wants to leave now and go to the meeting. But we've come a long way to play tonight, and if anyone wants to stay, we'll keep playing as long as we have an audience. We're going to take a short break now, and if anyone's still here when we get back, we'll just pick up where we left off."

Well, the saints be praised, I thought, at least somebody's got some sense around here; let's get on with it.

"Bill, your lip's bleeding," said Pam. "What did you do to it?" I reached up with my hand and came away with blood.

"Beats me," I replied.

Chapter 17

"Bill, they're having another meeting this afternoon over in Tarbles," Pam said when she returned from lunch the next day.

"Yeah? So what?"

"I think I'll go over." She paused. "Do you want to come along?"

"No," I said. I walked over to the window and looked over toward the front entrance to Tarbles Student Center. A large hastily hand-painted banner hung over the steps: Strike for Peace.

"You don't mind if I go, do you?" she asked.

"What the hell do I care?" I said impatiently. "Do what you like. It's a free country. I've got work to do." I sat down at the desk with my back to Pam and opened the first book I grabbed.

"Bill?"

"What?"

"Nothing," she said, kissing me on the back of the head. "I brought you some lunch. It's in my purse."

"Thanks," I said without looking up. "See ya later."

Strike for peace, I thought. Yeah, right. What the hell good will it do? Then I thought of the Cambodian invasion: Why? What the hell good would *that* do? What the hell good was anything?

After the announcement the previous night, two-thirds of the students in Clothier had left. But the Allman Brothers, true to their word, had gone on playing until nearly four-thirty A.M. for the small remaining audience. I'd been too tired to think by the time Pam and I had gotten back to her room, but I'd awakened around noon thinking about Cambodia. It didn't make sense. Why? What did they hope to gain? How do you wind down a war by invading another country? I hadn't gone to lunch—I knew the whole dining hall would be buzzing over the invasion; I didn't want to talk about it.

The afternoon crawled by interminably slowly. From time to time, I could hear muffled cheers and shouts coming through the open window from Tarbles. I stared at one book after another, but the words blurred on the pages like fresh ink in a thunderstorm.

What I saw was the newsreels of Allied soldiers rolling through French villages, the streets lined with cheering people, young girls in full skirts and puffy white blouses leaping out of the crowds, hugging the grinning grimy soldiers, thrusting fresh flowers into their hands, planting kisses on their stubbled cheeks, delirious with joy.

I saw the small Buddhist temple we'd discovered in a clearing one day up near the Horseshoe, knocking it down with a heavy wooden sawhorse, two scouts at a time wielding the sawhorse like a battering ram, beating against the walls until the concrete building had finally given up the struggle and surrendered.

I saw the cluster of small children begging food from the passing truck convoy headed north on the road to Dong Ha and Operation Lancaster along the DMZ, their tiny Asian eyes suddenly going round as quarters and white as virgin snow as the scouts rose up from the truck bed, hurling down small hard cans of C rations like missiles amid a hail of bloodcurdling shouts, tiny mouths flying open, tiny arms and legs flying in every direction, cans bouncing off chests and shoulders and heads, tiny bodies going down like sandbags.

I saw the photograph I'd taken off the body of a young Vietcong guerrilla after an ambush: seven young women in peasant garb, three standing, four kneeling, all holding automatic Russian assault rifles, all smiling with grim determination. And the young woman in the mortar pit in Hue. And the figure in black running along the tree line at the edge of the ricefield, the sharp crack of my rifle, the figure suddenly spinning through space like a scrap of paper caught in a gust of high wind. And the old man—the old man, his hands tied behind his back, going down as though he'd been struck on the back of the head by a flying brick.

The door opened and Pam stepped into the room. "Hi, babe," she said.

"Hello."

"Did you get a lot done?"

"Enough."

"Bill, you aren't angry, are you?"

"What for?" I said irritably. "No, I'm not angry."

"Do you want to go to supper?" she asked, sitting down on the bed.

"No," I said. I got up and kicked at a blouse lying on the floor. "Why the hell you gotta leave this place looking like a pigpen all the time?" I snapped. "I always end up picking up after you. Christ, you'd think you'd be old enough to clean up after yourself by now."

"Oh, come on, Bill," she said, reaching down and picking up the blouse.

"Oh, come on, yourself!" I shouted, suddenly whirling and kicking the large tin can of pretzels sitting on the floor by the closet. The can crumpled against the closet door, the lid flying off and the room instantly filled with a shower of pretzel fragments.

Pam laughed.

In a flash, I turned and struck her flush on the shoulder with a closed fist, hurling my whole body into the blow. It knocked her sprawling across the bed.

Utter silence.

She didn't scream. She didn't cry. She just lay there staring up at me with a look of abject, naked, raw terror in her eyes.

Oh, God almighty, what have I done? Here it was, here it was at last: Pam's eyes were the same eyes I'd seen in a thousand faces in a hundred villages, staring up at me in mute hatred as I towered over her, my whole body still cocked, ready to explode again. And this time there was no rifle, no uniform, no Sergeant Taggart barking orders, no mines, no snipers, no grenade ready to explode, no juggernaut momentum of a vast military bureaucracy out of control and bogged down in human quicksand, not a single excuse with which to defend myself.

So this is what you are, I thought. I felt dizzy and sick to my stomach. I was paralyzed. Boom, boom, boom, the blood pounded through my temples. I couldn't move, couldn't open my fist, couldn't uncock my arm.

And then I collapsed like a house of cards. "Pam, Pam!"— my arms reaching out for her—"Pam!" She brushed my hands

away as though they were vermin, and huddled tightly against
the wall.

"Get out," she growled in a low cold voice.

"Pam, baby, please forgive me, I'm sorry—"

"Get out! Leave me alone! Get out!"

"Pam, please, Pam—"

"Go away!" she shrieked at the top of her lungs, bursting into
loud gut-wrenching sobs, as though someone had torn her heart
out. "Pleeease! Go away!"

I stood up stiffly and walked out of the room. I don't know
where I went. I must have walked for eight hours. It was nearly
two A.M. when I finally reached my room in Pittenger. I sat down
at my desk and pulled out a glass and a bottle of whiskey.

When I woke up, it was late afternoon. I was lying on the
floor, the empty whiskey bottle lying beside me in a sticky pool
of dried whiskey. I had a large lump on my head. The radio was
on: " . . . students wounded, at least four killed. A spokesman
in the governor's office said that Guard troops had been called to
the campus the night before to quell violent protests in the wake
of the Cambodian invasion. This just in from Wall Street—"

What? What? I reached up and searched the dial for another
news broadcast. I got up and went down the hall to Chris Strain's
room. "What's this about students killed someplace? I just caught
the end of a news broadcast. Have you heard anything?"

"You haven't heard yet?"

"No," I said. "What? What happened?"

"You weren't at the strike meeting this afternoon?"

"No! What happened?"

"The Ohio National Guard shot down a dozen students at Kent
State University this afternoon. Killed four of them. Murdered
them in cold blood."

"Oh, Jesus," I said. It felt like someone had knocked the wind
out of me.

"You look like hell," said Chris. "Are you okay?"

"Yeah, yeah," I said, turning and walking out.

My head wasn't cut, but the bump was as big as an egg. I got
cleaned up, walked down the street to the drugstore, and bought
a newspaper. "Four Students Killed at Kent State," read the
headline. I sat down on the curb and read for a while. Then I got
up again and went back to my room.

It isn't enough to send us halfway around the world to die, I
thought. It isn't enough to turn us loose on Asians. Now you

are turning the soldiers loose on your own children. Now you are killing your own children in the streets of America. My throat constricted into a tight knot. I could hardly breathe.

One of the photographs accompanying the article showed a line of national guardsmen on the crest of a low hill. Another showed a young woman kneeling on the ground, her mouth twisted open in a scream, her face contorted with rage and anguish and shocked disbelief, her eyes swollen with tears, her arms outstretched toward the corpse of a man lying facedown in a pool of blood.

It was a photograph of Pam! Pam! And look there! Among the soldiers! That's me! The third one on the left! No! No!

And then I was crying. Dreams, dreams, broken dreams. How in God's name had my life come down to this? Why? Why? Why? Dear God, please, somebody. Was there no bottom to it? I must have cried for a solid half hour, maybe longer. I cried until I couldn't cry anymore. I cried until there was nothing left inside and my mind was more lucid than it had ever been before.

And then I knew. It was time—long past time—to put aside excuses and pride and vain illusions. Time to forget all that was irretrievably lost. Time to face up to the hard, cold, utterly bitter truth I'd tried to avoid for nearly three years. The war was a horrible mistake, and my beloved country was dying because of it. America was bleeding to death in the ricefields and jungles of Vietnam, and now the blood flowed in our own streets.

I did not want my country to die.

I had to do something.

It was time to stop the war.

And I would have to do it.

Chapter 18

Tarbles Student Center was jammed with people the next day. There were several hundred students, and many faculty members.

There were also representatives—complete with banners and information tables—from the Black Panthers, National Caucus of Labor Committees, New Mobilization, Students for a Democratic Society, American Friends Service Committee, Women Strike for Peace, Women's International League for Peace and Freedom, War Resisters League, and Fellowship of Reconciliation. I hesitated for a moment just outside the front door.

Did I really want to be here? Wasn't it a kind of betrayal? Less than three years earlier, my buddies and I had whiled away idle hours thinking up imaginative ways of dealing with the peaceniks and demonstrators: decapitation, castration, dynamite, boiling oil. We'd thought of everything: trampling them with elephants, shooting them into deep space, force-feeding them chocolate chip cookies, sending them to Russia in lead boats. Was I really going to become *one* of them now?

But I'd made up my mind. I took a deep breath and entered the building.

As I walked in, someone was in the midst of a speech. He was standing in the middle of the large main room with people seated on the floor all around him and still others perched on the balcony that ran around all four walls of the room. "We must act *now!* We must take this strike off the campuses and go out into Middle America where the votes are and *educate* the people. . . ."

I scanned the crowd nervously, almost bolting and running when I spotted Pam sitting with Faye and Pat Doyle, the woman who hadn't given me the time of day since I'd declined to join the November Moratorium. A vision of Pam's terror-stricken face rose up inside, grabbing my stomach and wrenching it violently. I hadn't seen her or talked to her for two days. The lump on my head still throbbed, and the cut on my lip was still tender. I forced myself to enter the room and sit down on the floor. If Pam had seen me, she gave no indication of it.

Speaker after speaker took the floor, asking for help in organizing, explaining this demonstration or that project, this group's activities and that group's point of view. What do we do? How do we do it? The tone of the assembly startled me. There was anger and tension. But there was also a tremendous unity, a sense of common purpose, a ferocious energy searching for constructive alternatives and solutions. Suggestions for violent action, when they arose at all, were greeted with hoots of derision and pleas for restraint: "If we do that, we're no better than they are!"

The emphasis was on dialogue and discussion: educate, rationalize, convince, convert.

I hadn't known what to expect. Would I be joining the ranks of Spiro T.'s pinhead pinkos and traitors? Would I end up in the midst of a Chicago-style pandemonious circus-turned-riot? Would someone thrust a Vietcong flag into my hands and tell me to deliver it to the White House? Certainly I hadn't expected to find so many people—so many divergent attitudes and opinions and ideas—all groping for some *sensible* direction that might lead to an end to the war.

Were these the crazies I would have relegated to the Furies of Hell only a few years earlier? Had their message changed, or had I not been listening? Had they become more human, or had I? As the afternoon wore on I found myself wanting to get up and speak, too. I had no idea what to say, but I wanted these people to know that I was with them, that I wanted what they wanted. Finally, still with no clear idea of what to say, I stood up and asked to be recognized.

"Most of you already know that I served in Vietnam," I began. I explained why I had enlisted, and what I had seen and done in Vietnam, and how I had tried for more than two years to ignore the war, hoping it would somehow just go away. I talked about a lot of things: the friends I'd lost, the resentment I'd felt toward my peers and classmates at Swarthmore, the difficulty of admitting that the war and my part in it had been a mistake, the urgent need I now felt to become involved. I must have talked for fifteen or twenty minutes, though I can't remember all that I said or how I said it.

What I remember is a multitude of faces all around me, intent, listening, staring in silence; my voice repeatedly wanting to break, so that I had to pause now and then to regain control of it; the people sitting on the floor of the balcony, their legs poking through the vertical supports of the picket-fence-like railing, seeming to dangle in space; the sound of an electric fan; the surge of pent-up emotions inside—fear, sadness, nervous exhilaration—rising and rolling through me like a great wave on the ocean. And I remember thinking: Is this what it's like to go to confession?

And then I was empty of words. I stood in the middle of the room for a moment longer. I was vaguely aware that aside from the fan, there was a total absence of noise or motion. I sat down again. I noticed that a girl sitting nearby was crying into a red

bandanna. I wondered why. Then a few people began to clap:
one here, one there, another one up in the balcony. Then all at
once, a great burst of applause exploded, sustaining itself at fever
pitch for many minutes like rolling thunder. It was hard to con-
nect the applause to myself or anything I had said. I felt light-
headed and giddy.

And then someone was kneeling in front of me and putting her
arms around my shoulders and drawing my head to her breasts.
Pam. Pam! I reached out and held on to her. "I love you, Pam;
I love you. Please don't leave me."

"I won't, Bill," she was saying. "I'll never leave me. Everything's going to be all right. You're wonderful. I love you." I
lifted my face and looked into hers. "Don't cry," she said.
"Everything's going to be all right." And then she leaned forward and kissed me deeply. The applause, which had at last
begun to die down, erupted anew, this time accompanied by
cheering, whistling, and good-natured catcalls.

Chapter 19

"But, Bill, we've hardly seen each other for two weeks!" Pam
pleaded. "Can't we just have a couple of hours to ourselves? It's
a beautiful day out. Let's go for a walk by the creek."

It was true. Since my first appearance at Tarbles, I'd been
going almost nonstop. Within minutes after I'd given my little
speech, I'd been deluged with requests to go here and help out
there: leafleting the workers at the local Westinghouse plant,
picketing the U.S. Army Induction Center in Philadelphia, speaking to the students and faculty of Nether Providence High School.
And when I wasn't on the road, I was in Tarbles attending meeting after endless meeting. Pam had tried to keep pace with me
for a few days, but had quickly tired of it.

"What's more important, Pam?" I asked. "Taking a walk or stopping this damned war?"

"That isn't fair," she said with a hurt look.

"Look, you wanted me to get involved," I said, "so I get involved—and now you *don't* want me to be involved. Make up your mind, will you?"

"Of course I want you to be involved," she argued. "I'm proud of you. Honestly. But you don't have to be a fanatic about it."

"Fanatic? What the hell do you mean by that?"

"Forget it. I'm sorry. Forget it."

"No. Why did you say that?" I insisted.

"Well, you're acting like you've got some kind of messiah complex or something," she said. "Like you think you're going to end the war all by yourself by next Tuesday. Don't you understand why everybody wants you to do all these things? You're their token Vietnam veteran, Bill. You're just their nigger, that's all."

"God damn you," I shouted, "you shut your mouth." I took a step toward her. She recoiled and put her hands up in front of her face.

"Don't you dare hit me! You asked me what I meant, and I told you. It's not my fault if you don't like it."

The worst part was that the thought had occurred to me already: that people were no more interested in Bill Ehrhart than they'd been two weeks earlier, that I was still only Swarthmore's real live Vietnam veteran and was only useful because I lent credibility to a bunch of academics and college kids. I'd tried not to think about it, and when I couldn't avoid it, I'd force myself to remember that it didn't matter; what mattered was stopping the war, and if these were the allies I had to work with, then so be it.

"I'm not going to hit you," I said. "Christ, what do you think I am?" Suddenly my stomach knotted as I thought about my own question. "Look, I'm sorry, but I've got to be doing this. I've been silent too long already. I'm going down to that rally at Widener College this afternoon. Do you want to come along or not?"

"No," said Pam.

"Suit yourself," I said. "I'll see you later."

The featured speaker at the rally that afternoon was Jane Fonda. I tried to listen to her, but I couldn't concentrate. I kept having flashbacks: How many times in Vietnam had we sworn to cut off Dr. Spock's penis and stuff it down Jane Fonda's throat if we ever got the chance? And now here she was, not a hundred feet away. I kept seeing this image of her up there, trying to talk with a huge cock stuffed into her face. "Mumble, mumble," she'd be saying, a look of terrified befuddlement on her face. And then Dr. Spock would appear, running around pulling his hair like Larry of the Three Stooges and screaming, "Give me back my dick, give me back my dick!" Once I even burst out laughing. The people around me must have thought I was wacko.

Later I noticed a group of guys standing beneath a banner reading Vietnam Veterans Against the War. I went over and began talking with them, and they quickly invited me to join them after the rally. We went to a basement room that served as their meeting place. There was a guy in a wheelchair, and he started crying, and a couple of other guys started crying, and all of them appeared to be three sheets to the wind on beer and pot, and they all began to rant about government conspiracies and war crimes and genocide. It made me very uneasy, like some sort of Bizarro World American Legion, and I left as quickly as civility allowed.

The next day, I was getting dressed in Pam's room when Pam said, "Bill, I'm going home today."

"What are you talking about?" I asked.

"I'm going home today," she said. "This afternoon. I called Dad yesterday, and he's picking me up around two."

"Why? When are you coming back?"

"Bill, I've finished everything but a couple of papers," she explained. "I can finish them at home and mail them in. I just want to get away from here."

"Why? What—why are you leaving? The term doesn't end for another week. We've got another week together."

"Together? When do I ever see you?"

"So that's it?" I said, shaking my head. "So you really do want me to choose between you and the war."

"No, Bill, can't you understand? I just want to get home. It's been a long year. I just want to get away from here for a while."

"You mean you just want to get away from me."

"It hasn't got anything to *do* with you. Please—"

"Nice of you to tell me now. Couldn't tell me last night, huh? Couldn't tell me three hours ago."

"I didn't want to get into an argument over it," she said. "I was afraid you'd just get angry. You frighten me when you're angry.''

"So you just run out on me at the last minute instead."

There was a knock on the door. "Bill, it's Pat Doyle. Are you ready to go yet?''

"Yeah, yeah, be right with you. I gotta go, Pam. Jesus, can't you even wait till I get back?''

"I'll ask Dad if he has time to wait. I don't know. It'll take me a while to pack, anyway. When will you be back?''

"One-thirty, two, two-thirty, I don't know. Pam, why are you doing this to me?''

"I'm not *doing* anything to you, Bill! I just want to go home. Can't you understand?''

"Bill," Pat hollered from the hall, "we really have to go. We'll be late.''

"Okay, okay!" I shouted. "Listen, Pam, you be here when I get back.''

Pat and I went over to Tarbles where we met an economics professor and another student. The four of us were going to speak to the Swarthmore Rotary Club that day. We walked across campus and through town to the Inglenook Restaurant where the Rotary met. I didn't feel comfortable with Pat. She hadn't said ten words to me from November until the day I'd given my little speech. But that afternoon, she'd come up to me all smiles, gushing something about how much I'd changed and how she never realized I had it in me, and I'd wanted to shout, "Hey, asshole, why didn't you ever bother to find out what I got in me?" But I'd kept my mouth shut, delivering a polite tight-lipped thank-you. It must have been fairly convincing; thereafter, she had practically adopted me, volunteering me for everything from picket duty to this speaking engagement. Now was not the time to argue about one's allies, I kept telling myself.

First the members of Rotary sang a few songs about fellowship and good cheer. Then we all had lunch. Then, one after another, Professor Pierce, Pat, and the other student went up to the podium and spoke. At last it was my turn.

"I would like you to understand at the outset," I began, reading from the notecards I'd prepared, "that I am a former Marine Corps sergeant honorably separated from active duty. I served thirteen months in Vietnam with the First Marine Division, earning the Purple Heart, the Navy Combat Action Ribbon, two Presidential Unit Citations, and the Good Conduct Medal.''

I paused to let my credentials sink in.

"I do not doubt for a moment the sincerity of our commitment to Vietnam. But based on my experience there, and the course of events since, I am deeply convinced that we cannot win this war without destroying Vietnam in the process. Believe me, if you really knew what was happening in Vietnam, you would understand that the basic rifleman in the field knows more than all the generals and politicians combined. I have seen unarmed men and women shot down on routine patrols and magically transformed into Vietcong guerrillas killed in action. I have seen whole hamlets destroyed by napalm because a single sniper fired a single shot at an American patrol. I have seen heavy artillery fired night after night into populated civilian areas because those areas were presumed to be hostile. And of course, in the face of such treatment, the prophecy is self-fulfilling. We set out to help the Vietnamese withstand the threat of communism, but everything we have done has only alienated the Vietnamese and driven them into the Communist camp. And who are these Communists? Are they Russians? Are they Chinese? No, they are the Vietnamese themselves. It is we who are the foreigners in Vietnam. We do not speak their language. We do not understand their culture. Moreover, the government we are backing has no support among the people, except for the wealthy and privileged who are wealthy and privileged at our expense and the expense of the Vietnamese people. That government is perceived as nothing more than an American puppet—and the perception is not without foundation. I have known of Saigon-appointed district chiefs who sold rice they were supposed to give away free. I have known Vietnamese national police who sold American weapons and equipment for their own profit. You must try to understand that it is us the Vietnamese wish to be liberated from, and thus we cannot liberate them. We can only conquer them—and I would hope that America is not a nation of conquerors."

My audience listened with impassive faces. I had no idea what they thought of what I was saying. I took a drink of water and continued:

"If all of this seems a little unbelievable, only think back to the Tet offensive of two years ago. For years we heard about the light at the end of the tunnel. What happened to that light? How was it possible, after three years of direct American combat support, three years of optimistic progress reports, for the Vietcong and North Vietnamese to launch so widespread and devastating

an offensive? I believe it was because they had at least the tacit
support of the people. I fought in Hue City against several thousand North Vietnamese regulars. There is no way so many soldiers could have been infiltrated into that city without *anyone*
having the slightest idea what was going on. *No one* can terrorize
the entire population of so large a city into such absolute and
unbroken silence. I had thought it was clearly understood two
years ago that the only reasonable course of action was disen-
gagement as soon as possible. But the invasion of Cambodia has
filled me with renewed fear that the Nixon administration has lost
sight of reality as badly as the Johnson administration before it.
While politicians negotiate the shapes of tables in Paris, and generals try to 'Vietnamize' an army that lacks all passion of belief,
the death and destruction continue unabated—indeed, are now
increased to alarmingly new levels. What purpose can be served
by the invasion of Cambodia? If we penetrate ten miles, the Vietnamese will only withdraw ten miles. If we advance ten miles
farther, they will only withdraw another ten miles into the impenetrable jungle. This isn't some isolated Pacific island. This
isn't like the boundary between Pennsylvania and Maryland. It's
jungle! Mountainous triple-canopied tropical rain forest. Hundreds
and thousands of miles of it. U.S. firepower and technology are
virtually useless, while the lightly armed and equipped Vietnamese can move when and where they want with virtual impunity.
Each time we advance, they need only withdraw and wait for us
to retreat. Will we commit another half million men to chase
them out of Cambodia? What then? Do we pursue them into
Thailand? And then on to Burma? How many more Americans
must die to justify the thousands that have already died? How
many more billions of dollars that could have been spent for the
needs of Americans will go up in useless smoke and flame in
Vietnam? There comes a time when American patriots must urge
peace instead of war. Henry David Thoreau went to jail rather
than pay taxes to support the American war in Mexico. Yet today
Thoreau is revered and respected. Who will be the heroes of the
Vietnam War? Men like me who fought there, or those who argue
for an end to further killing and senseless destruction? Those who
answer every broken illusion with still more violence, or those
who recognize that there are better places and better circumstances in which to defend the cause of freedom? When the most
powerful nation on earth ceaselessly pounds and pummels a nation of rice farmers and fishermen, where is the honor? Why are

we so determined to save the Vietnamese, who so clearly do not want or understand our help? Worst of all, the war in Vietnam is tearing our own country apart. The demonstrations and protests grow in number, size, and anger by the week, and the backlash response increases correspondingly—and now Americans are killing other Americans in the streets of America. It is time to stop trying to save Vietnam and begin trying to save America. I urge you with all my heart to do everything in your power to halt the invasion of Cambodia and bring an immediate end to the war in Vietnam. The finest tribute we can pay to the men who have already paid the ultimate price in Vietnam is to see to it that no more Americans have to pay that price for a cause that is already beyond recovery. No matter how noble our original intentions, the war in Vietnam has been a tragic mistake. But I would hope we are a noble enough people to admit our mistakes and do our best to correct them. We must not compound the tragedy of Vietnam by letting it continue. Thank you for your time and attention."

I emptied my water glass and sat down. There was a brief round of applause that barely qualified as polite. Then a tall thin elderly man with short gray hair raised his hand and was given the floor.

"As most of you already know," he began, "I'm a retired Army colonel. And I'd like *you* to understand, young fella, that *I* am a pacifist. *But,*" he added emphatically, punctuating the word with a bony index finger thrust decisively in my direction, "I am a pacifist with a *choice.*"

At some length, and with frequent references to God, the Founding Fathers, freedom, democracy, the United States Constitution, communism, atheism, apple pie and motherhood, Joseph Stalin, treason, the New York Yankees, welfare moochers, hippies, Puerto Ricans, dirty little rice-propelled slopes, heroes, cowards, and the Old Testament, the retired Army colonel went on to explain something which amounted to:

"I'm a pacifist so long as everybody else thinks exactly the way I think and believes exactly what I believe and recognizes that the policies, decisions, and actions of the U.S. government are the direct will of God delivered from on high by the Angel Gabriel. But if some son of a bitch disagrees in any way, shape, or form, I'll kick the living shit out of him with napalm and baseball bats and B-52s, and God will bless me for it."

I couldn't believe what I was hearing. This guy was a maniac, a lunatic! Without pausing, the retired Army colonel then went on to explain that he had served in Vietnam in 1954, that his son had served there in 1962, and that his grandnephew was serving there even at this very moment. "And I'm *proud,*" he concluded, staring directly at me as he drew his thin frame up to its full height like a bayonet balanced on its handle, "I'm *proud* that three generations of my family have defended the cause of freedom and served this country honorably in Vietnam."

The Swarthmore Rotary Club gave the retired Army colonel a standing ovation.

"Jesus Christ almighty, those assholes didn't hear a word I said," I fumed to Pat as we walked back to the college.

"What was that garbage about sincere commitments and noble mistakes you laid on those people?" Pat asked. "You don't really believe that crap, do you?"

"Hey, just get off my fuckin' back, lady!" I snapped. "You aren't ever satisfied, are you? I've had just about enough of you for one lifetime."

"Well, I was just asking," she sniffed. "You don't have to get testy about it." She stopped walking and stood there looking at me.

"Ah, go fuck yourself," I said, leaving her standing there.

When I got back to Pam's room, Pam was gone.

Chapter 20

The taxi ride from Treasure Island navy base to San Francisco airport had been a major disappointment, to say the least. I'd been waiting thirteen long months for my first glimpse of America, but the fog covering the entire Bay Area had been impenetrable. I hadn't been able to see a thing. On top of that, I'd had a cabbie who was convinced that we could win the war simply by sending the soldiers over for the duration. "Bet that would make you guys fight a little harder, wouldn't it?'' He'd bent my ear for ten straight minutes, and then I'd pretended to fall asleep. It was early March 1968.

Once inside the terminal, I immediately purchased a one-way ticket to Philadelphia and checked my seabag. The clerk asked if I wanted to check the captured rifle I was carrying, looking at it nervously, but I told her I'd carry it on. "Okay," she said hesitantly. "Your flight leaves at eleven forty-three; concourse D. Have a good flight."

Eleven forty-three A.M. I had three hours to kill. I bought a magazine at a newsstand and sat down in the middle of San Francisco airport. It was bustling with people. Men in business suits carrying briefcases. Women in skirts and matching jackets, many of the skirts short like the ones Dorrit had worn in Hong Kong. Miniskirts. Bare legs everywhere. It was enough to drive you crazy.

There were also a number of people, most of them more or less my age, dressed in faded blue jeans and denim workshirts and pieces of green utility uniforms with rank insignia on the sleeves. A young couple sat nearby on the floor against the wall, backpacks and rolled-up sleeping bags gathered about them like a fortress. Both had very long hair held out of their faces with brightly colored headbands, and strings of beads hung from their necks. When the woman moved, her breasts swung pleasantly beneath the loose-fitting workshirt. Her nipples poked at the faded blue material. No bra. It was enough to drive you crazy. I'd read about free love.

So these were the hippies, I thought. I couldn't remember ever having seen one before I'd left for Vietnam. Like the whole antiwar movement, the hippies and flower people seemed to have materialized out of nowhere during my absence from the World. In high school, I'd been reprimanded by the principal for allowing my hair to grow down over my ears and shirt collar. There had been no hippies in Perkasie. It had never occurred to Jenny *not* to wear a bra, much less to allow me to remove it, and the hem of her skirt had always reached her knees. When I'd enlisted, my picture had appeared in the local newspapers: the recruiter and I standing by the front door of Pennridge High School shaking hands.

I wondered if there were any hippies in Perkasie now. Hunched down behind my magazine, I watched the people in the airport coming and going, half expecting a band of placard-carrying flower people to surround me at any moment.

Out of the corner of my eye, I noticed a skinny bearded young man in blue jeans and an embroidered denim jacket. He wore a headband, and carried a brightly colored shoulder bag. I glanced up. He seemed to be headed straight for me. Oh, no, I thought, please don't. Go away. Just leave me alone.

"Peace, brother," he said, smiling broadly. He had freckles all over his face. 'How goes it?''

"Look, I don't want any trouble. I'm just waiting for a plane. You come lookin' for trouble, you're gonna get it.''

"Hey, be easy, friend," he said. "I noticed that rifle there. I'm kind of a gun buff; just wondered what kind it was.''

"Oh.''

"What kind is it?''

"Oh. MAS-36. French. It's pretty old; not in very good condition. I don't know why I kept it.''

"Maybe you could clean it up; get it plated or something. My granddaddy used to have a whole wall full of old guns—rifles and pistols, all kinds—had 'em all fixed up really nice. He owned a ranch in Montana. That's how I know about guns. Used to spend every summer there with him. Punchin' cattle. Playin' cowboy. Used to have the neatest times—like starring in my own TV western. Great place for a kid, Montana. Yippee-i-o-ki-yay!'' He sat down in the seat next to me and stuck out his hand. "My name's Rex. What's yours?''

"Bill," I said, shaking his hand tentatively.

"You're just back from Vietnam, I guess.''

"Yeah. That's where I got the rifle. I guess you could tell that.''

"I figured. Well, I'm glad you made it back okay. I guess you are, too! How long were you there?''

"Thirteen months.''

"Long time, huh?''

"Seems like forever . . . Rex. I used to dream about today like you dream about bein' a millionaire or winning a gold medal in the Olympics.'' I shook my head slowly.

"You get drafted?''

I let out a short snorting grunt through my nostrils. "No. No, I enlisted. Right outa high school. I volunteered. Seventeen.''

"Wow, that's heavy, Bill.''

A small wild laugh escaped from my throat before I even realized it was there. "It certainly is, Rex," I said. We both smiled as if we were sharing a secret, though I wasn't sure what it was.

"Why don't you get lost, freak."

We both looked up to see two middle-aged men in business suits standing right in front of us. They were glaring at Rex. "Beat it, freak," said the man on the left, who looked like a retired professional football player. "What are you bothering good people for?"

"He's not bothering me," I said as Rex stood up.

"It's okay," said Rex, addressing himself to me. "I've got a plane to catch, anyway."

"Go catch it," said the linebacker in the three-piece suit.

"He's not bothering me," I said.

"Nice talkin' with ya, Bill," Rex called back as he walked away. "I'm really glad you made it. Look out for yourself now, okay? Never know what you're gonna run into."

"You, too," I called, trying to wave around the bulk of the linebacker. The linebacker took a menacing step in Rex's direction.

"Peace, friend, peace." Rex laughed, lifting both hands in a V sign. "You're gonna give yourself an ulcer." He turned and skip-walked away, disappearing into the crowd.

"He wasn't bothering me," I said. "We were just talking."

"They oughta lock up every last one of those scum," said the linebacker. "Makes me sick to see 'em on the same planet with you boys. You got time for a drink, Sergeant?"

I didn't think I liked the linebacker or his partner very much, but I did want a drink.

"Yessir," I said quietly, "I've got time."

"No need to call me sir," said the linebacker as the three of us walked toward the nearest bar. "I'm just an old enlisted man, same as you. Corporal. Marines. Served in the Pacific. You know what they say: 'Once a Marine, always a Marine.'"

I'd heard the expression often enough; as we sat down I wondered vaguely if it was true. Both men ordered scotch on the rocks. I didn't like scotch. "Scotch on the rocks," I told the waitress. She questioned my age, but the linebacker slipped her a five-dollar bill and told her to run along.

"How old are you, anyway?" he asked.

"Nineteen—and a half."

"Goddamned crime; you're old enough to fight, then they try to tell ya you're not old enough to drink," the linebacker snorted.

"Nineteen, and you're a buck sergeant—quite a rack of ribbons you got there, too." He pointed to the double row of decorations on my left breast. "You must be one hell of a good Marine." It made me uncomfortable. I looked down at the table. "My name's Barton," he said. "This is Davis. You just back from Nam, aren't you?"

"Yessir—uh, yeah. Just got stateside this morning."

"Well, here's to you," said Barton, lifting his drink. "Take that weapon over there?"

"Yes."

"That musta been worth at least a stripe. You get the bastard that was carryin' it?"

"It was dark," I said. Our patrol had almost stumbled headlong into a Vietcong patrol, but we'd gotten off the path before they'd seen us. They'd walked right by, four of them, and Calloway and I had opened up and cut them down before any of them had had a chance to return fire. Calloway had been ecstatic. "Rifles!" he'd shouted. "We got 'em with weapons for once!" I was about to explain, then shrugged my shoulders. "I'm not sure who got him, me or Calloway."

"I know what you mean," said Davis, speaking for the first time. "Back on Iwo Jima—I was in the Marines, too—sometimes things got so wild you couldn't even keep score. Japs used to attack in human waves; suicide charges. Screamin' at the top of their lungs. All you had to do was lay there and mow 'em down. They just didn't care about dyin'. Die for the emperor and bow out smiling. The Vietnamese are like that too, aren't they? Just don't value life, Orientals. One less face they gotta feed."

Kharma, nirvana, reincarnation, banzai charges, Pork Chop Hill. Old women with black teeth and mouths full of betel nut; children with open running sores and flies; men with loose pajama legs pulled up, urinating in full view of the world; the strange clucking tongues; the empty faces. Asians aren't like us. It had been so easy to believe.

Then one day on a patrol near Hoi An, we'd come upon a funeral procession: two men carrying a small ornately carved casket, obviously that of a young child; a file of monks with shaved heads and flowing saffron robes, playing reed flutes and tiny cymbals; a dozen peasants behind them, some of them crying, two women wailing as though their insides had been torn out. I'd watched them pass, and later that night I'd almost thrown up at the memory of it. Their grief had seemed so real.

Now the memory of it made me feel sick all over again. "I don't know," I said. "I really don't know."

"They brainwash 'em," said Davis. "The Reds always brainwash their troops. Hop 'em up on dope and get 'em crazy for blood. I hear the VC go into a village and kill off everybody—everyone but the fighting-age men. Take the men and make 'em join the guerrillas. Isn't that right?"

"I never saw anything like that," I said. "I used to read about things like that before I enlisted, but I never saw anything like it while I was there."

"Well, it happens, believe me," said Davis, taking a gulp of his scotch and putting the glass back with a thump. "Happens all the time."

"You Americans are worse than the VC!" Sergeant Trinh had said the morning he'd told the battalion commander that he was through fighting for us. "Take your ignorance and go home!"

"What the hell do you know about it?" I burst out, half rising to my feet. "You don't have the foggiest notion what's going on over there. None of you do! We're the ones who waste villages! They don't have to twist any arms to get recruits—we do their goddamned recruiting for them!"

The two men stared at me in disbelief. "Hey, Sarge, don't get riled," said Barton. "We're on *your* side, remember? There's no call to get mad. Come on; sit down and have another drink. Hey, we appreciate what you been through."

"The hell you say. I got a plane to catch."

"Hey, your rifle," said Davis.

I didn't go back to get it. My head was spinning. I ducked into the nearest men's room, barely making it to the first urinal before I threw up.

"Are you all right, son?" There was a light touch on my shoulder. I spun around sharply. A stooped-over black man with curly gray hair took a quick step backwards, surprised by my sudden movement. He was dressed in coveralls and carried a push broom.

"I'm sorry," I said.

"Didn't mean to startle you. Are you all right?"

"Yeah. Yeah. I guess I ate somethin' bad or something."

"You want me to get a doctor?"

"No. I'm all right now. I'm just . . ." I flushed the urinal.

"You get yourself cleaned up; wash your mouth out. I'll go

get something to settle your stomach. You wait right here now; I'll be right back.''

Chapter 21

"Grab the wine!" I shouted.

Without looking up from his cards, Roger reached out with his right hand and steadied the half-gallon bottle, which had been just about to slide off the desk.

"Don't break my concentration," he said. "There! Building nines." I immediately scooped up the pile of cards. "Damn it, Ehrhart!" he hollered.

We were a day out of San Francisco, still bound for Portland, and we were riding heavy seas in a rainstorm. It was early evening.

"Looks like we're in for a rough night," I said. "This storm's still building. Did you see the main deck tonight?"

"Awash?" he asked.

"Yeah. Everything's under water but the catwalk. We got waves breaking against the forward hatches on the poop deck."

"Life at sea," Roger grunted. "So what happened to Pam, anyway?"

"Oh, we stumbled along for about half the summer. I was working for a guy building aluminum swimming pools—"

"Aluminum swimming pools?"

"Sure. You put up the walls with a screwdriver and a wrench like an Erector set, cover the bottom with sand, then drop in a big rubber liner and add water. Presto!"

"Doesn't sound too sturdy," he said.

"You get what you pay for," I replied. "Swimming pools for the low-rent crowd. Anyway, I'd go up and see her on weekends. Her father raced a sailboat on Long Island Sound and I got to be one of his regular crew. We worked together pretty well—me and him and another man—won the Long Island Sound championship for Ensign class boats, and we were going to enter the nationals until Pam threw in a monkey wrench. I think she'd been seeing her old boyfriend all summer. Anyway, she finally dropped the hammer a week before the nationals. I don't know who was more bummed out''—I laughed—''me or her dad. He really didn't want to take on a new crew member a week before the big race. Even offered to put me up in a hotel, so I wouldn't have to stay in the house with Pam.''

''Did you do it?''

''Hell, no. I was in no condition to deal with something like that—sailing with her father while she's in the backseat of somebody else's car gettin' it on. Then about a week later, I get laid off from my swimming pool job.''

''Damn,'' said Roger.

''Yeah,'' I laughed. ''I was a real mess. Spent about a month just lying in my room—I was staying with my parents that summer—cryin', bangin' my head against the wall. It's funny now, I guess, but I thought it was the end of the world.''

''Building fours,'' said Roger, ''and you leave 'em alone. Boy, she really stuck it to you, huh?''

''Oh, it wasn't her fault,'' I replied, scooping up Roger's pile of fours.

''I don't fucking believe it,'' Roger muttered.

''She was just a kid—and I was one wired-out head case. God knows what she thought she was in love with.''

''You ever see her again?'' asked Roger, groaning as he laid down the ace of hearts.

''Oh, sure. The next fall back at school, I was even sleeping with her again. Get this: She'd go away on weekends to visit her boyfriend and then on Sunday night, she'd come back and tumble into bed with me.'' I picked up the ace and a four with a five.

''Damn you, Ehrhart. Deal the next round. So why the hell did you put up with that kind of arrangement?''

''What could I do?'' I said. ''I was lonely. Man, I hated sleeping alone. It was like dying every night.''

''You must love it out here,'' Roger laughed.

''You get used to it after a while. 'Come hither, broken-hearted . . .' Anyway, it didn't go on like that for long. She started seeing another guy at Swarthmore and that was it for me.'' I let out a short laugh. ''Christ, when I found out about it, I went on one hell of a drunk. Sat in my room for two days and drank three or four bottles of apricot brandy. God, is that stuff nasty! Took me another three days to get rid of the hangover. A couple of times a day, Daniel or JC would stick his head in the door just to make sure I was still alive. Man, this ship is really rockin' and rollin'. I just hope this storm blows through before we get to Astoria; I'd sure as hell hate to try going over the bar in this stuff. When are we due?''

''We oughta reach the Columbia lightship sometime tomorrow night. Little casino,'' he beamed, picking up the two of spades.

''Add 'em up,'' I said, playing out the hand.

It wasn't even close. Roger grabbed the cards and bolted for the porthole. ''Don't!'' I shouted, but it was too late. In an instant, the porthole was open, Roger's face was drenched with rain and salt spray; half the cards had made it out the porthole, but the other half had been blown back in and were scattered all over Roger's cabin. Roger looked disgusted. ''I tried to warn you,'' I said.

''Fuck you,'' he replied. ''What time is it?''

''Quarter to eight.''

''I gotta go below. I'll see you later. Turn off the tape player when you leave.''

What a summer that had been, I thought after Roger had left. That last midnight run to Connecticut, running out of gas halfway there, waking up at six A.M. in the Casey driveway, driving away in tears.

And the nuisance I'd made of myself everywhere I went: Stop the war, we've got to stop the war—as though I could convince everyone in America.. There'd been Mrs. Kelly, who'd known me all my life, suddenly shrieking, ''My Sammy's a Marine helicopter pilot! He got shot down and won a Bronze Star! What's gotten *into* you, Billy Ehrhart? You're talking treason!'' And the cocktail party in Doylestown I'd been asked to leave: ''You're ruining everybody's evening, Bill; please keep your politics to yourself.'' I'd hardly been able to believe it. People *had* to listen to me! I'd *been* there! I was a veteran. I had really believed they would listen. I'd finished the summer working for minimum wage in a leather goods factory in South Philadelphia. My co-workers had avoided me like the plague.

I picked up the cards scattered around Roger's room, turned off the tape player, and headed down to my cabin to sleep, banging my shoulder against a hatchway when the ship suddenly pitched violently to starboard.

I was awakened about two A.M. by the twelve-to-four oiler, who told me that the second engineer wanted me down in the engineroom.

"What the fuck!" I mumbled. "What the hell does *he* want?"

"It ain't my idea," said the oiler. "Don't get mad at me."

I got dressed and went down to the engineroom. It was the second time I'd been down that night. About ten, Roger had called me down to help him clean up the paint locker. The heavy rolling of the ship had knocked several shelves of paint cans loose, and it had taken us until nearly midnight to secure them again.

"What is it?" I hollered to the Second above the noise of the engines.

"Come on, I'll show you," he shouted into my ear.

We walked the length of the engineroom, holding on tightly to the railings of the catwalks to keep from being pitched into the machinery, until we reached the steering gear room at the very stern of the ship. The massive rudder post came through the hull of the ship here, connecting to a series of powerful hydraulic gears controlled from the bridge.

But there was trouble in River City. The compartment was awash in about six inches of seawater mixed together with heavy grease, the whole slimy concoction sloshing back and forth from bulkhead to bulkhead as the ship rolled and pitched. It was clear that the packing seal around the rudder post had sprung a leak. Water was seeping in, bringing with it the grease that lubricated the bearings. It was also clear that the leak was not serious and that we were certainly in no danger of sinking.

"This," shouted the second engineer, gesturing around the compartment.

I couldn't believe I'd been dragged out of bed for this. I stood there looking at the mess, wondering what it had to do with me. "So what do you want?" I hollered.

"See if you can clean it up," he shouted.

"You aren't serious!" I hollered back. He *couldn't* be serious, I thought.

He looked at me as though I'd just blasphemed. "Yes, I'm serious."

"How?" I shouted. He pointed to a mop and bucket banging around in the swill like a couple of deadly projectiles. Oh, Jesus, Joseph, and Mary, I thought, a mop and bucket? It would take a four-inch pump to make any difference at all. But by the time I turned around, the Second was already headed back toward the maneuvering platform. I hollered after him, but he didn't hear me, which was probably just as well.

The merchant marine isn't like the Marine Corps. You don't salute people, and you don't have to call officers sir, and you can quit any time you want. But I didn't want to quit, and I didn't want to get fired, and as with any job, if you don't do what you're told, you'll get fired. The guy was out of his mind, I was dead tired, and the ship was bucking like a wild stallion. But I had no choice but to go through the motions.

I stepped over the high sill into the compartment—and immediately slipped in the greasy water and fell down, wallowing like a pig in the mud. That fucking shitbag dirtball asshole son-of-a-bitch bastard, I thought. He really *was* going to get me killed.

And then it dawned on me. By company work rules, because I'd already put in a regular eight-hour day, and had worked overtime from ten to midnight, and was now working from two to God-knew-when, by the time I'd report for my regular shift in the morning, I'd have been on *triple overtime* since midnight. The company hated triple overtime. When somebody turned in triple overtime, the big bosses in Philadelphia would freak out and make life very unpleasant for the captain and the chief engineer for allowing someone to get into a triple overtime situation. The second engineer, who was new to the company, obviously did not understand this. But I did. And it dawned on me that I had the second engineer by the family jewels.

Suddenly, I felt great! Yippee! First, I slid around on my hands and knees collecting the mop and bucket and securing them before they did me bodily harm. Then I rigged up a couple of safety lines so I could work without falling down every two seconds. And then I started to mop. Oh, it was ridiculous. I got nowhere at all. But I was having the time of my life, imagining the chief engineer's face the next morning when I would tell him I was on triple OT. I even started to whistle.

About four A.M., the second engineer showed up and told me to knock off. "I guess it isn't doing much good," he hollered.

"It certainly isn't," I hollered back. I went up to my cabin and slept for a few hours, then reported for my regular shift.

When I told the chief the situation, his mouth dropped open and his cigar fell out. "Get the hell out of here and don't come back for twenty-four hours," he spluttered. "Go get some sleep, and come see me in my cabin this afternoon when you wake up."

"So, well, uh, Ehrhart," said the chief that afternoon, "Pretty rough night, huh?"

"Yessir," I grinned.

"Well, uh, look," he said. He was clearly uncomfortable. "I'm going to be straight with you, Ehrhart. You know how the company feels about triple overtime."

"Yessir, I do," I replied, "but apparently the second engineer doesn't."

"Well, yes, that's what I wanted to talk to you about. Look, I don't want to have to report this," he said. "Now, you've got a right to it, I'm not arguing that, but it's going to cause a lot of trouble—"

"Chief, I'm sorry about that, but it's not my fault—"

"I know, I know."

"That dumb son of a bitch coulda gotten me *killed* down there. And then there *really* woulda been some trouble."

"I understand that you're angry, Ehrhart," said the chief, stoking on another cigar. "You certainly have every right to be. It was a stupid thing to do. But I'm asking you, as a personal favor to me, how about if we just let this triple overtime stuff slide, and I'll write in enough extra regular overtime over the next couple of weeks so you end up with the same amount of money." I sat there scratching my chin and thinking. "I'll even throw in a few extra hours," the chief added.

"Well, gee, Chief," I said, "that's sounds fair enough—but you know what I really want?"

"What?" asked the chief hesitantly.

"I want this not to happen again. This second engineer, you know?" I said. "You know what I mean?"

The chief couldn't quite suppress a grin. "Yeah, I think I know what you mean," he said. "Don't worry. It won't happen again. He'll be gone just as soon as we can get a replacement. Probably up at Cherry Point."

"Fine," I beamed. "You got a deal. And you don't have to give me any extra hours. Just give me what I've got coming." And then I laughed. "Jesus, Chief, you shoulda seen it down there. The whole damned steering gear room was covered with grease! The guy had me in there with a mop and bucket, for Chrissake!"

"I know, I know," the chief laughed, grabbing his forehead between his thumb and index finger.

"Hell's bells," I said.

"Well, go back to bed and don't go anywhere *near* the engineroom until morning, okay?"

"Say, listen, Chief, as long as I'm here. Do you mind if I ask you a question?"

"No, what?"

"You don't have to answer this if it's none of my business," I said, "but Roger told me you retired from the Navy because they were going to send you to Vietnam. I was just wondering why." The chief's expression turned serious. "Like I said," I added, "you don't have to tell me if you don't want. I'm just curious."

"You were there, weren't you?" the chief asked.

"Yeah."

"You think I'm some kind of slacker for not going?"

"Oh, no, Chief, not at all. Believe me, if I had been old enough to know any better, I sure as hell wouldn't have gone either. Hell, after I got out, when I was in college, I was writing CO recommendations for friends of mine."

"Yeah? Well, I'll tell ya," said the chief, leaning back in his chair and puffing on the cigar, "I put twenty-three years in the Navy. Served in Korea. I was with the fleet that landed the Marines in Lebanon in 1958. Blockaded Cuba in sixty-two. But I never could make heads or tails of what was going on in Vietnam. Just seemed like chickenshit to me. I couldn't see how anything going on there was worth a single American life. Every year, they had a new excuse for being there, and none of them ever sounded very convincing. You're gonna ask people to fight a war, then you ought to be able to tell them what you're askin' them to die for. I don't think anybody ever knew. I've got a wife and three kids. By the time I got my orders in sixty-nine, I was eligible for retirement anyway. I could take this job with ARCO—get this paycheck plus my retirement—or I could go to Vietnam. Which would you have done?"

"You made the right decision, Chief," I replied.

"Doesn't bother you that you went and I didn't?"

"Hell, no," I said. "That's what I call the Sore Loser Complex. I got past that a long time ago. Bothers me that *I* went—bothers the hell out of me, actually—but it certainly doesn't bother me that you *didn't*. More power to ya, Chief."

Chapter 22

"Hey, Billy!" said Daniel Kaufman, walking into my room and sticking out his hand. "Good to see you."

"Hi, Daniel! Wanna drink? I was just about to mix up a whiskey sour."

"Well, well," said Daniel as we shook hands, "don't mind if I do."

Daniel was over six feet tall, but his most distinguishing feature was his body hair. He was covered with it. He had no shirt on, and the hair on his shoulders and back and stomach and sides was nearly as thick as the hair on his head. He looked like a woolly mammoth.

"There's ice in JC's refrigerator," I said, handing him two plastic glasses.

Though I wasn't looking forward to seeing Pam again, I was happy to be back at school that fall of 1970. I'd been made a proctor for third-floor Dana Hall, and had been given a nice outside single room with a deep bay window overlooking the woods and Crum Meadow at the edge of the campus. Though Bart Lewis had graduated, JC Mooney and Daniel, both members of DU I'd gotten to know a little the previous year, had singles just across the hall from me. And I was feeling more confident academically since my grades for the first two semesters had turned out to be pretty good.

The arrival of my second-semester freshman grades, in fact, had been about the only bright spot all summer. Between losing Pam, getting laid off from my job building pools, and having to commute eighty miles a day for half the summer to work for minimum wage for the Ice Leather Company, I hadn't had much fun. And in spite of Kent State, and the ensuing protests, and the obvious military failure of the Cambodian invasion, the war had continued to hammer away relentlessly. I'd hardly had a civil word to say to anyone who didn't agree that the war should be ended immediately. Living with my parents had been especially difficult since they didn't seem to understand anything I was trying to say, and virtually everything I had to say was delivered at high decibel levels.

Daniel came back with the ice and a Baggie filled with marijuana. "Wanna get stoned?" he asked.

"I can't," I replied. "I gotta meet all the new freshmen on the hall today—and their parents. Couple of them have already been around, but most of 'em haven't shown yet. I gotta check 'em into their rooms."

"So what?" said Daniel. He started to roll a joint. I shrugged my shoulders, and he kept rolling. "How was your summer? You see any of Pam?"

"Yeah, for a while—till she dumped me. She finally figured out I was crazy," I said. Daniel looked puzzled, but didn't inquire further. "The way it goes," I added. He passed me a lighted joint, and I took several deep drags from it. "How was your summer?" I asked.

In half an hour, between the booze and the grass, we were both loaded. Several times we were interrupted by timid-looking freshmen and their anxious-looking parents. Each time, I'd immediately go to the door, trying to intercept them before they could enter the room and smell the smoke and alcohol. I was having a lot of trouble talking, and I was convinced that my condition must be obvious.

"Don't worry about it," said Daniel. "They don't know their assholes from a hole in the ground."

"Christ, this is hard work," I said, checking another name off my list. "I shouldn't have gotten stoned. Are you sure I don't look stoned? Who were those people anyway? Christ, I can't even remember their names. I just met 'em!"

" 'Oh, honey; oh, dear; we can't leave our little baby with those—those ruffians!' " Daniel screeched, imitating a worried mother. We both roared. I felt light-headed and giddy.

"Are you *sure* I don't look stoned?" I asked.

"Paranoia," Daniel bellowed in a deep voice. "Hey, let's go to the president's tea."

"God, no; I'll get fired my first day on the job."

"Come on, let's go."

"Like this?" I said, gesturing at our clothes. Daniel had put on a torn sleeveless T-shirt in deference to the parents who kept dropping in looking for the proctor. I was wearing a brightly colored tie-dyed Wallace Beery-style shirt that looked like fluorescent long underwear. Though I had never grown my beard back after my trip to Florida, we both had mustaches and very long hair. Mine was held out of my face by a rainbow-colored headband.

"Hell, yes," Daniel replied. "Nobody'll know the difference. Let's go. They'll probably have some good munchies. I'm starved."

So was I. We got up and weaved our way across campus toward the president's house, where President Cramer was holding an outdoor reception for the new students and their parents.

"Where the hell is it?" Daniel laughed as we went thrashing into a thick hedge behind Dr. Cramer's house.

"Ouch!" I shouted. "Watch the fucking branches."

All of a sudden we both burst through the hedge and found ourselves standing just behind the receiving line in Dr. Cramer's yard. I could have reached out and shaken Dr. Cramer's hand—if he hadn't already been shaking hands with some parent. He was flanked by Dean Williams, Dean Bradley, Dean Lawford, Vice President Cruse, and every other heavyweight in the administration, all of whom were also shaking hands with people. The whole receiving line had stopped midsentence and turned around to see what all the commotion was. They were all dressed in coats and ties or Sunday dresses. Dean Williams looked like he was about to laugh, but all of the others looked like death warmed over. There was dead silence. If looks could kill, Cruse would have dropped us cold in our tracks. Oh, shit, I thought, I'm finished.

"Oops," said Daniel.

"Er, uh, excuse us," I stammered. "We got lost."

We both beat it around the end of the receiving line, our shoulders hunched over in an attempt to hide, and disappeared into the crowd of well-dressed people standing around on the lawn.

"Oh, Jesus Christ, Daniel," I said. "There goes my ass."

"Did you see their faces?" Daniel howled.

In spite of my absolute conviction that I had just been relieved of my proctor's job, I couldn't help laughing, too. "I thought Betty Lawford was gonna crap in her drawers on the spot," I giggled.

"Screw 'em," said Daniel. "Where's the chow?"

"Over there," I said, pointing to one of the sophomore women who were serving as hostesses, walking around with trays of cookies and punch. "We'll take that," I said, approaching her. She gave me an astonished look but didn't argue as I lifted the tray from her hands. We emptied the half-dozen remaining cups of punch instantly, then started on the cookies.

"Not bad," Daniel mumbled through a mouthful, crumbs flying as he tried to talk.

"Mumph," I replied, my mouth too full even to try. We cleaned off the tray in two minutes and handed it to a very surprised freshman with a nametag I didn't bother to read.

"As long as we're here, let's be useful," said Daniel. He grabbed another tray from a passing hostess. "Here, gimme that," he said. "Go get yourself another one." He proceeded to walk up to a small knot of parents and students. "Anybody want a cookie?" He grinned broadly.

I lifted a tray from another hostess. She started to protest, but I cut her off. "Get lost," I said, "you're fired." I joined Daniel, who was by now on his second or third group of people. "Have some punch. Have a cookie," I said, pushing the tray in front of me as I went.

"Try one of these," said Daniel to a startled woman in a flowered hat.

"They're delicious," I said, balancing my tray in one hand as I reached out with the other hand, grabbed the cookie Daniel was pointing to, and popped it in my mouth. "Oh, here's another one just like it," I said, pointing to my tray and then gesturing to the woman. "Take it; it's yours. No charge. Hey, mister, want a cookie?"

Chapter 23

"Hey, wake up, it's nearly midnight." Gerry Griffith, the new guy, was gently nudging me. "Wake up. What the hell is that?" It was his first night on perimeter guard duty.

I rubbed the sleep out of my eyes and stood up in the open bunker. Gerry was pointing toward the east. "What?" I asked.

"That red streak," he said. It was gone, but I could see the lights of an airplane circling in the sky far out over the dunes, maybe six or seven miles, out near the ocean. I was awake now.

"Keep watching," I said. The lights continued to circle over the same spot. The aircraft was too far away to hear the engines. Suddenly a brilliant red streak silently began to descend toward the earth until it connected the flashing lights to the ground below with a solid bar of color. Many seconds later, as the flashing lights and red bar continued to move like a spotlight sweeping the sky from a fixed point on the ground, a sound like the dull buzz of a dentist's slow-speed drill came floating lazily through the humid night air. Sound and image appeared to be synchronized for a while. Then the red streak slowly fell away from the circling lights and disappeared into the earth, leaving the thick sound humming alone in a black vacuum. Finally, long after the lights had stopped circling and begun to move off in a straight line toward the south, the sound abruptly stopped.

"That's Puff the Magic Dragon," I said. "The gunship."

"What's that?"

"Air Force C-47 with Vulcan cannons." I explained that the old transport plane, a military version of the DC-3, had been converted into a flying battleship by mounting three Vulcan cannons along one side of the fuselage. Since the guns were in fixed mounts, they could only be aimed by tilting the entire aircraft toward the ground and circling over the target. Each of the three cannons could fire six thousand bullets per minute.

"That's eighteen thousand rounds a minute, my man," I said, "three hundred bullets per second. Chops up anything and everything like mincemeat: fields, forests, mangroves, water buffalo, hooches, people. Everything. Takes a patch of redwood forest the size of a football field and turns it into matchsticks before you can hitch up the horses. I've seen places where Puff's left his calling card. Unbelievable. Looks like a freshly plowed field ready for planting. I saw a body once, got chopped up by Puff. You wouldn't have known it had ever been a human being. Just a pile of pulp stuck to little pieces of cement and straw that used to be the guy's hooch—or her hooch, absolutely no way to tell the difference. It was so gross it wasn't even sickening. It was just there, like litter or something.''

"Jesus fucking Christ," Gerry whistled. "Puff the Magic Dragon?"

"That's what they call it."

Well down on the southeastern horizon now, the lights began circling again. Then the red streak, like a bar of hot steel just off the rolling mill, stabbed deliberately into the earth.

"What are they shooting at?" asked Gerry.

"God knows. Whatever's there."

We were both silent for a while, just watching. Then Gerry began to sing the Peter, Paul, and Mary song very softly, "Puff the Magic Dragon lived by the sea . . .''

Chapter 24

"Here's to the Third-Floor Dana Beer Cartel," said JC, hoisting a beer.

"Here's to the Grand Vizier of Third-Floor Dana," said Daniel, hoisting another beer and nodding grandly to me.

"Here's to the Grand Vizier's Economic Adviser," I said, tipping my beer toward Daniel. We clicked the bottles together and drank. "This is a great idea."

"Brilliant," added JC.

"Thank you, thank you," said Daniel.

And it was, too. It had all begun a week earlier. The three of us had begun drinking one Wednesday night because nobody felt like studying, but just when we'd been getting warmed up, we'd run out of fuel. It had been too late to go out and buy more. We'd all gone to bed feeling cheated, as though we'd been robbed of a golden opportunity.

The next day, Daniel had collared me in the bathroom. "I've got the problem solved, Billy. Here's what we do. Each of us buys a case of beer, all at the same time. Every Wednesday night, we drink one case. That gives the guy who paid for that case three full weeks to scrounge up the money for a replacement. In the meantime, we've already got the two other cases for the next two weeks."

It was a stroke of genius. We'd even drawn up a written charter with the terms clearly stated, each of us committed to buying a case of beer every third week. We'd all signed the charter before making the first run to the beer store, and tonight was the formal inauguration of the cartel.

"I'm glad we got rid of blackballing," I said as we sat in JC's room listening to music. The previous day, DU had voted to dispense with the traditional procedure by which any one member could block an invitation to a new person to join simply by saying that he didn't want that person. Henceforth, anyone that a simple majority of the fraternity wanted would be invited to join.

"You realize you almost got blackballed last year?" Daniel laughed.

"What do you mean?" I asked.

"Ask Mike Morris about it," said Daniel.

"Why Mike? What are you talking about?"

"Never mind. Just ask Mike sometime," Daniel replied, chuckling softly. "Put on another record, JC."

"What do you want?"

"Led Zeppelin."

"Hey, Billy," said JC, "what's this shit with Pam Casey and Carl DeWitt?" I tried not to wince.

"Fuck if I know," I said. "I've been wondering who's the aberration in her life, me or DeWitt."

"Are you kidding?" Daniel piped in. "The guy's a total schlepp. He's got the personality of a laboratory test tube. Beats me what Casey sees in him."

Daniel and JC didn't know about the fiasco on the ski slopes, or the fiasco in Florida, or the time I'd slugged Pam in the wake of the Cambodian invasion. I opened three more beers and passed them around.

"Is that why you got so drunk the other week?" JC laughed, his long brown hair shaking down over the shoulders of his thin six-foot frame.

"Fuck, no. I was just in a bad mood."

"Bad mood?" said Daniel. With a sinking feeling, I thought he was about to pursue the question of motivation. "You had one foot in the grave and the other in a bottle. We thought you were dying or something.''

"Felt like I was for a while there," I laughed. "Man, I'll tell ya, that's the last time I go toe to toe with apricot brandy." I held my head, feigning a hangover, and we all laughed. I was relieved to let the matter go at that.

Two hours later, we finished off the case of beer allotted for the first week.

"What do we do now?" I asked. "I'm not tired yet."

"Let's have another beer," JC suggested.

"What about the cartel?" asked Daniel, waving the charter.

"Who's gonna miss a couple of beers?" said JC.

"Hell, this is an inaugural ball, isn't it?" I added.

"Right," said Daniel.

"Come in!" JC hollered.

I hadn't heard anyone knocking. Ever since an NVA antitank rocket had blown up four feet from me in Hue City during the Tet offensive nearly three years earlier, spraying me with shrapnel and nearly taking my head off, I'd had trouble hearing. It wasn't so bad most of the time, but in a place like the dining hall where there was lots of background noise, or here in JC's room with the stereo going, it was hard work just to follow the immediate conversation. I hadn't heard the knock at the door.

A skinny freshman stuck his head in the door and looked around timidly. "Excuse me," he said. It was the kid that lived just below JC. His eyes finally settled on me, and he motioned to me. "Can I see you for a minute?" he asked. I got up unsteadily and walked out into the hall.

"Lock yourself out of your room?" I asked. All proctors had master keys.

"No. Uh, I'm trying to sleep, and, uh, that music is really loud. It's one o'clock. Do you think you could get them to turn it down some? My alarm clock just fell off the shelf and hit me on the head."

I tried not to laugh. "Sure, Frazer, sure. Don't worry about it. Go back to bed." I went back into the room and burst out laughing. "The vibrations from your speakers just knocked Frazer's alarm clock off his shelf," I said. "It hit him on the head."

"Fuck him," said Daniel.

"That goddamned nerd is up here every other night complaining about my music," said JC. "Why doesn't he buy a pair of earplugs?"

"Beats me," I shrugged, sitting down and opening another beer.

By two-thirty, we were nearing the end of the second case.

'Listen, guys," I said, "I got an eight o'clock class this morning. I better pack it in."

"What for?" JC asked. "You never go to that class anyway."

"That's not true," I protested. "I've been there three times. Christ, why the hell did anybody ever invent eight o'clock classes?"

"Why the hell did you sign up for it, sucker?" said Daniel.

"I didn't," I replied. "I signed up for an eleven-thirty class. Parker was the instructor. How was I supposed to know the guy's a fossil? I went to the first class, and he didn't say anything worth listening to for fifty minutes. Well, hell, I thought, it's the first class; nobody's read anything yet. What's he supposed to say? Second day, about halfway through the class, he *still* hadn't said jack squat, and it dawned on me that he never *was* going to say anything worth listening to. So I just got up in the middle of his lecture and said, 'Excuse me, I have a dentist appointment,' and I walked out. The only other section I could get into was Kestler's. An eight o'clock with Kestler or an eleven-thirty with Parker."

"Nice choice," said JC.

"There it is," I said. "Anyway, I've been doing all the reading. I got a B on the midterm, so what the hell."

"So you don't need to go to class," said Daniel. "Have another beer."

"That's the last bottle for this case," said JC, popping it open.

"Now what?" I said.

"I got an idea," said Daniel, breaking into a wide grin. "JC shouldn't have to put up with all this harassment from that nerd Frazer. Let's fix his ass." Daniel explained his plan, and we all roared our approval.

"Christ, you guys," I said, wiping the tears out of my eyes, "I'm supposed to be the proctor."

"Don't worry, Billy," said Daniel, "JC and I'll take care of everything."

"Okay," I said, "let's go. I'll supervise."

"Don't touch anything," said JC.

"Not me. I'm the proctor."

We all got up, weaving unsteadily, and headed for the second floor, checking trash cans as we went.

"Here's a good one," said JC. "It's almost half full. Looks like some coffee grounds, pizza crust, a banana peel—"

"Grab it," said Daniel. JC slid the white covering sheath off and the two of them carried the twenty-five-gallon canister into the shower stall. They turned on the water and filled up the can. Then they maneuvered the can back into the hall and down to Frazer's room. They leaned the can over and propped it against Frazer's door, so that it would tumble into the room when the door was opened, spilling its contents. Then they both banged loudly on the door, and we all ran like hell.

We were lying in JC's room howling when Frazer came bursting in all puffed up like an angry cat. "What do you people think you're doing?" he shouted.

"What are you talking about?" asked Daniel, his face suddenly blank.

"You know what I'm talking about!" he shouted.

"Hold your voice down," I said. "You'll wake up the whole dorm. People are trying to sleep, for Chrissake. Have a little consideration, will you?"

"Consideration?"

"Quit shouting," I said, this time more forcefully.

"You've got a lot of nerve telling me about consideration," he said in a much quieter voice. "You're supposed to be a proctor!"

"He *is* the proctor," JC grinned.

"He's the Grand Vizier!" said Daniel.

"I don't know what the hell you're talking about, Frazer," I said. "*You've* got a lot of nerve barging in here in the middle of the night accusing us of God knows what. Would you mind explaining?"

"Oh, sure, I suppose you don't know anything about the water and garbage somebody just dumped in my room," said Frazer, a wise-guy smirk on his face.

"Garbage?" said Daniel.

"What garbage?" asked JC, pulling at his muttonchop sideburns.

"I didn't do a thing," I said.

"Get off it," said Frazer. "I know it was you guys. There's nobody else awake in the whole dorm, and I come up here and find you all laughing."

"Billy just told a joke," said JC. "You wanna hear it?"

"Very funny," said Frazer.

"Listen, Frazer," I said, "I didn't do a goddamned thing, and Daniel and JC have been with me all night. And that's that."

"Well, we'll see what Dean Bradley has to say about it."

"This discussion is over, asshole," said Daniel. "Go howl at the moon."

"Don't think you're going to get away with this—"

"I said get lost," Daniel growled, beginning to rise.

Frazer's eyes got big and white and round, and then he vanished. We all burst out laughing again.

"No sense of humor," said Daniel.

"I need another beer," said JC.

"So do I," I said.

"Me, too," said Daniel.

We started in on the third case. It was three-fifteen. By six-fifteen, the third case was gone.

"That's the last of the beer," said JC after we finished toasting the sunrise with a stirring rendition of "The Star-Spangled Banner" that had some guy in first-floor Hallowell screaming out his window for us to shut up.

"No sense of patriotism," I said. "What do we do now?"

"I don't understand it," said Daniel, scratching the hair on his chest. "I had it all figured out. The cartel shoulda worked."

"Let's go eat breakfast," said JC.

"I'm starved," I said.

"I can eat fitty eggs!" JC shouted.

"Let's go," said Daniel.

But JC couldn't eat fifty eggs. Between the three of us, we only managed to eat forty-seven soft-boiled eggs. That in itself was quite a feat, however. You got two eggs to a serving. Seconds were allowed. Thirds were frowned on, but if you begged hard, you could usually get them. After that, you were on your own. We put our coats back on so we'd look like different people. We got other people to go back for us. We pulled our coats way up around our necks and hunched our shoulders and turned our collars up. We snuck up to the serving line, snatched eggs, and ran for it. "Hey! Hey, it's *them* again!"

"I can't eat any more."

"Me neither."

"I'm stuffed."

"Hey, it's almost eight o'clock," I said. "Let's go to my political science class."

"You're joking," said Daniel.

"We're not even in it," said JC.

"So what?" I said.

And off we went. Daniel chickened out just as we were going into the classroom, but JC and I trooped in and sat down in the front row, where I always sat because it made it easier to hear. Professor Kestler never batted an eyelash.

Kestler was having an open affair that autumn with another political science professor named Ann Harris, who happened to be the wife of the chairman of the religion department. About five minutes into the class, JC tapped me on the shoulder and passed me a note. "Does Rob Kestler suck Ann Harris's dagnarbles?" it said. I burst out laughing. Then I fell asleep. JC said later that he started giggling when he saw the pen slip out of my limp hand and fall to the floor. That was the last thing he could remember.

Chapter 25

Plopfwhoosh. Plopfwhoosh. Mortars!

I opened my eyes in the darkness to the sound of mortar rounds leaving their tubes. *Plopfwhoosh. Plopfwhoosh. Plopfwhoosh.* My heart suddenly dropped into my stomach, my body already diving for the fighting hole before I was awake enough to tell myself to move. Shouts of "Incoming! Incoming!" rose all around me as I hit the hole, tucking myself up under my helmet and flak jacket in a fetal position. *Plopfwhoosh. Plopfwhoosh.* You could hear the rounds gently rising through their high trajectories, the tone of the dull whistle changing audibly as the first rounds hit the top of their arc and began the descent toward earth. Other rounds were still going out: *plopfwhoosh, plopfwhoosh.* A dozen more rounds left their tubes before the first rounds began impacting. *Plopfwhoosh, plopfwhoosh, plopfwhoosh.* I waited for the rounds to start dropping in, my body shivering, my teeth chattering uncontrollably, my thoughts frozen into a soundless scream.

Shells began to burst all around me, louder than the loudest fireworks of a Fourth of July fantasy, the blasts stifling the scream that had never emerged from my throat. You could hear jagged pieces of hot steel tearing at the darkness. Cascades of dirt and sand, and clots of debris, rained down into my fighting hole, pounding an irregular rhythm against my helmet and flak jacket, striking my arms and legs. I curled up even more tightly, burying my face in the dirt, my whole body tight as steel wire, my fingernails digging into the palms of my clenched fists. Jesus, shit, Mother, fuck, fuck, stop it!

We took twenty or thirty rounds in two, maybe three, minutes. When the explosions finally stopped, a familiar eerie silence fell over everything, broken only by groaning men and screaming men and frantic shouts of "Corpsman!" I could hear Sergeant Seagrave nearby, moving among the scouts' positions: "Anybody hit? You guys all right?"

I stuck my head up. "Yeah. I'm okay."

Chapter 26

"Why wait?" I shouted to Daniel above the music. "If we leave tonight, we can be in Pittsburgh by sunup. We can take turns driving, and sleep in the car."

"What about Clyde and Doris?" Daniel asked.

"I'll call 'em and tell 'em to be ready by two A.M."

Daniel looked at me, his eyebrows furrowed in thought. Then he broke into a broad grin and said, "Well, let's get rolling."

It was the beginning of Christmas vacation, December 1970. Classes were over, and we were in the middle of one of Rick Keiter's famous 1950s parties, at which Kite played 45 RPM records of Elvis Presley, the Platters, Dion and the Belmonts,

Little Richard, Smokey and the Miracles, and the Delphonics, while everybody danced and got roaring drunk. Daniel and I had been planning to leave the next morning for a seventeen-day run to the West Coast and back.

But as the party had progressed into the night, I had gotten increasingly anxious to get on the road. I loved the feel of a full tank of gas and the open highway stretching away in front of me. Where I was at any given moment was almost always, finally, empty and unhappy. But one never knew what lay down the road. Somewhere out there, just beyond the range of the headlights, just beyond the horizon, possibility still existed. Who knows? Who knows? On the highway, there was always hope. Driving, for me, had become a kind of addiction.

"Why wait?" I said to Daniel.

"Let's get rolling," he replied.

By two-thirty, we were loaded and ready to go. Four people plus luggage in a Volkswagen Beetle is no small trick, but we were dropping Doris in Pittsburgh and Clyde in St. Louis. I put the car in reverse, started to back out of the parking lot beside Dana Hall, and ran into a tree.

"Ambushed," I said. "Did you see where that tree came from?"

"Oh, God," said Clyde.

"Nice work, Billy," said Daniel.

"Are you sure you're sober enough to drive?" Doris asked.

"Sure, great, never felt better, no problem. Just lemme get out of this parking lot where I got a little room to maneuver."

Forty-five minutes later, we were on the Pennsylvania Turnpike heading west. Clyde and Doris were fast asleep in the backseat.

"Did you bring any beer?" I asked Daniel.

"No, but I've got something else."

"What?"

"Arab candy," he beamed, rooting around in the pack wedged between his legs and the floorboard. "I learned how to make it when I was in Israel. It's honey and hashish rolled into balls and coated with powdered sugar. Ah, there it is." He pulled out a glass jar and opened it, sticking his hand in. "Shit," he said, "it melted." He held up the jar, and in the dim light from the dashboard, I could see that the jar was filled with a milky brown gooey liquid.

"Nice work, Daniel."

"Well, we can drink it," he said, putting the jar to his mouth.

"Gimme some," I said.

As the miles rolled on we began to hit the tunnels on the turnpike: Blue Mountain, Allegheny—seven of them in all. As we entered each tunnel, Daniel would say, "Hey, Billy, maybe this tunnel goes straight to California."

"Far out, man! All we gotta do is drive in at this end and come out the other side in California." It never seemed to work, but we kept hoping.

We reached Doris's house the next morning. Her mother made breakfast for us, and then offered us a room for a few hours.

"Can't stop now," we said. "Gotta get to California."

California. The promised land. I'd been sixteen the first time I'd gone to California. A high school buddy and I had taken a train to Chicago, and a bus from there to Los Angeles, finally ending up in Fullerton, just south of L.A. Within three days we'd found a fifteen-dollar-a-week room in a seedy hotel populated mainly by transient fruit pickers, and jobs as laborers in an aluminum sliding door factory.

What a summer it had been. The Beach Boys. Surf's up! Huntington Pier. Balboa Ballroom. Hollywood. Disneyland. Freeways like nothing you ever saw back east. Taco stands, and supermarkets that never closed. Tijuana, Mexico—a real eye-opener for a sixteen-year-old kid who'd never been farther away from home than Harrisburg. I'd even met a real California girl (as in "I wish they all could be California girls") with a swimming pool in her backyard and a real bikini, not the conservative "two-piece" suits you saw on the beaches of New Jersey that summer of 1965. The Watts riots occurred while we were there, but I hadn't thought much about it except to wonder how anyone could act that way.

We reached Clyde's house by early evening. His mother fed us a steak dinner and offered us a bedroom for the night.

"Can't stop now," we said. "Gotta get to California." So Clyde's mom packed us a bunch of sandwiches and fruit, and off we went into the night.

California. All through my senior year of high school, I'd dreamed of going back to California. I'd even applied to and been accepted by UCLA. But in the spring of 1966, I'd changed my mind and decided to enlist in the Marines instead. The decision had taken almost everyone but me by surprise: an honor roll student three years running, National Honor Society, student council vice president. Why the Marines? I'd had to do some persuading to get my parents to agree, and they had to agree because I was only seventeen and couldn't enlist unless they signed the enlistment contract, too. We'd talked about it for a long time one day, but finally I'd said, "Is this the way you raised me? To let other parents' children fight America's wars?" That hadn't been the way they'd raised me, and that had ended the discussion.

One day at school a few weeks before I'd graduated, Karen King had come up to me in the hall. "You're really joining the Marines?" she'd asked.

"Yes."

"They'll send you to Vietnam. You could get killed."

"I know," I'd replied, gazing over her shoulder into the distance.

That spring of 1966, I'd also met Jenny. By the time I'd gotten my orders for Vietnam, we were talking marriage. And by the time I'd gotten back to California, it was January 1967, and I was in staging at Camp Pendleton, just down the road from Fullerton and my last stateside stop before Vietnam. I'd gone to visit my California girl a few times, but had spent most of the time telling her about Jenny and showing her pictures of Jenny and talking Marine jargon like "Take it to the Cong" and "Kick ass and take names, in that order."

"Why are you so darned eager to go to Vietnam and get yourself killed?" my California girl had asked the last night I'd been with her. The question had offended me.

"Listen, Lydia," I'd replied, "I don't know what people believe around here, but back home we believe that you owe something to your country. I consider it a blessing and a privilege to be an American citizen, and when I have kids, I want them to be blessed, too. Freedom doesn't come cheap, you know. If you want it, you have to fight for it. Where the hell would we be if our fathers and grandfathers hadn't been willing to make sacrifices? We'd still be an English colony. Or we'd all be Nazis. And if we don't fight in Vietnam, we'll end up being Communists. Maybe not us, but our children or grandchildren. Is that what you want? I don't."

Later, Lydia had driven me back to Pendleton. "Something's happening here," Buffalo Springfield had sung on the car radio.

"And I got to beware." I liked the song. It didn't occur to me that Buffalo Springfield might be on Lydia's side, not mine.

As Daniel and I left Oklahoma behind and cruised into Texas, I found myself wondering what had ever become of Lydia. The last I'd heard, she'd married an Army officer. Strange world, I thought.

"Hey, Billy," said Daniel, "you notice anything strange?"

"You been reading my mind?" I asked. Daniel looked perplexed. "Never mind," I said. "No, I don't notice anything strange. Should I? Is my fly open or what?"

"Look around. Look at the cows. I've been watching the cows for the last two days. Black ones, brown ones, tan ones. But there's no white ones. Have you noticed any white cows in the past two days?"

"Well, no, not that I can remember," I said. "Damn, you're right. We *haven't* seen any white cows."

"I wonder where they all are," said Daniel.

"Beats me," I said. "We got any food left?"

"A couple of sandwiches and some fruit."

"No white cows?"

"No white cows."

"Gimme a sandwich."

"How come you didn't go out for swimming this year?" Daniel asked.

"Hell, I did water ballet again," I replied. "That's enough exercise for one year. I don't know, really. I really like Jamie McAdams—you know, the coach—but I just didn't feel like it. Too much hassle to be straight every afternoon for practice, I guess. Too much like work. I wish we had some beer. Let's get some beer."

"Where?" Daniel shrugged. We were out in the middle of Nowhere, Texas, headed for Nowhere, New Mexico.

"Must be a place around here somewhere," I said. "Damn well better be. We're gonna need gas in another seventy-five miles or so."

"Sure is a big country," said Daniel, gesturing at the vast expanse of wide-open prairie we were crossing.

"Sure is," I said. "Big and empty."

"Well, when we get to the Rockies, we'll have a little scenery at least."

"It's empty there, too," I said.

I thought of the first time I'd driven this road back in August of 1965, heading east at the end of that glorious summer in California. It hadn't been an interstate highway then, just a two-lane road, U.S. Route 66. We'd bought an old 1949 Chevy for sixty-nine dollars the day before we'd left. We'd lost the top luggage rack on the Los Angeles Freeway. The carburetor had nearly fallen off in Barstow. The stars in the sky above the California high desert that first night had been so incredibly numerous and vivid that I'd nearly crashed trying to look at them, and we'd finally pulled off the road and sat there on the warm engine hood just gazing up at all those awesome stars. I'd never imagined there could be so many stars. I'd sat there in utter disbelief, not wanting to move, wanting to take in as much of that magnificent shimmering white on black as my mind could possibly hold.

The next day, we'd blown the Chevy's engine near Santa Rosa, New Mexico. We'd immediately bought a 1958 English Vauxhall for eighty-seven dollars and what was left of the Chevy, and continued on. Swimming in the Red River. Surfing in Galveston. Eating apple pie on a street corner in the French Quarter of New Orleans. The Vauxhall had finally given up the ghost in a swamp on the Georgia–South Carolina border, and we'd hitchhiked the last six hundred miles, arriving in Ocean City, New Jersey, on Labor Day weekend to the wonder and envy of our friends. It had all been new and fresh and exciting: the amber waves of grain, the purple mountains' majesty, the alabaster cities. America, America.

Of course, there had been the Mexican prostitute with the dynamite body and the pockmarked face who'd lived down the hall from us in the transient hotel in Fullerton. And the Watts riots. And the two white men in Louisiana who'd chased off the two black men who'd stopped to help us fix a flat tire, shoving one of the blacks to the ground and shouting, ''Get away from these white boys, nigger,'' before kindly fixing our flat themselves and treating us to breakfast. And the sheriff in South Carolina who'd been about to throw us in jail for vagrancy until we'd managed to convince him that we weren't ''nigger-loving Freedom Riders,'' but were only all-American high school kids headed home after a long summer.

But those images hadn't been able to intrude for long or very deeply. What did they mean to a sixteen-year-old kid from Small-town, U.S.A.? They'd simply been stories to tell my friends back home. Just more adventures in a summer jammed full of adventures. Marco Polo on the road to China.

"Why didn't you get an FM radio in this thing?" Daniel complained as he switched from one country-and-western station to another before turning the radio off.

"Because this is your basic economy model. I paid cash for this machine—blood money—the money I saved in Vietnam. Cost me two thousand and twenty-one dollars, taxes, tags, and drive it away. I made it with about ten bucks to spare. Hell, I didn't even get a cigarette lighter because it cost fifteen bucks extra. Who needs the fancy stuff, anyway? The little bear gets me where I wanna go; that's all I need. You wanna walk?"

"I'm going to sleep," Daniel replied, crawling into the backseat. "Wake me up when you get tired of driving."

During the night, we reached the Arizona border. We had to stop at some kind of checkpoint, which turned out to be an agricultural inspection station.

"You boys carrying any fruit?" asked a uniformed inspector.

"An apple and an orange," said Daniel from the backseat, holding up the fruit.

"I'll have to take the apple," said the inspector. "You're not allowed to bring this into the state."

"What's the matter with apples?" I said as we drove on.

"Beats me," said Daniel. "Don't knock yourself out worrying about it."

"Don't they like apples in Arizona?" I said. "How can they have apple pie without apples? How can they be real Americans without apple pie?"

"I'm going back to sleep," said Daniel.

We hit a snowstorm that night, but I had some chains, so we were able to keep going. By morning, we were well across Arizona, closing in on the Bear State Republic. Daniel was driving.

"Hey, look!" I suddenly shouted, pointing off to the right. "White cows!"

Daniel stood on the brakes, and we both jumped out of the car and stared at them. There was a whole field full of them. An enormous field. There must have been a thousand cows in it, and they were all white. Every last one of them.

"Well, I'll be damned," said Daniel.

"Now we know where all the white cows are."

"How did they get here?"

"Damned if I know," I said. "I guess they walked. Man, this is a weird state. All the white cows in America, and no apples. Let's get the hell out of here."

An hour later, we crossed into California, where we encountered another agricultural inspection station.

"Here we go again," I said.

"Got any fruit?" asked the uniformed agricultural inspector.

"Just an orange," said Daniel. "They took our apple in Arizona."

"Let me see it," he replied. I handed him the orange and he looked at it closely, turning it slowly in his hand as though it were a globe of the world.

"What are you looking for?" asked Daniel. "Track marks?"

"I'll have to keep this," said the inspector. "You can't bring citrus fruit into California."

"Oh, no!" I said. "You can't do this to us. They already took our apple. The orange is all we've got left. It's our breakfast. Can we eat it?"

"I'm sorry," said the inspector, "but you can't have it."

"We'll eat it right here," I said, "right before your very eyes."

"Don't give me a hard time, fellas," said the inspector, a hard edge to his voice. "Just move along; you're holding up traffic."

"Asshole," I said as we drove away.

"How were we supposed to know our orange was a junkie?" said Daniel.

"Whadda they got against fruit out here, anyway?" I said.

From the border crossing at Needles, the highway rose sharply into the California mountains. We soon topped the summit and found ourselves gazing down into a broad valley that stretched north and south to the horizons. On the other side of the valley lay another range of mountains.

"California!" I shouted.

"When's Didi expecting us?" Daniel asked.

"Not today, that's for sure," I said. "We'd better call her from the next town. Let's get some beer, too."

"Sure was nice of her to invite us to crash at her parents' place," said Daniel.

"She's a neat lady," I said. I was anxious to see her.

I'd met Didi Barnesly at school about a month earlier. She was a sophomore also, but had taken a year off and hadn't been there my freshman year. Though I'd only recently met her, I'd noticed her almost from the first day of the new school year. She was not the kind of woman that passed unnoticed. She had very long brown hair that was always combed out and flying loose in the wind, a round elegant face, and large breasts that clearly stood straight out with no artificial support. She seldom wore anything but old-fashioned dresses with full, floor-length skirts, and in cold weather she wore a heavy cape instead of a coat. I'd noticed her all right, but it had taken me a long time to find a way to meet her.

In the meantime, after Pam had finally stopped sleeping with me, I'd had only a few one-night stands that had left me feeling guilty and disgusted with myself. It was a constant battle between my near-obsessive fear of sleeping alone and my battered sense of self-respect. I did not care to trust anyone the way I had trusted Jenny or Pam. Even Dorrit, my beautiful Danish faerie queene, had failed me in the end, persuading me that I had to go back to Vietnam and then dying a horrible death in a back alley in Hong Kong. I wanted desperately and I didn't want at all, and I didn't know how to cope with it.

But in spite of myself, Didi Barnesly had continued to fascinate me. I'd see her eating in the dining hall, or gliding across campus with her hair rippling and her skirt rustling in the breeze. What is she like, I'd wonder. And then one day I'd come out of the dining hall and seen her walking alone toward Parrish, and I'd gotten a wild hair up my backside and decided what the hell, why not?

"Hi," I'd said, catching up to her as casually as possible. "Excuse me for barging in uninvited. My name is Bill Ehrhart."

"I know who you are," she'd responded with an enigmatic look.

"You do?"

"Yes."

"Oh. Well, I was just wondering, it's a nice day and all. I was just going to go for a walk in the Crum. Would you like to come along?"

But as soon as the words were out of my mouth, I had suddenly remembered the woman in San Francisco Airport my first morning back from Vietnam. My stomach tightened at the memory: me and a pretty American girl sitting at a booth drinking Coca-Cola, smiling and smiling, a simple welcome home from the alien ricefields and sand barrens and jungles of Asia. I'd rehearsed the scene a thousand times through the endless days and nights alone in Vietnam: the Coke, the smiles, perhaps a brief touching of hands before we'd go our separate ways. Sitting in the airport in my uniform that morning, I'd finally screwed up my courage and asked a young woman in a green dress to join me. But something had gone wrong; it hadn't worked the way I'd always imagined it would. She'd turned white as a sheet immediately, and I'd thought she was going to scream or call the cops, and I'd started talking a mile a minute, trying to get her to understand that I meant no harm, but she'd turned away, almost running, and I'd been left standing there, embarrassed and humiliated.

Had I done it again, I'd wondered, standing there on the lawn in front of Parrish, my heart pounding to beat the band. But after a moment of thought, Didi had smiled and replied, "It *is* a beautiful day, and I'd love to go for a walk with you." We had walked all afternoon through the woods and meadow along Crum Creek.

And we had spent a lot of time together in the month since then. Lying together on the cold rocks above Crum Creek. Listening to Gregorian chants by candlelight in her room in Parrish. Sitting side by side in my bay window in Dana overlooking the woods and the meadow and the railroad tracks.

Naming the prince of hearts as my card, she'd read my tarot, saying that I would always be a stranger in the world because I would always see the world not for what it was, but for what it ought to be. "You don't belong to this world," she'd said that night, studying the cards. "You belong to a world where flowers are always in bloom and love never falters. You are too kind for this world, too gentle, too honest. Your only defense is your vision, which is both a curse and a blessing. You will spend your life trying to make others see what you see. Few will, and you will be lonely. But you will never surrender because your vision is true and you are incapable of denying it. You have a beautiful heart."

I had thought that night of the old woman in the ricefield, hearing the crack of my rifle. I had thought of Pam, too. Too kind, I had thought, too gentle? Without attempting to explain, I had cried softly for a long time, my face buried between Didi's breasts while she held me tightly, rocking me like a baby and singing of tea and oranges that come all the way from China. She was a strange and beautiful woman. Almost mystical. I loved her.

"Do you believe this highway?" said Daniel, intruding on my thoughts as he gestured at the sixteen lanes of traffic on the San Bernardino Freeway.

"California! Land of the freeway. Yippee!" I was excited

about seeing Didi again. When she'd learned Daniel and I were traveling west for Christmas, she'd insisted that we visit her at her parents' place in Laguna Beach. I had willingly agreed.

"How much farther to Didi's?" Daniel asked, opening another can of Olympia beer. "I'm stiff as a board."

"So am I. Another hour maybe," I replied. "It's not far. Gimme another beer, will you? Fuckin' A, man, coast to coast in fifty-five hours! That's truckin'!"

"My back hurts," said Daniel.

"Hang in there, pal. In another hour, we'll be swimming in the Pacific Ocean!"

Chapter 27

I walked out of the battalion mailroom holding Jenny's letter as though it were the Host. I hadn't heard from her in more than a month of twisting turning nightmares and vivid daydreams played out in slow motion: automobiles wrinkling like tinfoil under the force of high-speed impact, trapped bodies screaming, sirens and ambulances, hospitals, the deathly stillness of white sheets and nurses, cancer, leukemia, knives and threats in dark alleys on moonless nights. I walked slowly to the intelligence shop in the command bunker and sat down. I opened the letter.

"Dearest Bill," it began, "I guess you're wondering why I haven't written. I just didn't know how to explain." What followed was less an explanation than a simple farewell—brief, alien, and distant—less than half a page. "Please forgive me," it concluded. "I pray God will protect you and keep you safe. You'll always be special to me. Jenny."

I couldn't make sense of it. I was prepared for horrible bodily injury, had already imagined myself spending a life caring for a woman with one leg, a blind woman, a woman confined to a wheelchair. Death I could have understood. Anything. But this.

This isn't possible, I thought. This isn't *possible!* Eight fucking months! Long letters. Passionate letters. Filled with every imaginable endearment. A perfect chain, like a rosary, a lifeline, a beacon. Something beautiful in the midst of the inescapable ugliness. Gone just like that? This isn't possible, I thought.

"What'sa matter, Corporal Ehrhart?" asked Gunny Johnson. I looked up. He and Lieutenant Kaiser were both staring at me.

"What? What? Nothing."

"You're white as a ghost, boy," said the lieutenant. "You look like you got the DTs. Are you feelin' okay?"

"What? Yeah, sure. Nothing."

"What is it?" the lieutenant persisted. "Bad news from home?"

No! No! No! *Please,* no! "What? I don't—what, sir?"

"Go lie down, boy," said Lieutenant Kaiser.

"What?"

"Go lie down," said Johnson.

I got up and walked out into the bright hot light. I started across the sand toward the tents, stumbled, righted myself, turned toward the high berm that surrounded the perimeter, walked to the top, and sat down, staring up Highway 28 toward Danang, where the big Freedom Birds took off every day heading for the World.

Chapter 28

"Hey!" I shouted. "This is the Oakland Bridge! We're headed back into San Francisco again!"

"Oh, no!" Daniel giggled. "We missed the turn again."

"What the hell kind of navigator are you? That's the second time we've missed it. Where's the map?"

"Right here," Daniel replied, laughing and waving the map in my face.

"Get it out of my face!" I shouted. I was laughing, too. "I can't see where the hell I'm going. Look out."

"Here it is," said Daniel, stabbing at the map with his finger. "The turn's supposed to be right here. Maybe they moved it."

"Who moved it?"

"I don't know."

"Look!" I hollered. "There's the signpost up ahead. Your next stop—the Twilight Zone!"

"What do we do?" asked Daniel.

"Well, I guess we go around and try again."

"Maybe we should stop off at Gold's and have another brownie."

"Oh, Christ, no! I can hardly see straight as it is."

"Good brownies." Daniel grinned as we started across San Francisco again toward the Golden Gate Bridge.

We'd spent three days with Didi, getting tan and enjoying the luxury of swimming in the ocean in December before roaring off again in the middle of the night toward northern California. We'd reached San Francisco about noon, only to discover that Jack Gold, a friend from Swarthmore who lived in San Francisco, wouldn't be in until midafternoon.

"What do we do for two hours?" I said.

"Let's get tattoos."

"Okay."

Daniel had gotten a scorpion; I'd gotten USMC.

"Why'd you get a scorpion?" I'd asked.

"I dunno. Why'd you get USMC?"

"I dunno. Let's see if Gold's home yet."

Jack had greeted us at the door with a dish of hash brownies. "Have one," he'd said. "They're excellent. Have a couple!" Daniel and I hadn't eaten anything for eighteen hours, and it took only about forty-five minutes for the brownies to send us into orbit. We'd spent the rest of the afternoon assaulting the Golds' refrigerator, attempting with great success to reduce its contents to rubble, and then we'd roared off again in search of Sacramento, where we were supposed to spend Christmas with one of my older brothers.

But we were having a little trouble finding the way. We'd already circled the north bay twice via the Golden Gate, San Rafael, and Oakland Bay bridges. On the third trip around, however, we finally found the road to Sacramento.

"Did you see that sign?" I roared at Daniel. "It was as big

as a barn! How the hell could you miss it?'' Daniel grinned
sheepishly and shrugged his shoulders. ''You're fired,'' I said.

''I'm stoned,'' he said.

''Good brownies,'' I said as we drove into the gathering darkness.

My brother Rob was two and a half years older than me. He
was an Air Force lieutenant. The last time I'd seen him, nearly
three years earlier, we'd both still been in Vietnam—me fresh out
of Hue City and just about to leave, him only a month into his
tour. There'd been an indoor movie theater at the radar site where
he worked, and we'd gone to the show one night. It had started
with a recording of ''The Star-Spangled Banner'' accompanied
by a film of an American flag blowing in the breeze, and everyone in the theater had stood at attention.

''You know,'' Rob had said as we'd sat down, ''it doesn't
matter how many times I hear that song, it still gets to me.''

Both the song and his remark had filled me with a terrible
confusion that I hadn't wanted to deal with.

''Want some popcorn?'' I'd replied.

''I was just about to give up on you guys,'' said Rob when
we finally reached his place an hour and a half later.

Daniel and I looked at each other and laughed. ''We got stuck
in the Twilight Zone,'' I said. ''This is Daniel Kaufman. My
brother Rob.''

''There's beer in the refrigerator,'' said Rob. ''You want to
take a shower before we go? When's the last time you had a
haircut?'' He batted my long hair with his fingertips. I couldn't
tell if he was teasing or not.

''About six months ago. On that crummy GI Bill I'm getting,
I can't *afford* haircuts.''

''Bitter, bitter,'' said Rob.

''Yeah, well, there's Spiro T. all the time flapping his lips
about how grateful America is to its Vietnam veterans. So what
do they give us when it comes time for school? A couple of
balloons and a bag of peanuts. Christ, World War Two and Korean vets got tuition, room and board, books, and seventy-five
dollars a month spending money. Grateful nation, my ass.''

''Life's a bitch,'' said Rob.

''Yeah. So where are we going tonight?''

''To a party.''

''Oh, yeah? What kind of party?''

"An Air Force officer-type party," he said. "It's just a few guys from the base, and their wives and girlfriends."

"Are they gonna let me and Daniel in?"

"Not to worry," Rob replied. "I got you a couple of safe-conduct passes."

When we got to the party, Rob introduced us. Some people didn't seem to bat an eyelash; others looked a little skeptical of our long hair and headbands. I wondered if any of the older men were Rob's superior officers. I didn't particularly want to ship-wreck his career. I was nervous at first, finding it hard to think of anything to say, but after a few drinks all around, Daniel and I seemed to ease our way into the crowd pretty comfortably. Actually, they seemed like ordinary folks mostly, except that all the men had short hair and most of the women had a lot of makeup and elaborate hairdos.

I was sitting at the kitchen table with several men when the man next to me turned toward me and said, "Rob tells me you were in the Marines."

"Yeah, I was. Three years."

"Never be able to guess from looking at you," he said good-naturedly.

"No, I guess not"—I laughed, getting a little nervous again—"but I've been out for a year and a half."

"You were in Nam, weren't you?"

"Yeah."

"Where were you?"

"All over I Corps," I replied. "I was with First Battalion, First Marines. We were down around Hoi An, below Danang, for about eight months. Then we went up north around the DMZ—Quang Tri, Con Thien, all over."

"What were you doing?"

"I was supposed to be an intelligence assistant, but the battalion scouts were part of our section, so I ended up doing double duty most of the time. They figured out they could get an extra scout that way without having to report it on the table of organization."

"You see much action?" he persisted.

I felt ambivalent about the conversation. I wanted to impress these guys with my military record, so that they wouldn't think Rob's brother was just another hippie flake. But I was afraid it would turn into a political discussion, which would probably end up doing Rob no good at all.

"What?" I asked.

"Did you see much action?"

"Enough. All in all, I'd just as soon be here."

"Rob said you earned the Purple Heart during the Tet offensive," interjected an older man with silver hair.

"Yeah, but it was no big deal, really."

"What happened?" asked the younger man beside me.

"Oh, I just got stupid one day up in Hue City. Spent the whole morning firing from the same window of the house we were in. It was a rookie mistake. I shoulda known better after twelve months—I did know better, but I just lost my concentration. Thinkin' about the Freedom Bird, or some damn thing. NVA gunner across the street decided he didn't like me and took a shot at me with a B-40 rocket. I lucked out of it, though. Got sprayed with a little shrapnel and had my bell rung pretty good, that was all."

"Well, the Purple Heart's something to be proud of," said a blond-haired man at the end of the table.

"What for?" I laughed. "Seems kind of like the booby prize to me. All you gotta do is be in the wrong place at the wrong time. Sort of like getting a medal for standing on the railroad tracks with a train coming."

"You really feel that way?" asked the blond.

"Well, yeah," I said. "If I'd had my head and ass wired together, I wouldn't have gotten hit. I make a stupid mistake, and I get a medal for it. How much sense does that make? It makes about as much sense as the war does." The last sentence just sort of tumbled out of my mouth before I could stop it.

"You think the war doesn't make any sense?" asked the older man.

"Well," I said, pausing to think, "I don't want to offend anybody. Everybody's entitled to his opinion. But as far as I'm concerned, it's the wrong war in the wrong place at the wrong time. It seems clear to me that we're not doing anybody any good there. I think our involvement was a mistake, and I don't see what good it does to perpetuate it."

"Well, I don't disagree with you," said the older man, much to my surprise, "but I don't think we can afford to withdraw precipitately. Nixon's going in the right direction."

"Maybe so," I replied, "but he's taking his sweet time about it. It's one thing to withdraw precipitately, but he's making a big production out of pulling out U.S. troops while actually widening the war.''

"That's crap!" said the blond. "He's already cut U.S. troop strength in half since he's been in office."

"And invaded Cambodia, and jacked up the air war drastically," I responded. "All he's doing is trading American lives for Vietnamese lives. Look at the casualty figures. Haven't enough people died already? It's about time we just recognize the situation for the mess that it is, and stop fooling around, for Chrissake."

"And what about the POWs?" asked the blond, clearly agitated.

Christ, this is exactly what I had wanted to avoid, I thought. Once again, I was stuck someplace I didn't want to be, and there didn't seem to be any way out.

"Well, what about 'em?" I asked. It suddenly occurred to me that some of the prisoners might actually be friends and colleagues of these men. After all, most of the POWs were pilots shot down over North Vietnam.

"Are we supposed to just abandon them?" asked the blond.

"Of course not," I said. "But I'd be willing to bet that if we said, 'Okay, North Vietnamese, we're going home now; all you have to do is hand over our men, and we'll pack up and go home,' they'd be perfectly willing to hand them over and wave good-bye. What do they want 'em for once we're gone?"

"Well," snorted the blond, "it's certainly clear that you don't know much about Communists."

"And I suppose you do!" I said. "I'll tell you something, mister. I spent thirteen months down in the ricefields. I pulled fifteen major combat operations. I was at Con Thien and Hue. I didn't kill people from ten thousand feet up. When I killed people, I had to point my rifle at 'em and pull the trigger and watch 'em crumple up and die. What have you done lately?"

"What's that got to do with—"

"So don't tell me who understands what! That's what it's got to do with. Communism, schmommunism, that doesn't mean fuck-all. All those people want is to be left alone. They want people to stop dropping bombs on them, and wrecking their homes, and destroying their crops, and beating them up and killing them. Christ, if I were Vietnamese, I'd be a Vietcong, too."

"I don't have to listen to this garbage," the blond snapped.

He got up abruptly and stalked off. "You're a disgrace to the nation," he muttered over his shoulder.

That did it! I got up quickly to go after him, but the man sitting beside me grabbed my arm and pulled me back down. "Let it go," he said quietly. "A close friend of his is being held prisoner in the north."

"Well, I'm sorry about that," I said, my head spinning from anger and alcohol, "but it doesn't change the facts. There's no way we're gonna win that war. And the longer we stay, the more POWs there are. How many more thousands are going to die for a few hundred POWs? That makes a hell of a lot of sense, doesn't it?"

"Some of us don't disagree with a lot of what you're saying," said the silver-haired older man. "But it's a damned difficult situation. We *have* made a commitment to the South Vietnamese government. We've got to try to give them a chance to defend themselves before we pull out."

"It's a nice thought," I said, "but it's never gonna happen. There wouldn't be any Saigon government if we weren't there, and the minute we leave, it's going to collapse, whether we stay six more months or ten more years. Thieu has virtually no support out in the ricefields and villages where it counts. I saw it with my own eyes. I lived in the middle of it. The Vietnamese people hate us—and with good reason. And the Saigon government is perceived—rightly so, in my opinion—as nothing but a puppet of the Americans. What the Vietnamese are trying to defend themselves against is *us*. And the longer we stay, the worse it's going to get."

"You may be right," said the older man, "but I think the government's doing the best it can with a difficult situation. Nixon isn't the one that got us into Vietnam, you know."

"Maybe not," I said, "but he's the one that promised to get us out."

"I think he's doing the best he can." The older man sighed. "Anyway, it's out of *our* hands. He'll do what he's going to do, and there's not much we can do about it."

"But it's *not* out of our hands," I replied. "Isn't this supposed to be a government of the people, by the people, for the people? And *we're* the people, for Chrissake. What the hell's going on in this country if the government won't listen to the people?"

Chapter 29

"You got everything in your cabin secured?" Roger asked as he strapped on his lifejacket.

"I hope so," I shrugged, a gesture that lifted my own lifejacket up around my ears. "I guess I'll find out, won't I? Christ, I can't believe we're going over the bar in this weather—and at night, no less. What'd they do, put the second engineer in charge of the whole ship?"

Crossing Columbia Bar is no easy task under the best of conditions. Except for the Outer Banks of North Carolina, it has claimed more ships and lives than any other section of the North American coast. The complex interaction of centuries of silt deposit, ocean tides, inexorable wave action, and powerful river currents has built up a bar at the mouth of the river nearly a mile square. Within this so-called potato patch, currents and crosscurrents rip and tear at each other and at the silt and sand on the bottom, constantly closing old channels and opening new ones. Those same currents play havoc with any vessel that ventures onto the bar, and even big ships like the *Endeavor* could be hurled around as easily as driftwood. Running aground, getting turned sideways and swamped, and even breaking apart were all very real possibilities as we neared the Columbia lightship and the mouth of the river that night. It didn't help any that the storm we'd been riding for the previous two days was still with us.

"Don't worry about it," said Roger. "We've done it before."

"Oh, sure," I said. "No big deal. That's why the captain's got us all up at one A.M., dressed in lifejackets and ready to abandon ship."

"Where's your sense of adventure?"

"I had all the adventure I need for this week down in the steering gear room last night."

"I heard about that," Roger chuckled, shaking his head. "I also hear the second engineer's gonna get the gate when we get to Bellingham."

"That's what the chief tells me. We made a little deal. He fires the Second, and I don't make him report the triple OT."

"Well, I told you that guy wouldn't last too much longer," said Roger. "That's not the first time he's screwed up. You wanna play some casino?"

"Yeah, okay. I don't know why you keep trying to play this game."

"You can't keep winning forever," said Roger, taking out a fresh deck of cards and beginning to shuffle. "Come on, luck, be a lady tonight."

"You sexist pig, Roger. Luck's an eighty-year-old bag lady from Fishtown, Philadelphia, and you couldn't get to first base with her if you were the last bum on the Broad Street subway."

"We'll see about that."

"Deal," I said.

"So tell me, did your brother ever get in any trouble for that party you and your pal crashed?" Roger asked as he dealt the first round.

"I guess not," I said, studying my cards. "He never said anything to me about it, and he's still in the Air Force. Even made captain. He's teaching history now at the Air Force Academy in Colorado Springs."

"Well, that was some trip you guys had," said Roger. "I wish I'd have done a few things like that while I had the chance."

"Oh, that was just for starters," I said. "We weren't even halfway home yet."

"Ten of diamonds!" Roger shouted. "And it's mine."

"Won't do you any good."

"We'll see, we'll see. So what else happened?"

"Well, the day after Christmas, Daniel and I headed back down to Didi's place for a few more days. Rob came with us because he wanted to see a friend of his in San Diego. All the way down, we kept hearing on the radio about some rock concert in Laguna Beach that had gotten out of hand—the cops supposedly had all the roads into town blocked off, and they weren't letting anybody in except people who lived there—"

"Couldn't you tell them you were visiting—"

"Wait a minute, just listen. That wasn't the problem. See, Gold had given us a bag of marijuana for the trip back, and we were afraid they'd search us and find the stuff. Which is not what we needed, especially with my brother in the car. He didn't even smoke the stuff, you know, and there's his career passing before his eyes. Finally, about ten miles from Laguna, we figured we had to do something. Well, we couldn't smoke it all that fast, and we couldn't bring ourselves to throw it out, so we ate it."

"Yuck."

"Yeah. Like eating sawdust. So you know what? By the time we got to Laguna, there weren't any roadblocks. No cops. Nothin'. We just cruised right in. And that's not even the worst part. The worst part was that we didn't even get a buzz off the stuff. Doesn't do a thing for you unless you heat it first—cook it or burn it or something. But we hadda find that out the hard way. And that was our whole stash for the trip east."

At the end of the first hand, Roger was leading eight to three. "I told you this was going to be my game!" he said.

"We got a long way to go yet," I replied, shuffling the cards and dealing the second hand.

"So then what happened?"

"Well, we spent a few more days with Didi. Drove up into the high desert around Joshua Tree National Monument and had a snowball fight stripped to the waist. It was like sixty degrees, and there's snow all over the place. I'd never seen anything like it before."

"Didi stripped to the waist?"

"No, asshole, snow and hot weather at the same time. Anyway, Didi left her blouse on."

"Too bad."

"The way it goes," I said. "Hell, one morning I went into the bathroom, and here's this hand-lettered greeting card in my shaving kit reading 'Didi loves you,' and I couldn't do anything about it because we were staying at her parents' house. Somebody was always around. One of her sisters, or Daniel, or her brother, or her mom or dad. I was goin' nuts. I didn't even get a chance to ask her if she'd written the note."

"Did she?" asked Roger.

"Yeah, but I didn't find out for sure until after we'd all gotten back to Swarthmore. Anyway, I'd made arrangements to stop off and visit some guy I'd been good friends with when I was in that fighter squadron in Japan and the Philippines—Smitty, the big Swede, the guy that threw the potato salad all over me at that squadron picnic?"

"Oh, yeah."

"He was stationed in Yuma, Arizona, by this time, going for twenty years. So Daniel and I roared out of Laguna Beach and drove all day and half the night to get there. Stayed for two days, and the only thing that got a little awkward was that every time I started to talk about Vietnam or politics and stuff, he'd find some excuse to change the subject. Never got mad or argued with me. Just changed the subject. Otherwise, we had a nice time. It wasn't until later that I figured out a few things."

"Like what?"

"Like we stayed there for two days and two nights, and never left the house. Didn't go to the store, or the movies, or the NCO club, or anywhere. We didn't even sit out on the patio in the backyard. And what I figured out later is that he didn't want anybody to see him with us. We must have embarrassed him, you know, like he was afraid of what people would think if they saw him with two hippie types. Geez, I felt really bad about it afterwards. I mean, I really liked Smitty; we'd been good friends back in the old days."

"You ever hear from him again?" asked Roger.

"Nope."

"Too bad."

"Yeah," I shrugged. "This is cards. He musta thought I'd gone right off the deep end."

"Hadn't he been in Vietnam?"

"Oh, yeah, he'd been there. But he was Air Wing. All he'd done was fix the electrical systems on F-4s at Danang airfield. It really wasn't all that much different from stateside."

"You never talked to him about it when you were stationed together?"

"Not so much," I replied. "Vietnam was still just one big hurt-locker back then. Mostly, I just didn't talk about it."

"That's the hand," said Roger. "Count 'em up."

"I got nine," I said. "That makes it twelve to ten, my lead."

"Damn."

"Your deal."

"Have you ever seen anybody else that you knew back then?"

"Yeah. A couple of guys. It took me a couple more experiences like that to figure out that it's best just to leave the past where it is."

"Bad news, huh?"

"Not *bad* so much as *sad*, actually. Just sad. You see people that you care about but you haven't seen for a long time, and what you see isn't at all like what you remember, and you go away wondering what the hell happened. People change. Maybe I've changed more than they have, I don't know. Man, one of the guys I saw—I'd known him when we were both stationed in North Carolina, but I hadn't seen him for nearly three years. He was a student at Ohio State by then, and I stopped to see him on the way home from the Indianapolis Five Hundred in the spring of 1971, about five months after I saw Smitty. Turns out he's president of the OSU Vietnam Veterans Club—and I'm not talking Vietnam Veterans Against the War, either; I'm talking Neanderthal here, real caveman stuff. He spent the whole night telling me how he and the rest of the guys in his club would go to antiwar rallies and beat up demonstrators. And I'm sitting there in his living room with my long hair and rainbow headband and beads. Christ almighty. I have no idea what he thought of me, but it sure didn't cramp his storytelling style."

"Jesus. Building nines," said Roger, putting down a five on top of a four.

—"Thanks," I said, picking up the pile with a nine of my own.

"Goddamn it!"

"Be nice."

"So how did that guy end up so different from you?" Roger asked.

"Beats me." I shrugged. "I guess everybody that went through Vietnam came out of it differently. It's a hard thing to admit that your own government sucker-punched you. I guess a lot of guys just can't cope with it. Look at all the Vietnam veterans ending up in prison, ending up as junkies or suicides, ending up with less-than-honorable discharges. You just can't tell me that somehow my whole generation turned out to be nothing but a bunch of fuckups. All those guys are hurtin' inside. They got burned and they don't know how to deal with it. Most guys short-circuit along the way, one way or another. Guys like my friend at Ohio State, I don't think they've ever asked themselves even the most basic questions about what really happened in Vietnam, or why. They'd rather go on believing—God, I don't know what. That it wasn't for nothing. That it was some kind of noble cause that the doves and the peaceniks screwed up. Fuck if I know what they believe. All I know is that I got a lot of fond memories of a lot of people I knew back then, and I hope a lot of them have fond memories of me, and I'd just as soon leave it that way."

"You haven't seen anybody else, huh? Never saw anybody you were with in Vietnam?"

"One other guy, my best buddy from Vietnam. I visited him a couple of months after I was at Ohio State. It wasn't a bad visit, actually, but it wasn't great. All we had in common was something that neither of us wanted very much to remember. After that, I stopped trying. I never should have tried in the first place, but I seem to have to learn everything the hard way."

Just then the propeller stopped turning and the ship began to bob up and down fiercely as it drifted to a stop. The bobbing motion was very different—and much more violent—than rolling while the ship was under way.

"Hey, we've reached the bar," said Roger. "Come here. You gotta watch the pilot come aboard."

"I've seen the Columbia pilot before," I said.

"Not in weather like this, you haven't. This is amazing. Get over here. And grab those two vents. If we put 'em in, it'll help keep the rain out. You gotta open the portholes to watch this."

"You're crazy. It's pouring out there."

"No, no, it works. I'll show you. Hurry up."

I picked up the two rubber vents and brought them over. They fit right into the open portholes, jutting out into the night like little rubber awnings. They didn't exactly keep you entirely dry, but they worked surprisingly well. As I stuck my head out of the porthole, I could see the beam from the Columbia lightship sweeping eerily through the storm. Then two big floodlights were turned on up on the bridge of the *Endeavor*, lighting up the whole starboard side of the ship and the patch of ocean between the ship and the pilot boat. Rain fell in torrents from low boiling clouds, and the black sea thrashed and heaved angrily.

The Columbia River pilot boat was unlike any other on the West Coast run. Most pilot boats came right up alongside the tanker to deposit the pilot. But the Columbia boat had a system and a design especially made for the rough waters that regularly prevailed off Columbia Bar. It was larger than most pilot boats, and its stern was shaped into a flat ramp that angled right down to water level. At the top of the ramp, a smaller double-ended motorized dory rode piggyback on the deck of the pilot boat.

As I watched, three men in yellow raingear struggled out of the pilot boat's cabin, precariously made their way along the heaving, tossing deck to the dory, and rolled back the canvas tarp that covered the open launch. Then two of the men climbed into the dory while the third man positioned himself on the deck of the pilot boat at the dory's bow. The dory's helmsman signaled with his hand, and the man on deck then released a hook attached to the dory's bow. The dory slid swiftly down the ramp and into the water, where it immediately began bobbing up and down like a cork gone berserk. One moment it would be perched atop the crest of a wave; the next moment, it would drop down into a trough, completely disappearing from view, only to reappear at the top of the next wave.

In this up-and-down fashion, the little dory made its way toward the tanker, which was also heaving and rolling, but in a completely different rhythm and pattern from the dory. Looking along the hull of the ship toward the bridge, I could see a rope ladder hanging over the side of the *Endeavor*. As the ship rolled to starboard the ladder would swing way out from the side of the ship, and as the ship rolled back to port the ladder would come slamming back in against the hull. That a tiny dory only 12 to 15 feet long was going to attempt to come alongside a 642-foot tanker in weather and seas like this was utterly insane. That a man was actually going to attempt to transfer himself from dory to ship by means of a wildly swinging rope ladder was even crazier.

But that is exactly what they did. It took two tries for the pilot—standing up in the dory, no less—to grab the ladder, the helmsman of the dory meanwhile miraculously keeping his boat in close without colliding with the ship. Once the pilot grabbed the ladder, the dory was instantly gone, pulling away before an errant wave could splinter it against the steel hull, and leaving the pilot hanging on to the ladder thirty feet or more below the safety of the main deck. One moment, the pilot would be dangling in space as the ship rolled to starboard; the next moment, as the ship rolled back to port, he'd go slamming back against the steel hull.

In the meantime, the dory was fighting its way back to the pilot boat. When the helmsman got close to the pilot boat, he lined himself up with the stern ramp, gunned the engine to full power, and scooted right up the ramp, getting about two-thirds of the way up the ramp before coming to a halt. At precisely that moment, the man at the top of the ramp, who had never left his post, leaned out with the hook and deftly snagged the ring on the bow of the dory. Then he quickly started up a winch that hauled the dory the rest of the way up the ramp. The moment the dory was securely in place, the two men covered it with the canvas again, worked their way forward along the deck, and disappeared into the cabin.

I had been so engrossed in watching the retrieval operation that I had momentarily forgotten about the pilot. I looked forward toward the bridge and the ladder just in time to see the pilot being helped over the edge of the deck. Somehow he had managed to make it up the ladder without falling off.

"Jesus Christ," I whistled. "Those guys are all crazy."

"Pretty darned good, aren't they?" Roger grinned.

"Well, yeah, they're pretty amazing, but Jesus, that's a hell of a way to make a living."

"Those guys are the best boathandlers I've ever seen anywhere in the world," said Roger. Soon we could hear the engines beginning to crank up deep in the bowels of the ship, and then the ship began vibrating as the propeller bit into the sea. "Well, hold on to your cookies, boy, here we go. Better shut the portholes."

"Gimme a towel," I said. "I'm soaked."

You could tell the exact moment that the ship entered the "potato patch" over the bar. We immediately began to pitch and roll violently, bucking and shuddering as though the ship were being twisted and wrenched six different ways at once. It was more severe than anything I'd felt since coming aboard, even during the previous times we'd crossed the bar. During one succession of three waves that hit one right after the other from the same direction, we must have been heeled over at least forty-five degrees. I thought for sure that we were going all the way over.

"Yahoo!" Roger hollered as we both clung to his bed to keep from being thrown against the starboard bulkhead.

"Holy Moses, man. This ain't at *all* what I had in mind when I volunteered for sea duty."

Chapter 30

What the heck's this, I wondered as I opened my mailbox in Parrish and pulled out a large blue envelope. It had clearly come through campus mail: there was no stamp and no return address. I walked outside, sat down on the step, and opened it. It contained a valentine from Didi. Well, I'll be damned, I thought. I'd completely forgotten that today was Valentine's Day, February 14, 1971.

She'd obviously taken a lot of time and care with it, too. Handmade from colored construction paper and paper lace, it had a collage of magazine photos pasted on the outside, and inside was a hand-lettered poem she'd written called "In Your Window":

The day can't end
before I show you the sunset,
before you show me where the moon will rise.
The night can't begin
until we understand the words
of the language of silence here in your room.

From your window I saw you sit easy on your bunker,
watching the red-gold rockets
the way the headlight patterns
spilling off the walls of your room
feed the empty night just now.

When a man speaks to a woman,
and only for a moment, shocked,
they stare across a darkened room
alone.

Didi, Didi. What was in her head, I wondered. Alone among all the women I dealt with, she seemed to understand me for what I was. Unlike other women—and most men, for that matter—she seemed neither enamored with nor frightened by the ex-Marine sergeant who'd come back to Planet Earth a stranger. And she seemed to accept what she understood—all of it. She ignored nothing and invented nothing. Being with her was a kind of amnesty.

Yet we hadn't become lovers—not yet at least—much to my dismay. Often she would sit with me in my window overlooking the Crum until late into the night, holding me in the silence seldom broken by words and never broken by mindless chatter. But always, in the end, she would go, leaving me to choose between lowering myself down alone once again into the coffin of sleep or going off to one or another of several women who did not understand me at all but were willing to share their beds with me.

God knows what those women thought or expected or wanted. I knew that it had little to do with me, but I didn't care. It was only that some nights, when I lost my nerve completely, I was willing to degrade myself and degrade those women rather than face the nightmares alone. Morning always brought shame and humiliation, but night always came back again, bringing with it terrors beyond all reason. Some nights I could cope with it; some nights I couldn't.

I read Didi's poem one more time, lightly rubbing the card with my fingertips, put it back in the envelope, and walked over to the swimming pool. Jamie McAdams, the men's swimming coach, was just turning out the lights.

"Hi, Jamie," I said uneasily.

"Well, Father, how are you?" he said, pumping my hand with both of his. He always called me Father because I was the oldest guy on the swimming team—or had been when I'd been on the team the previous year. "What are you up to these days?" he asked, his round face a little red and beaming with warmth. Over sixty years old, he stood about five feet three inches tall, and carried more weight than he should have around the middle, though he wasn't obese by any means. He looked like a good-natured elf. "Where have you been keeping yourself?"

"Oh, just around."

"Well, I certainly have missed you this season."

"That's what I wanted to talk to you about, Jamie," I said, shifting my weight uncomfortably. "Have you got a few minutes we can talk?"

"Sure, sure, Father. Come on in. What's on your mind?"

"Well, I'll tell you. I know it's kind of late in the season, but, well, I was just wondering, you know, if maybe I could be on the team for the rest of the season."

"Well, well," said Jamie, lifting his eyebrows.

"You wouldn't even have to let me swim in the meets. I'd be happy just to practice with the team."

Even more than that, I just wanted to be around Jamie. He made me feel good. He was one of the gentlest, most sensitive men I'd ever known. There weren't many people that I felt comfortable with, but Jamie was one of them, and I'd missed him very much since last season. I kept that part of my thoughts to myself, however.

"Oh, I think we ought to be able to find a place for you in the lineup." He smiled. "We don't exactly have people begging to swim the two-hundred butterfly."

"Gee, thanks, Jamie!" I really hadn't expected it to be so easy. "I don't know what to say. Thanks a lot."

"Well, I'm glad to see you again, Father," he replied. "It's about time you get your keister back in the water!" Then his face turned more serious. "You know, Father, I've thought about you a lot this season. Why didn't you come out in November?"

"I don't know, Jamie," I said slowly, "I really don't know. I just didn't feel like it. I worked pretty hard last year, and I was still doing times that were slower than what I was doing when I was fifteen. I guess I was feeling discouraged."

"So you're getting older," Jamie laughed. "So what? You know I don't care how fast you go. I just—" His voice cracked suddenly and his eyes got misty, and when he began talking again, he was using that blustering gravelly voice he always used when he didn't want you to think he was getting emotional. "I just like to see you guys in there enjoying yourselves. My goodness, Father, the way these—what do you call 'em—these professors pile on the work around here, you gotta do *something* to unwind. Otherwise you'd *never* have any fun." He paused, and when he started speaking again, his voice was normal. "Especially you, Father. You need to have some fun." He put his arm around me and patted my shoulder. "You've been having a tough time, haven't you?"

"Yeah, Jamie, I have," I replied. "It's hard sometimes. Really hard."

"Well, I knew there was something wrong when you didn't show

158 MARKING TIME

up for practice back in November. Anybody who drinks bourbon with his coach the night before the championship one year and doesn't come out for the team the next year, well, I know *something's* wrong. Father, you keep it all bottled up inside yourself,'' he said, looking at me intently, ''but I could see it last year. To tell you the truth, I wasn't all that surprised when you didn't come out for the team this fall.'' My eyebrows raised involuntarily. ''Oh, sure,'' he continued, ''I've learned a few things in sixty-three years. Young whippersnapper like you can't pull one over on me. Which side of the bed do you think I get up on?''

''I missed you, Jamie,'' I suddenly blurted out, leaning over and hugging him tightly.

''I've missed you, too, son. Now get out of here,'' he said, his voice turning gravelly again, ''and come back for practice tomorrow.''

Chapter 31

After a morning of digging, and filling and stacking sandbags, the cool water of the river felt gloriously liberating. The clouds had broken and the sun was shining. The water was clean. Stripped to the buff, the scouts splashed and flopped around like seals. The current was so swift that you had to swim upstream just to stay in place. Just a few meters offshore, the water must have been at least five meters deep; I dove for the bottom, but couldn't touch it. Though the river was about forty meters wide, we all stayed close to the west bank since the east bank was ungarrisoned and unguarded.

The sharp slap of bullets striking the water came a split second before the sound of the shots. ''Sniper!'' several guys hollered at once.

The warning was unnecessary. With the first report, the splash party broke up, scouts heading for the riverbank like frantic tadpoles. Seagrave and Amagasu, who'd been standing watch on the west bank, opened fire immediately. I was out of the water and halfway up the sandy bank when someone hollered, "Aymes is still in the river! He's hit!" Still scrambling up the bank, I looked back. Aymes lay facedown in the water, his arms floating limply on the surface of the river, the current already carrying him swiftly south. I raced back down the bank and dove in. By now other Marines, attracted by the gunfire, lay on the top of the riverbank firing toward the trees and bushes on the opposite side. I swam after Aymes, holding my head up as high as I could to keep him in sight, stroking for all I was worth.

The level of fire quickly rose to a bristling storm of small arms and exploding grenades from M-79 grenade launchers. I reached Aymes and grabbed for his chin as I had been taught to do only two summers before in Red Cross lifesaving. I pulled his head up, reached across his chest with my other hand, and took him in a cross-chest carry. As I did, a red-gray ooze spilled down over my arm and I almost threw up right there in the water. It was Aymes's brain. There was a hole the size of my fist where his right eye should have been. The current swept us out toward the middle of the river. Already we were a hundred meters south of where we had been swimming.

"Throw me a line! Throw me a line!" I hollered. I couldn't tell if we were still taking fire. I used Aymes's body as a shield. A rope fell across us; I fumbled for it and caught hold, tied it around Aymes's chest, and held on as we were pulled ashore. A corpsman was already waiting. "Forget it, Doc," I said as we hauled Aymes's body out of the water and up over the top of the bank to safety. "He's dead."

The firing had stopped. I went down to the river again, knelt down, and washed the remains of Aymes off my arm and shoulder. I threw up into the river, watching the slime drift away swiftly in little swirls and widening streaks. I washed the sour taste out of my mouth. I was still stark naked. I looked across at the opposite bank, but there was no one there, and no sign that anyone had ever been there.

Chapter 32

"Thanks for the valentine," I said, reaching out and touching Didi's knee gently. She covered my hand with both of hers.

"You're very welcome," she said. "I'm glad you like it."

We were sitting facing each other in the bay window in my room in Dana, our backs against opposite walls, our knees drawn up, and our feet intertwined. It was dark, but I hadn't turned on the light. The bare black trees outside, many of them towering over the three-story dormitory, swayed eerily in the wind.

"Can you really picture me in Vietnam?" I asked.

"Yes. At least I can picture what I imagine. I don't really know if what I see in my head is what it was really like." She brought my hand up to her lips and kissed it, then put it back on her knee. A car drove by slowly on the campus road below the dorm, the beam from its headlights, broken and scattered by the trees, momentarily filling the room with moving patterns of light and shadow.

"Billy, who's Dorrit?" Didi asked after a long silence.

"Where did you hear that name?" I asked, startled.

"Last week when you fell asleep in my room, you called out her name three times."

"No kidding?" I took a deep breath and exhaled slowly. "She was a woman I met in Hong Kong when I was on R and R. I met her on the street the second night I was there—just walked up to her and grabbed her arm and begged her to let me talk to her for a while. Boy, I was really drunk. I don't know why she didn't knock me down and run."

"She could tell you were a sweetie," Didi laughed.

"I don't know about that, but anyway, she didn't. I ended up spending five days with her."

"She wasn't Chinese, was she?"

"No, Danish. She was a commercial artist. Worked for some advertising company there. Talk about dreams. Only Hollywood would ever have believed it. There I was, eight months into my tour in Vietnam, five months still to go, just turned nineteen, my high school sweetheart had just sent me a Dear John letter a month earlier, I'm in a strange city full of bars and prostitutes specializing in taking lonely naive suckers like me straight to the cleaners—and out of nowhere, suddenly there's Dorrit. Wow. They hadda be the five most beautiful days of my life, all strung together back to back. Under the circumstances, I probably would have fallen head over heels for Godzilla, but she certainly wasn't Godzilla. She was—well, she was almost an angel."

"Was she a natural blonde?" Didi asked, jostling my knee playfully.

"Of course." I laughed. "Classic Scandinavian. Very beautiful. And very kind and gentle. The morning I was supposed to go back, I woke up with her lying beside me and the hotel bellboy banging on the door shouting that the military bus was downstairs waiting to take me back to the airport. And I looked at her, and I thought about five more months in the middle of all that madness, and I told the bellboy to go to hell and take the bus with him. I was all set to desert. I think I really would have done it, too."

"Why didn't you?"

"Dorrit talked me out of it. She wouldn't let me. Oh, it wasn't like she *wanted* me to go back to Vietnam and maybe get my head blown off. She was crying, and I was crying, and it was really a scene. But she said I couldn't throw away my whole life just for five months—just to avoid going back to Vietnam for five more months. You know, how I'd probably get caught and put in prison, and even if I didn't, I'd be a fugitive for the rest of my life, and I'd never be able to go home again, and stuff like that. And I suppose she was right. But I'm not really sure anymore. The more time passes, the more I wonder."

We lapsed back into silence for a while, Didi still holding my hand in place on her knee. The Media Local rumbled through the woods below the dorm, the beam from its headlight broken into a dozen constantly changing shafts by the tree trunks.

"Do you ever hear from her?"

"She's dead now," I said. "She was raped and tortured and murdered in some godforsaken back alley one night."

"Oh, Billy. I'm sorry."

"Funny, the way things work out sometimes. I ended up surviving, and Dorrit didn't." My eyes had filled with tears, and when I blinked, they began to roll slowly down my cheeks. I looked away from Didi into the darkness of the room.

"It's all right to cry, Billy."

My head dropped to my chest, and my shoulders began to shake up and down in a series of deep, soundless sobs. Didi encircled me with her arms, and cradled my head on her shoulder. After a while, I stopped crying, but we stayed like that, our bodies intertwined, for a long time.

"It's very late," she said finally. "I have to go."

"Please stay tonight." I tightened my grip on her.

"I can't stay, Billy."

"Please, Didi. Don't make me beg."

"It wouldn't make any difference," she said, taking my head between her hands. "Billy, Billy. If I sleep with you tonight, what about tomorrow night? And the night after that? I'm not what you need, Billy. I do love you—very, very much. But I've got problems of my own—" Her voice faltered momentarily. "We're like two comets streaking through the universe. If we get too close, we'll burn each other out, and there'll be nothing left of either of us."

Chapter 33

The column was halted again—God knew why, and only God cared. We were sitting beside the trail smoking and taking it easy when two of the scouts burst out of the bushes nearby. "Come here and look what we found," they shouted. Not fifty meters away was a small one-room temple built in a clearing among the trees. It was made of plain concrete with a dull red tile roof, but inside, brightly colored tapestries hung from the walls, and an ornately carved altar stood against one wall. Various kinds of pottery stood on the altar, some of it containing incense sticks. There was no one around, but someone had recently been making repairs to the roof. A sawhorse and some other equipment leaned against the back of the building.

"What is it?" asked Wally.

"It's a church, asshole," said Mogerty.

"Let's knock it down," said Hoffy, dragging the heavy sawhorse around front.

"What for?" asked Wally.

"Why not?" said Hoffy. "Grab the other end of this." Wally and Hoffy picked up the wooden sawhorse, counted to three, took a running start, and crashed the sawhorse against the wall of the temple. They both fell down and came up cursing and shaking their stinging hands. "Jesus, that sucker's solid," said Hoffy.

"Not like that," said Morgan. "Do it this way. Come on, Bill." We picked up the sawhorse and placed one end of it against the wall. "Draw it back and swing it forward," he said, "like this: heave ho!" The sawhorse banged against the wall. Heave ho!" he shouted again. The sawhorse banged against the wall again. "Heave ho!" everybody shouted in unison. "Heave ho! Heave ho!" The sawhorse broke through the wall, knocking a hole about two feet in diameter. "Like that, Hoffy," said Morgan, dusting off his hands on his pants.

Wally and Hoffy picked up the sawhorse and positioned it about two feet to the left of the hole. "Heave ho!" they shouted. "Heave ho!" everybody shouted. "Heave ho! Heave ho! Heave ho!" Another chunk of the wall fell in. "Hooray!" everybody shouted. Wally and Hoffy bowed to each other, then to the rest of the scouts. Mogerty and Barnes picked up the sawhorse: "Heave ho!"

In this fashion, taking turns by twos, we proceeded along one wall, knocked out the corner, worked our way down the next wall, knocked out that corner, and started down the third wall. It looked like a large mechanical beaver had gone berserk on the building. "Heave ho! Heave ho!" *Crrrack!* The roof shuddered. "Heave ho! Heave ho!" *Crrraaack!*

Everybody scattered as the whole top half of the temple began to heel down slowly onto the broken walls. Then the roof tore away from the one remaining good wall, banged down on the three broken walls, split in half, and fell in on itself, crashing to the floor of the temple in a roar of dust and rubble. The crowd of spectators from Alpha Company that had by this time gathered to watch leaped to their feet, cheering and applauding. The scouts shook hands all around.

Chapter 34

As the helicopter touched down on the crude landing zone hacked into heavy brush, it was besieged by a formless undisciplined mob of ARVN soldiers. Indeed, the soldiers were openly mutinous, pushing and shoving each other in a frantic attempt to gain space aboard the aircraft. An American air crewman, standing in the chopper's open doorway, tried to maintain some semblance of order, but he was quickly pushed aside by the mob, the chopper instantly writhing with bodies like some dead carcass infested with maggots. In a kind of panic, the chopper began lifting off again only moments after it touched down, trying to escape the melee.

Burdened with too much weight, the aircraft made a slow and precarious ascent, as if at any moment it would collapse out of the sky. An ARVN soldier fell or was pushed from the door, tumbling down onto the soldiers crowded below, their arms still outstretched toward the slowly rising chopper. At least a dozen soldiers clung to the chopper's landing skids. Some of them also fell off, their fingers smashed by the rifle butt wielded by the American crewman, who had fought his way back to the door and was frantically trying to lighten the impossibly heavy load. Others were pulled off by the soldiers still on the ground. A few managed to hang on, dangling from the skids, their legs kicking at thin air.

"So much for Vietnamization," I said, gesturing toward the television set.

A few weeks earlier, in February 1971, South Vietnamese army soldiers, supported by American air and artillery, had crossed the border into Laos in a Cambodian-style invasion. The stated purpose had been to cut the Ho Chi Minh Trail and stop North Vietnamese army infiltration into South Vietnam. It was, Pentagon and White House sources had said, to be a major test for ARVN forces, a demonstration that Nixon's policy of Vietnamization was succeeding.

But by now, only a few weeks later, the operation had crumbled into what was obviously a disaster. For several days, television screens had been filled with scenes of ARVN troops streaming pell-mell out of Laos back into South Vietnam aboard overloaded helicopters, overloaded trucks, overloaded tanks and jeeps, and even on foot. Many of the soldiers were without weapons or equipment of any kind, having abandoned everything in their headlong flight from the battleground. It had turned into a fiasco, a debacle.

Yet American government spokespeople refused to admit it. Even now as we sat watching in the living room of the DU house, Ron Ziegler, Nixon's press secretary, came on the air to explain to reporters that the operation had achieved its objectives, and that a planned withdrawal was proceeding in an orderly and systematic manner.

"You lying fucking asshole!" I shouted at the screen, shaking my fist in frustration. "It's a goddamned rout! I can't believe this crap. How can the guy keep a straight face, for cryin' out loud? Change the damned channel, will you? I can't watch any more of this garbage."

"Swill time!" hollered Mark Jacobs as he and another DU came in, their arms loaded with shopping bags. In one bag were several pints of two-hundred-proof grain alcohol; in the others were several dozen cans of unsweetened orange and grapefruit juice. Within minutes, the contents of all of the containers had been emptied into a large plastic garbage can, and Jacobs was stirring the concoction with a two-by-four plank. "Belly up, folks," he said, cackling like one of the witches in *Macbeth.*

"You hear about the Calley verdict?" asked Fred Charles as I dipped my cup into the vat.

"Yeah, I heard," I said.

"What did you think?"

"Didn't surprise me any," I said, taking a drink. "I coulda told you the verdict two years ago. Christ, what a farce. You can't tell me his superiors didn't know what he was up to. Hell, they ordered him to do it. Maybe not in so many words, but you can bet they made it clear from the word go that his job was to produce a body count. And that's exactly what he did.''

"What do you think they should have done with him?" asked Fred.

"It isn't what they should have done with him that's the problem," I said. "It's what they shoulda done with everybody else that pisses me off. Medina and the rest of Calley's superiors—right on up to the White House. They're all responsible, just as much as Calley is. Listen, for all I know the guy's probably a cold-blooded creep. I'm not saying they shoulda given him a medal. But given the way things are over there, what Calley did was inevitable. It's the whole damned war that's wrong, not just what one guy did or didn't do. The whole damned government shoulda been on trial.''

"Fat chance," said Mike Morris, who had been listening to the conversation.

"Yeh," I said, "fat chance."

"Still think Nixon's trying to end the war?" Mike asked.

"Gimme a break, will ya?"

The house was filling up with DUs now. The fraternity had reserved one of the small private dining rooms in Sharples for the Friday evening meal, and we were just getting primed before going off to dinner. For nearly an hour, I poured down glass after glass of grain punch. By the time we left for dinner, I was loaded. We took the plastic vat of punch with us, sneaking it in a back door. I continued to drink through the meal.

In the middle of dinner, the door to the dining room opened and two female students started to walk in carrying trays of food. They hadn't realized that the room had been reserved for DU. They stopped dead in their tracks when they saw us. I immediately leaped to my feet and pulled my pants down. One of the women let out a short scream, then stifled it, and the two of them backed out the door in awkward haste. As the door closed we could hear at least one of the trays clattering to the bare floor just beyond the door. The room erupted in a loud round of applause.

A little while later, Kathleen, the matronly silver-haired woman who supervised the dining hall, came into the room looking very stern. "You boys are making too much noise," she scolded. "If you can't be more quiet, you'll have to leave." I leaped up onto the table right in front of her, turned my back to her, dropped my pants, bent over, and gave her a full moon. When I stood up

again, the room was filled with laughter and applause, and Kathleen was gone.

Sometime after that, the door opened again and Didi walked
in. She was wearing an especially lovely long dress, and her hair
flowed over her shoulders and halfway down her back. She was
perfectly radiant. The whole room rapidly fell silent as people
became aware of her presence.

"Oh, Billy," she smiled. "We're supposed to have a date
tonight, remember?" I sat there staring at her through a drunken
fog, trying to remember. "I'll be waiting for you in my room
when you're ready for me."

"Oh, yeah," I said, "I'll be right over."

She smiled again very seductively as she left, pulling the door
closed behind her. There was dead silence for a moment. Then
the room exploded in a hail of whistles, clapping, and catcalls,
all directed at me.

By about two-thirty in the morning, I found myself in JC's
room with JC, Mike Morris, and Archie Davison. We were all
loaded. I wasn't entirely sure what had happened to the previous
seven hours. "Let's raid Willets," I suggested. Willets was one
of the women's dorms.

"How do we get in?" asked JC. "It's locked after midnight."

"Leave it to me," I said. When we got to Willets, there were
still several lights on in first-floor rooms. I picked one at random
and knocked on it. A woman came and looked out, saw my
Swarthmore letter jacket, and opened the window.

"Excuse me," I explained, "I was studying with Martha Dolan today and I left some books in her room. I'm going home for
the weekend early this morning and I need to take one of the
books with me for an exam on Monday."

"Do you want me to see if she's awake?" she asked.

"Oh, no," I replied, "you don't have to bother. If you could
just let me in, I'll do it."

"Okay," she said, "come around to the lobby door."

"Go down to the fire exit and wait for me," I said to the other
guys as I passed by where they were hiding on my way to the
door. As soon as the woman who'd let me in had gone, I went
down to the fire door and let in JC, Mike, and Archie. "Up to
the third floor," I said. "We'll run down the third floor, back up
the second floor, and back out this door. Ready? Let's go."

We burst into the third-floor corridor, shouting and hollering
like maniacs as we ran down the hall banging on some doors and

kicking others with our feet. I kicked a few of them open, shattering locks or hinges in the process. We got to the other end of the third floor, raced down the stairs, and repeated the process on the second floor. Then we leaped down the steps and bolted into the night, leaving audible pandemonium and confusion behind us. We ran toward Tarbles Student Center, diving headfirst under a large fir tree whose branches drooped to the ground, providing a perfect hiding place.

"Wonder how long it'll take campus security to get here," JC laughed. We were all panting for breath.

"Those old farts?" I said, almost choking on my own laughter. "Christ, if we were dangerous, those girls'd be in a world of trouble right about now."

"Say, Bill," Mike giggled, "weren't you supposed to have a date with Didi tonight?"

"Oh, shit," I said.

Chapter 35

I had no clear idea why I was going to Washington, D.C. I didn't know where I would go or what I would do. As the miles rolled on I had to fight the urge to turn my car around and drive back to Swarthmore, to get back into bed and forget the whole thing.

For nearly a year and a half, I had steadfastly refused to demonstrate in the streets. Even after I had become personally convinced that the war must be ended, even after I'd begun to speak out against the war privately and in public, I had not been able to join the thousands of others who regularly took to the streets.

Had it been some gut recall of those leaflets I'd picked up in the field in Vietnam depicting the October 1967 march on the Pentagon, the sickening sense of betrayal that had swept over me? Did I still associate the demonstrations with the pandemonium that had taken place in Chicago that summer of 1968? Was it cowardice, a fear of being shot down in cold blood like those students at Kent State, and later at Jackson State in Mississippi? Or did I see it, finally, as an act of unjustifiable defiance, a kind of treason against the government I had always been taught to believe in and the country I still desperately wanted to love?

And why had I decided to go on this particular Saturday morning in April 1971? What had caused me to wake up this morning, get dressed, climb into my car, and head south, as though the decision had been made somewhere beyond consciousness while I slept? I didn't know that either, and I was no longer as certain of my decision as I had been two hours earlier. Not a soul knew where I was now, or what my intentions were. I could turn back, and no one would be the wiser.

Still, I had to do *something*. Day in and day out, the war never let up. And the longer it went on, the more I'd begun to read and investigate, and the more disturbing it had all become.

I'd learned that the eighty-eight years of French colonial rule in Vietnam had been harsh and cruel; that the Americans had supported Ho Chi Minh and his Vietminh guerrillas with arms and equipment and training during World War Two, and in return, Ho's forces had provided the Americans with intelligence and had helped to rescue downed American pilots; that an OSS officer named Archimedes Patti, Washington's man in Indochina, had urged the U.S. to recognize Ho at the end of the war, arguing that Ho was an independence leader first, a Communist only after that; that Ho had spent years trying to gain American support for Vietnamese independence, beginning as far back as 1919; that instead of recognizing Ho at the end of World War Two, the U.S. had supported the French claim to Indochina, and had ultimately paid three-fourths of the French war bill for the First Indochina War; that North and South Vietnam were nothing more than an artificial construction of the Western powers, created at Geneva in 1954; that Ngo Dinh Diem had not been a "miracle of democracy," but rather a tyrant hated by all but the Americans and a few upper-class French-educated Vietnamese Catholics. And I'd seen with my own eyes the filth and corruption and brutality of the Saigon regime, first under Nguyen Cao Ky, then under Nguyen Van Thieu.

Why hadn't I been told any of this before I'd gone to Vietnam? No one had even suggested these things. Not my teachers or my government or the *Time* magazine I'd read religiously during my last three years of high school and even during my tour in Vietnam. I'd had to learn it all on my own, most of it years after I'd left Vietnam. Had people been so ignorant, or had I been lied to deliberately?

Were Richard Nixon and his administration acting with the best of intentions, no matter how misplaced those intentions might be, or had lying become a way of life? How could anyone say that the invasion of Cambodia had been a success? The war in Vietnam had not slowed even for a moment. Prince Norodom Sihanouk had been overthrown by a military dictator, and a civil war that had not existed before the invasion was now raging in Cambodia, and Cambodia had been drawn into the vortex of Vietnam with a vengeance. And how could anyone even begin to suggest that the invasion of Laos had been a success? Had been anything other than an utter disaster? It seemed clear that the government was lying—blatantly, nakedly, openly lying.

God, what a terrible thought. George Washington and Abraham Lincoln. Tom Paine and Thomas Jefferson and John F. Kennedy. John Paul Jones, the Gettysburg Address, the Halls of Montezuma, Guadalcanal and the Bill of Rights, Remember the *Maine* and Damn the Torpedoes. *My whole life!* Everything I believed in. Was it all a lie? Or had we gone horribly wrong somewhere? It made my heart want to explode with pain. The day I'd graduated from Marine boot camp had been the proudest moment of my life.

When I'd first come in contact with members of Vietnam Veterans Against the War, they'd struck me as being totally unhinged, the whole lot of them with one foot in the psycho ward. But in the year since, I'd had to wonder long and hard. Wasn't I as crazy as they were? Were any of us *really* crazy? It was the war that was crazy, and we had brought the craziness home with us. Something was terribly wrong.

And something was wrong, too, when the government professed admiration and gratitude for its veterans but gave us a GI Bill that hardly covered the cost of textbooks, and refused treatment at VA hospitals for veterans suffering from drug addictions picked up in Vietnam and stress disorders resulting from the war; when Vietnam veterans who petitioned for peace were told by their own representatives in Congress that they weren't really veterans at all—or if they were, then they must have been dishonorably discharged; when those who died were extolled as heroes, while those who lived and now wanted to put an end to the dying were ignored or told we were a disgrace to the nation; when Nixon was willing to continue to sacrifice the lives of thousands of working-class draftees in order to rescue a handful of college-educated career-oriented professional pilots who knew long before they'd ever been shot down exactly what they were risking and who could have resigned at any time. Christ, sometimes it made me so angry I could hardly think straight.

Yet I hadn't been able to bring myself to join VVAW. Only a few weeks ago, VVAW had staged a large demonstration in Washington. Thousands of veterans had come to return their military decorations to Congress. Few people in the government wanted to listen. Instead, they built a fence around the Capitol, and the veterans—their voices choked with emotion, their faces streaked with tears—had had to hurl their medals over the fence from a distance onto the lower steps of the building.

I'd had a few contacts with VVAW since that abortive visit to the Widener chapter a year earlier, and several vets I knew had asked me to join them in turning in their medals. I'd taken my medals out from the box in which I kept them in the back of the bottom drawer of my desk. I'd held them in my hands, one by one, like pieces of gold or rare old heirlooms, considering them.

From the time I was a little boy, I'd wanted a medal. A Red Badge of Courage. A sign that I was a hero in the company of Stephen Decatur and Alvin York. Now that I had them, what did they mean? I could never hang them on my wall in a tasteful wooden display case, tacitly saying to friends and visitors, "Look, this is what I've done for my country; this is the man I am." I could never be proud of them. But after a long while, perhaps as long as an hour, I'd put the medals back into their box and put the box back in the drawer, and the day had come and gone, and I had said nothing, not even to myself.

But if I hadn't been willing to go to Washington then, why go now? What had tipped the scales in the few weeks since? Perhaps it was the shame I felt at being unwilling to relinquish the worthless baubles of dead dreams, at lacking the courage to join my fellow veterans in an act more noble than anything I had ever done to earn those glittering trinkets. I didn't know.

When I got to Washington, the city was jammed with people. I had to park several miles from the main demonstration site in front of the Lincoln Memorial. As I walked through streets full of people carrying signs and banners, the jostle and press of the crowds made me feel claustrophobic, and the ranks of riot police made me feel nervous, trapped, and naked. I tried not to think about anything.

I could get no closer to the speakers' platform than the Washington Monument. The mall between the monument and the Lincoln Memorial was as crowded as the Jersey shore on Memorial Day weekend. I walked around wondering where to go or what to do, trying not to step on people. Far away on the speakers' platform, someone was giving a speech. I couldn't tell who it was, and the loudspeakers conveyed only a coarse, indistinct parody of a voice. Around me, people sat listening to rock and roll music on tape players and radios, smoking marijuana, talking, laughing, and arguing. The whole place had the air of a festival, but the feeling of claustrophobia wouldn't let go.

After a while, a man with a bullhorn came walking through the crowd nearby, announcing that there would be a demonstration at the Justice Department in support of someone I'd never heard of who was apparently on trial for refusing the draft. I decided to go, partly out of curiosity, partly to escape the overwhelming crowd that left me feeling lost and vulnerable.

At the Justice Department building, there were several hundred people sitting on the steps. In between speakers, the crowd sang "We Shall Overcome" and chanted "Hell, no, we won't go." I tried to join in, but I felt uncomfortable and out of place. It reminded me of orientation week my first year at Swarthmore when I'd spent an afternoon surrounded by strangers and children rolling down a grassy hill on the lawn, trying to belong and feeling hopelessly awkward and ridiculous. What in the world was I doing here in Washington, I wondered.

Suddenly a voice bellowed from a bullhorn off to my left: "This is an illegal demonstration!" I turned to look. The voice belonged to a policeman. Behind him, completely blocking the end of the street, stood a solid line of cops, all carrying long black billy clubs and riot shields, and dressed in visored helmets and what appeared to be flak jackets. My stomach tightened into a small hard knot. Christ, I didn't want any trouble. "This is an illegal demonstration," the voice bellowed again. "You have two minutes to clear the area."

Demonstrators around me began to shout and jeer at the police, hurling obscenities and calling them pigs and Nazis. Jesus Christ almighty, I thought frantically, what the hell are these kids trying to do, get us all killed? Those cops are armed! One of the demonstrators took the speakers' bullhorn and replied to the cops:

"We are covered under the permit issued to New Mobilization, and under the First Amendment to the United States Constitution. We are breaking no law. This is a nonviolent demonstration. You have no right to order us to leave."

"This is an illegal demonstration," the policeman said again. It was not a reply. It sounded like a recording. It was clear that the cop had no interest in debating the matter. "You have one minute to clear the area." The crowd was still shouting and jeering. These people could do whatever the hell they wanted, I thought; I was frightened, and I was getting out of here. What the hell had I come here for, anyway? Didn't I already have enough trouble without going around looking for more? I turned to the right, hoping to make it to the opposite end of the street from the line of cops.

Jesus fucking Christ! The opposite end of the street was also blocked by a line of cops in riot gear! Where had they come from? What was going on here? Others in the crowd also seemed to notice, almost simultaneously with my own realization, that both ends of the street were now blocked off. There was now no avenue of escape. The shouting and jeering continued, but a few people were also screaming. The crowd began to mill around in confusion.

"This is an illegal demonstration. You are under arrest," said the cop with the bullhorn. Immediately, both lines of police began to close in at a trot, shields held up and billy clubs raised to strike. Jesus God almighty! What the hell was happening? We hadn't done anything wrong! We hadn't done *anything!* The cops were *attacking!* They hadn't even given us a *chance* to leave.

The whole crowd seemed to panic at once. Someone on the steps behind me pushed me down. I got up, stumbled, and began to run, but there was nowhere to go. People were shouting and running and screaming. Cops were among the crowd now, swinging their clubs like baseball bats. Their visors were down, and you couldn't see their faces, but you could hear them swearing and shouting, "You motherfuckers—you fucking traitors." People were falling down, or being knocked down by clubs or shields. Cops were kicking people on the ground. Two cops held a man faceup across the hood of a car while a third cop clubbed him repeatedly in his exposed stomach. A cop swung his club at me. I ducked and ran. Another one grabbed for me but missed. I didn't wait for him to try again. There were small battles raging all around me. Battles? No, these weren't battles; they were mas-

sacres. The demonstrators were utterly helpless. *I* was helpless.
I couldn't think. It was all happening too quickly. What the hell?
What the hell! A weapon—just give me a weapon—anything, a
car aerial, a hubcap, something to strike back with. *God*, give
me a weapon! "You fucking pigs!" It was my voice. "You filthy
Nazis! You fucking filthy pigs!" My face was wet. Was it blood
or was I crying?

Sirens! There were more cops coming! I made a headlong dash
for the end of the street. I got hit on the back, but I kept running.
Directly in front of me, a young woman lay on the ground
screaming and trying to cover her face and head as a cop with
his back to me bent over her, hitting her repeatedly with his club.
He was making no attempt to arrest her. He was simply beating
on her. I was running. I lowered my shoulder and barreled straight
into the small of his back, sending him sprawling. I grabbed the
woman by her collar and waistband. "Get up!" I shouted. "Get
up! Run, goddamn it!" She was bleeding heavily from cuts on
her face and head. She didn't seem to know what was happening.
Christ, I hit a cop, I thought; I *gotta* get outa here! "Get up!" I
screamed. The woman wasn't responding.

I was about to let her go when another man grabbed her under
the left arm. "Come on!" he shouted. I grabbed her right armpit
and we took off, dragging her with us. That cop must have gotten
up by now. I kept waiting for his club to come down on my
head, to split my skull open and splatter my brains all over the
capital of the United States of America. It was like waiting out
a mortar attack: you knew it was coming, you'd heard the rounds
leave their tubes, you knew they were up there somewhere, arc-
ing slowly up toward the top of their flight and beginning their
descent, you knew they were coming back down again, but you
didn't know where or when. All you could do was wait, wait,
wait with your stomach jammed up into your mouth and your
guts screaming for mercy.

It was just like the war—only this time I had no weapon, no
flak jacket or helmet, no way to defend myself, no protection of
any kind. Was this what it felt like to be a peasant in Vietnam,
I wondered, wanting to throw up.

Chapter 36

"Please don't talk like that, Bill," said my mother.

"Well, that's what they are!" I said. "They're nothing but a bunch of pigs!"

"You don't have to shout at me," she replied.

"Well, you weren't there, Mom. You don't believe me, do you? I'm tellin' you, it happened just the way I explained it. We weren't doing a damned—a darn thing illegal. Just making a lot of noise. And those *pigs* just plain attacked us. Like a bunch of SS storm troopers."

"I'm not saying they didn't," she replied, "but I just can't believe you didn't do something to provoke them. Look at the way you're talking to me. You sound like you're just spoiling for a fight."

I threw up my hands in exasperation and walked out of the kitchen. How could my parents possibly believe it, I realized sadly. Already in their early fifties, they'd grown up in the Depression and come of age during that noblest of all American crusades, the Second World War. If the United States had committed itself to Vietnam, then there must be a good reason for it. They'd even allowed me to pass up college and enlist in the Marines at seventeen, and the reluctance they'd initially expressed had had no political basis. Indeed, up to that point in my life, my view of the world and America's place in the world had been theirs too, and my values had been as much theirs as they'd been my own. They'd risked three sons in Vietnam. How could they believe me now? I wouldn't have believed it either if I hadn't had my face rubbed in it repeatedly over the past four years.

How difficult it was to be around them these days. I loved them, and I didn't doubt their love for me. But every conversation for the past several years always seemed to end up as an unresolved argument, my father storming out in anger, my mother sitting there in stoic silence. Whatever patience and tolerance I possessed—which was very little anymore—seemed always to vanish in my own home. And I would go away again, feeling ashamed and angry that I couldn't find the self-control to be more considerate of my own parents. But I wanted them to *understand,* and they didn't.

"Can you stay for supper?" Mom asked, coming into the living room.

"No," I replied, "I've got to get back to school early. We've got a DU meeting tonight. Mom, can't you see what this war is doing? Nixon's out of control. He's completely obsessed. It's just *got* to be stopped—and stopped *now.*"

"You weren't talking like this when you first came back from Vietnam," said Mom. I could feel my internal temperature rising again. I struggled to keep the lid on it.

"What was I supposed to say then? What *could* I say? Come on, Mom, you know darned well I was messed up—and you knew it then—and the heck with what I was saying."

Three years earlier, when I'd volunteered to go back to Vietnam in the spring of 1968 less than two months after I'd gotten back to the States, I'd put off telling her until the last minute. I'd been afraid of what the news might do to her. I'd already survived one tour, my older brother had left for Vietnam in January, and my oldest brother had orders to go in July. But I couldn't put it off forever, and when I'd finally told her—much to my eternal amazement—she hadn't batted an eyelash. She was clearly not surprised at all. "I could see it coming the first week you were home," was all she'd said. How she'd guessed, I didn't know. I'd never shared any of my private doubts or fears with her. Perhaps it was some sort of intuition only a mother can possess. However she knew, she hadn't argued with me then, and she didn't argue with me now.

"Besides," I continued, "Nixon wasn't president then—and I didn't know then what I know now."

Mom shook her head slowly but didn't say anything. I wondered what she was thinking.

"Listen, I gotta get rolling," I said. "I wanna stop by the cycle shop and see Max for a few minutes. I haven't seen him in a long time."

"That would be nice," she said. "I haven't seen him around

much. Ellen says he's almost never home anymore. She's worried about him.'' Ellen was Max's mother.

"Another one of the walking wounded," I said.

Again, she didn't argue. Her expression said that she didn't know what to think. "Tell him to stop in and see us," she said.

"I will. Where's Dad?"

"Over at the hospital visiting. I thought he'd be back by now."

"Well, tell him I said good-bye, okay?" I kissed Mom on the cheek and left.

When I got to the motorcycle shop where Max worked, he was just getting ready to leave. Max and I had grown up together. When we were little kids—eight, nine, ten years old—he and I and Jeff Alison had spent a lot of time together. But Max was two years older, and as we'd grown up we'd begun to travel in different circles. He'd hung around with "the tough guys," but we'd remained fond of each other, and the tough guys had never given me any trouble because they all knew I was Max's friend.

Max had dropped out of high school without graduating and had enlisted in the Marines, eventually spending twenty-five months in Vietnam. Incredibly, we'd run into each other three times during my thirteen months in Vietnam. The third time had been the most remarkable. I'd been driving a jeep on a road near Quang Tri. We'd been in a hurry because the road wasn't secure—nothing was ever secure in Vietnam—and suddenly we'd found our way blocked by a stalled truck. I'd leaped from the jeep cursing, ready to shoot the truck driver for forcing us to come to an indefinite halt out in the open. But the driver turned out to be Max, and we'd had a regular hometown reunion right there in the road while the other Marines stood around scratching their heads and nervously eyeing the nearby trees and fields.

"Bill!" said Max now as I entered the cycle shop. "Long time, no see. How ya been?"

"Not bad, I guess," I replied, shaking his outstretched hand. I told him about school, and he filled me in on life in Perkasie. "The place never changes," he laughed. "Same old quiet little hick town."

"Yeah. My parents just can't believe there's a real world out there with great big ugly teeth. Nobody in this place can."

"How are your parents?"

"Pretty good. You oughta stop by and see 'em sometime. Mom asked about you."

"Well, they're good people," said Max.

"Yeah, they are," I replied. "I'm sure having a hard time dealin' with 'em, though."

"What's the problem?"

"Aw, I don't know," I said slowly. "They just refuse to believe how fucked up this country is. They just don't see it. *Won't* see it."

"Can you blame 'em?" Max asked. "This is Perkasie."

"It isn't just Perkasie, Max. It's everywhere. Fuckin' Nixon's Silent Majority have their heads up their asses so far they can tickle their own tonsils."

"The way it is," said Max, shrugging his shoulders.

"Maynard, why did you keep going back?"

"To Nam? Hell, you know what it's like bein' a stateside jarhead. I couldn't take the Mickey Mouse. At least they left me alone over there. I don't think I polished my boots once in two years."

"What do you think now?" I asked. "Would you do it again?"

He paused and gazed out the showroom window. "What difference does it make now?" He shrugged. "You think too much. Come on, I'll buy you a beer."

"No, I can't," I said, "I gotta get back to school. I got a meeting tonight. Listen, classes'll be over in a few weeks. I'll call you when I get home. Maybe we can go to the beach for a weekend, okay?"

"Sure," he said. "Gimme a call." We walked out to my car.

"You still driving a cycle?" I asked.

"Yep," he grinned, pointing to a big Harley-Davidson parked beside the building.

"Well, take it easy, will you?"

"Don't worry about me, boy," he laughed. "I can take care of myself." He put his arm around my back and squeezed my shoulder.

I got in the car and headed out of town, but as I passed the Mayflower Bar, I decided to grab a six-pack of beer for the road. I zipped up to the curb and parked. Though the Mayflower was a permanent fixture in town, I'd never been inside. It was a shot-and-beer joint with little attraction for anyone under forty. But all bars in Pennsylvania sell six-packs to go, and that was all I wanted at the moment.

There was a polka playing on the jukebox, but conversation among the eight or nine middle-aged patrons stopped abruptly when I walked in. Everyone seemed to be staring at me. I wondered vaguely if my fly was open, but didn't look down. So what if it was?

"Gimme a six-pack of Rolling Rock to go, please," I said to the bartender.

He looked at me for a moment, then replied slowly, "You don't look like you need a beer, sonny boy; you look like you need a haircut."

Oh, shit, I thought, just what I needed. "Any law against long hair?" I asked.

"You got an LCB card?" asked the bartender, ignoring my question. Strictly speaking, when you turn twenty-one in Pennsylvania, you're supposed to apply for a Liquor Control Board identification card, but I'd never bothered to get one because it cost four dollars and I had two IDs already.

"No," I replied, "but I've got a service ID—Marine Corps— and my driver's license." I had the Marine ID because technically I was still an inactive reserve until April 1972; all enlistment contracts were for six years, to be fulfilled in some combination of active duty, active reserve, and inactive reserve. I took both cards from my wallet and laid them on the bar.

"Well, this must be a phony ID," said the bartender, picking up the service ID. "Fella in this picture can't be you. Look at the nice haircut." He showed the card to the customers sitting nearby. "This doesn't look like you at all."

By this time, the other customers had begun a steady stream of comments among themselves, loud enough for me to hear:

"Pretty cute, isn't she?"

"Wonder if she's got as much hair on her pussy."

"That's not a girl; that's a queer."

I could feel my face getting red with anger and I had to work to restrain myself, but I just stood there while the bartender picked up the driver's license and studied it. "There's no photo on this thing. You coulda stolen it, for all I know."

"I didn't steal it," I said, my face and neck tightening. "It's mine."

Several customers oohed and aahed in mock wonder. The bartender looked at the card awhile longer, letting his customers get in their last licks. Then he said, "Sorry, sonny, can't serve you unless you have an LCB card." He broke into a broad grin, and everybody in the Mayflower Bar began to laugh.

I was burning inside by this time, but I picked up the two cards and silently started for the door. Then somebody said very loudly, "Hey, sweetheart, why don't you go across the street to Andy's Barbershop and get a haircut? I'll pay for it."

I stopped and turned around quickly. "Why don't you go fuck yourself?" I said. The place went silent again except for the jukebox, and a man at the bar began to stand up. "That's right, motherfucker, just step right over here and we'll find out damned quick if I'm a queer or an ex-Marine sergeant." The man remained standing, but didn't move. "Come on, motherfucker! You ain't afraid of a queer, are you?" I started back toward the bar. "Let's go, you asshole!"

"That's enough, mister," the bartender said, holding up his hand and pointing at me with one finger. "You better get out of here before I call the cops."

"Oh, yeah, call the cops!" I shouted. "What do we got here, ten to one? And you gotta call the cops. You chickens. You spineless assholes. Tough bunch of talkers we got here, huh? Come on, let's go," I said, my voice now low and menacing, my arms in front of me and my hands motioning repeatedly in a gesture of invitation as I took a few steps toward the bar. "You shitbag cocksuckers. Come on! Let's dance."

Nobody moved except the bartender, who reached for the phone and started to dial without taking his eyes off me. I stood there a moment longer. Who would show up? Chief Nellis? I thought of the night a dozen years before when Jeff Alison, Larry Carroll, and I had put three raw eggs through the window of the chief's patrol car, and he'd chased us through the backyards of Perkasie, his ponderous body bouncing in several directions at once, his gun drawn, his shouts of "Stop or I'll shoot" met with hoots of derisive childish laugher as we'd scrambled over fences he had a better chance of bowling through than climbing. And then I thought of those hard remorseless cops in Washington only a few days earlier. Times had changed, I thought. Maybe this time Chief Nellis would really shoot.

These were the people I'd gone to Vietnam for, I thought. "You weren't worth it," I said, and I turned around and left.

Chapter 37

Those pimps! Those sewer scum! Those arrogant, murderous liars! Those . . . those—Christ in heaven! I'd been turning it over and over in my mind for more than a week, and I still couldn't find words vile enough to describe them. Even the whole lush vocabulary I'd learned in the Marines was inadequate. The magnitude of betrayal was beyond all possible belief—except that it was true; it was all there in black and white, unavoidable at last, outrageous, obscene. As I drove northwest through the Lake of the Woods toward the vast Canadian prairie beyond, I wanted just to keep driving forever.

My sophomore year at Swarthmore had ended six weeks earlier. Didi had gone back to California to deal with her own problems—problems she had sometimes referred to vaguely but had never explained to me. Perhaps she was tired of the East, tired of Swarthmore, tired of I didn't know what, but this time she was gone for good, she'd said. In a way, I'd been relieved to see her go. The combination of her loving tenderness and constant refusals had become a kind of madness. I'd gone back to building swimming pools again.

Then in late June, thanks to a man named Daniel Ellsberg, *The Pentagon Papers* found the light of day; I'd bought a paperback copy of the *New York Times* edition and begun to read.

It had been a journey through an unholy house of horrors where all one's worst fears and darkest nightmares had suddenly become reality, hard, cold, and immutable; where all of the ugliest questions that had first arisen in the ricefields and jungles of Vietnam had suddenly been answered in the starkest and most unmerciful terms; where everything I had believed in for eighteen years and had desperately tried to cling to through four more years of pestilence and famine had suddenly crumbled into ashes—ashes so thick you could hardly breathe, bitter, dry, and suffocating.

A mistake? Vietnam a mistake? My God, it had been a calculated, deliberate attempt to hammer the world by brute force into the shape perceived by vain, duplicitous power brokers. And the depths to which they had sunk, dragging us all down with them, were almost unfathomable. America, America, God cast his shame on thee.

Our construction crew had been building pools in the Washington, D.C., area and living in a motel in Silver Spring, Maryland. The night I'd finished the book, I'd quit the job on the spot, collected my pay, thrown my belongings into a Howard Johnson's pillowcase, and hit the road. It had been eleven P.M. I'd had no idea where I was headed. All I'd wanted was a tank full of gas and a lot of miles, miles and miles and miles of open road, thousands of them. Drive. Don't think, just drive.

Except for a few days in Milwaukee with Bart Lewis, I'd been driving for a week, sleeping in the car by the side of the road when I couldn't stay awake any longer.

But I couldn't stop thinking. Everywhere I went, there were ghosts all around me. Maloney, Roddenbery, Calloway, Scanlon, Pelinski, Dodd, Basinski, Rowe, Talbot, Aymes, Stemkowski, Bannerman, Krebs, Thurston, Falcone, Wommack. All dead. Kenny with his arm gone. Gerry with his knee smashed. Captain B with both thighbones shattered by a fifty-caliber machine-gun bullet. Staff Sergeant Trinh with his father dead from a Japanese bullet and his sister dead from a French mine and his mother dead from an American artillery shell and his beloved Vietnam in blistering ruins and his heart broken forever. The forests stripped of their leaves, the fields stripped of their rice, the villages drowning in billowing orange-black clouds of napalm. For what? And the old woman in the ricefield, and the old man on Barrier Island, and the small boy in the marketplace in Hoi An: dead. All of them, dead.

And for what? For what? For a pack of dissembling criminals who'd defined morality as whatever they could get away with. For a bunch of cold-blooded murdering liars in three-piece suits and uniforms with stars who'd dined on fine white porcelain plates while year after year they'd sent the children of the gullible halfway around the world to wage war on a nation of peasant rice farmers and fisherpeople who had never wanted anything but their own country free of foreigners, who had wanted only to grow their crops and catch their fish and live. If only I had known when it had mattered.

Here was the evidence that Ho Chi Minh had begged Truman seven times in 1945 and 1946 to help his people gain their freedom from the French—he'd even offered to put the country under United Nations trusteeship—and he had not even received the courtesy of a reply.

Here was the 1948 intelligence report that could find no evidence that Ho was taking his orders from Moscow or Peking or anyone but the Vietnamese.

Here were the sabotoge and propaganda teams of Colonel Edward Lansdale sent into North Vietnam even before the 1954 Geneva accords were signed, spiking the engines of the Hanoi bus system, spreading dire rumors of murder and mayhem if Ho Chi Minh took control, the calculated violations and deliberate efforts to undermine the accords even as the U.S. government publicly promised the world it would abide by them.

Here was Eisenhower's support for Diem's refusal to hold the reunification elections promised in the Geneva accords.

Here were the glowing public statements of progress and plenty in South Vietnam while what little land the peasants had received from the Vietminh during the French Indochina War was taken away from them by Diem and given to his northern Catholic supporters, and elections were rigged or abolished, and peasants were forced to build and live in virtual concentration camps, and thousands were arrested and murdered by secret police, and U.S. government analysts consistently reported repression, corruption, and deterioration all through the 1950s while U.S. aid and support and guidance continued unabated.

Here were the orders from North Vietnam to the southern cadre not to engage in armed resistance, the spontaneous rebellion of the people themselves against Diem, the gradually evolving decision of the southern cadre to support the people rather than lose them, and only reluctantly and after the fact, the North Vietnamese decision in the late fifties to support the southern insurgency.

Here were the first U.S. combat advisers surreptitiously sent to Vietnam in 1961 by Kennedy with no public announcement and no public knowledge.

Here was the U.S. government's direct connivance in the overthrow of Diem.

Here were the secret commando raids against North Vietnam planned, directed, and supported by the U.S. government.

Here were the plans for bombing the north more than a year before they were executed, the power brokers waiting, waiting for the chance, the excuse, some pretext the American people would believe to justify unleashing the bombers. And the intelligence estimates stating that the bombing would do no good, could do no good against an agrarian economy, and that anyway the North Vietnamese were not in control of the southern rebellion and could not stop it even if they chose to, which they undoubtedly would not.

Here was what became the Gulf of Tonkin resolution that would give Lyndon Johnson carte blanche to do as he pleased in Vietnam, already written and waiting six months before the USS *Maddox* was attacked—not while on routine patrol in international waters as Congress and the American people were told, but while sailing in direct support of secret Saigon-government raids on North Vietnamese coastal installations.

Here was the evidence that the years of negotiations and temporary bombing halts had been no more than public-relations ploys designed to dupe the American people into supporting the ever-increasing escalation of the war, the offers to the North Vietnamese made in the full calculating knowledge that the terms would be found unacceptable.

And even after the Tet offensive of January 1968 had finally revealed the utter bankruptcy of it all, even to the power brokers, here was the iron refusal to acknowledge the inability of the United States to impose its self-centered, arrogant will on another people by force of arms, the shifting of gears from one kind of tactic to another that had allowed Richard Nixon to pursue the war with the same relentless recklessness that had possessed all of the others before him, and he was indeed pursuing it with a vengeance.

Oh, it was all here in *The Pentagon Papers*. All of it, and much more. Page after page after endless page of it. Vile. Immoral. Despicable. Obscene. Never once in all those years had they questioned their ultimate aims. Never once had they considered that the Vietnamese might not be malleable enough to conform to their blind, willful fantasies. Never once had they told the truth—to me, or to anyone.

I'd been a fool, ignorant and naive. A sucker. For such men, I had become a murderer. For such men, I had forfeited my honor, my self-respect, and my humanity. For such men, I had been willing to lay down my life. And I had been nothing more to them than a hired gun, a triggerman, a stooge, a tool to be used and discarded, an insignificant statistic. Even as the years since I'd left Vietnam had passed, even as the doubts had grown, I had never imagined that the truth could be so ugly. Yet here it was—not some rhetorical diatribe from the Weathermen, not some antiwar pamphlet from the Quakers, but the government's own account, commissioned by Robert S. McNamara, secretary of defense for Presidents Kennedy and Johnson. Christ in heaven, I thought as I drove west along the Trans-Canadian Highway, if there was one single shred of justice left anywhere in all the universe, may all their stone-cold bloodless hearts roast in hell forever.

Winnipeg had long since come and gone. Brandon, Virden, Moosomin, Wolseley, Regina. Towns and wheatfields and miles and days flowed like a slow river across the continent. I was heading for Moose Jaw, Saskatchewan. Moose Jaw! Lumber-jacks. Mounties. Dogsleds. Plank sidewalks. Sergeant Preston and his trusty husky, King. Why not? Where the hell else did I have to go? For three days I bore hard across the Canadian plains with single-minded determination. Moose Jaw. Maybe I would even stay there. What was there to go home to? A bunch of turds who'd stolen or shattered every dream I'd ever believed in. A bunch of pigs trying to beat my brains out. A bunch of rummies in a bar who weren't worth the filthy paper I flushed down the toilet. Fuck 'em all. I'd rather be a fur trapper.

But Moose Jaw turned out to be a small town much like Perkasie with paved streets and concrete sidewalks and electric streetlights and not a Mountie to be seen anywhere. Fifteen hundred miles for a mirror image of Americana in the middle of a wheatfield? It figures, I thought. I bought a six-pack of Labatt's beer and a Moose Jaw, Saskatchewan, souvenir bottle opener with an enamel Canadian maple leaf on the handle and left town thirty minutes after I'd arrived. I'd spotted a place on the map that sounded interesting: only two hundred and eighty-four miles due west to Medicine Hat, Alberta. Wigwams. Buffalo. Pemmi-can. I could be there by midnight.

Chapter 38

"But why, Bill?" asked Roger. "I don't disbelieve you, but why would anybody *do* all that?" He had put down his cards, and he was looking at me intently.

"Well, for starters, it's not a matter of believing or disbelieving," I replied, reaching up to the shelf above my desk and pulling down a dog-eared copy of *The Pentagon Papers*. "It's all right here," I said, plopping the book down on the pile of cards between us.

"Okay, but why? What made 'em do it?"

"I don't really know for sure," I said. "Not exactly. But I've got some pretty clear ideas about it."

"Like what?"

"Well, for one thing, the United States has been doing stuff like this for a long, long time—since even before we were the United States. Man, I'll tell ya, I thought *The Pentagon Papers* were the last straw. Was *I* ever in for a big surprise. That was just the beginning, Roger. Look at the Indians—Native Americans, really; Indians is just a name Christopher Columbus gave 'em because he didn't know where the hell he was—anyway, nowadays everybody shakes their heads and says, 'Oh, yeah, the Indians got a raw deal; sure was too bad what happened to 'em.' But how many people really know just how bad a deal they got? I don't suppose you've ever read this book, have you?" I reached up and pulled down a copy of *Bury My Heart at Wounded Knee*. "It's a history of broken promises, greed, treachery, and murder. It's unbelievable, Roger. We'd do things like stick Native Americans on barren reservations in the middle of nowhere and leave 'em there until they were starving half to death, and then when they left the reservations to hunt for food, we'd kill 'em. One time, we even gave 'em army blankets deliberately infested with smallpox. Nice, huh? Give 'em a reservation 'forever and ever,' then discover gold on it, and kick 'em out again. All kinds of stuff like that. And this book is just what happened *after* we drove 'em all west of the Mississippi—the ones that were still alive, that is; a lot of the eastern tribes we completely exterminated— this book doesn't even begin until around the 1860s. The colonial governor of Pennsylvania used to pay bounties for Indian scalps. Roger Williams got exiled from Massachusetts Colony for claiming that Native Americans ought to be paid for their land. Here's another classic, Roger. Ever hear of the Trail of Tears?''

''No,'' he replied.

''I didn't think so. They don't teach you stuff like this in school. Well, here's the way it worked. Native Americans were told, 'Okay, you wanna stay here, you gotta live like whites.' So the Cherokee nation, down in Georgia, they decide, 'Well, if that's the way they want it, that's the way we'll play it—which they thought was a pretty smart move because they could see what was happening to the tribes that weren't catching on to Whitey's system. So they set up a whole society with a written language, a constitution, government institutions like courts and a legislature, schools, everything. Next thing you know, white settlers wanted the land. State of Georgia says the Cherokee have to go. Do the Cherokee go to war? Oh, no. They ain't fools. They're gonna play it by Whitey's rules all the way. They take it to court—and the Supreme Court of the United States says they can stay, Georgia has no legal right to expel them or take their land. Then along comes Andrew Jackson, president of the United States—who made his reputation as an Indian fighter—and Jackson says, 'Fuck you, Supreme Court, I'm not going to enforce your decision, and there's nothing you can do about it.' A flagrant violation of the U.S. Constitution and the explicit responsibilities of the president—only there wasn't anything the court could do about it because most Americans didn't give a damn about the law or the Indians. Middle of the night, in come the soldiers, round up all the Cherokee without any warning, and send 'em all packing to Oklahoma Territory. In the middle of the winter this is. No food, no blankets. Something like three-quarters of 'em never made it. That's why it's called the Trail of Tears.''

''Jesus.''

''Oh, Christ, that's nothing, Roger,'' I said, standing up and beginning to pace back and forth in the cabin. "You ever heard of a man named Colonel John M. Chivington?"

"No."

"He was the guy that massacred a whole Cheyenne village of old men, women, and children at a place called Sand Creek in Colorado. First he told all the braves they could go hunt buffalo. Then, when the braves were gone, he and his Colorado militia rode in at daybreak and killed everybody that was left. Seven hundred fully armed cavalrymen against thirty-five braves, twenty-five old men, and four hundred women and children. Get this, I love this part. The chief, Black Kettle, he had a big American flag flying over his tepee, and when he saw the soldiers coming, he just stood there under that flag waiting for the soldiers with open arms. The Great White Father back in Washington had told him that as long as he flew that flag, he and his people would be safe. He even ran up a white flag when the soldiers didn't seem to notice the good old Stars and Stripes and started shooting; he thought there must be some kind of mistake. And when it was all over, Chivington's men made tobacco pouches out of people's scrotums."

I walked over to the porthole and leaned against the ledge beneath it, staring out at the darkness. Roger didn't say anything.

"Listen, you wanna finish this hand or not?" I finally asked, turning around.

"What's the hurry?" said Roger. "You're winning again anyway." He reached for the bottle of Annie Greensprings Peach Creek wine and poured himself a glass. "You want some?"

"Sure," I replied, walking back to the desk and sitting down. I pushed a glass toward him. "You heard anything about going into dry dock when we get to Seattle?"

"Yeah. We got a crack in one of the propeller blades they gotta fix."

"Oh, great, that's nice. And if the damned thing snaps off before we get there?"

"It won't," Roger laughed. "It's not that bad. But it needs to be fixed before it does get that bad. We'll be in Seattle by tomorrow morning."

We'd reached Portland on the last day of 1973. It had been a short turnaround, and we'd sailed the next morning, crossing Columbia Bar in good weather and with no difficulty. We were now steaming north along the Washington coast.

"So go on," said Roger. "This is fascinating."

"I guess that's one word you could use to describe it," I said. "Anyway, the point is, Whitey was going to get his way and that was that. We stole the whole American southwest from Mexico in the 1840s—unilaterally moved the Mexican-American border south about fifty miles and then claimed they had Mexican soldiers on American soil and invaded them—then threatened to go to war with Britain over the Pacific Northwest. Ended up with the whole continent from coast to coast by the 1850s—except for a few redskins which were no problem, just kill 'em. The only reason we didn't start building an overseas empire until the late 1800s is that we didn't need one. We had a built-in empire right here, as much as we could handle at the time—new markets, new sources of raw materials, new territory, all in one package. American business didn't need to expand any farther until they'd exhausted all the possibilities right here."

"You think it's all a question of business?"

"Well, in a general way, yeah. Or perhaps more accurately, greed. Greed for land, greed for gold and silver, greed for timber and iron and copper, greed for anything you can make a buck on, and the cheaper the better. Business, basically. Dollars and cents. Listen to this," I said, grabbing another book and flipping through it until I'd found what I wanted. "This is General Smedley Butler, two-time Medal of Honor winner, testifying before Congress in 1935:

" 'I spent thirty-three years and four months in active service as a member of our country's most agile military force, the Marine Corps. And during that period I spent most of my time being a high-class muscleman for Big Business. I helped in the raping of half a dozen Central American republics for the benefit of Wall Street. I helped purify Nicaragua for the international banking house of Brown Brothers in 1909–12. I brought light to the Dominican Republic for American sugar interests in 1916. I helped get Honduras *right* for American fruit companies in 1903.'

"And this isn't some bleeding-heart liberal handwringer talking here," I said, waving the book, "this is a Marine Corps general. Hell, Roger, the Spanish-American War was nothing but a naked grab for overseas territory. The Spanish empire—what was left of it—was a decrepit ruin by the 1890s. Easy pickings. All we needed to do was pick a fight, which is exactly what we did. First, we eliminate import tariffs on Cuban sugar, which induces the Spaniards to jack up Cuban sugar production. Cuba's a Spanish colony at the time. Then, a couple of years later, we suddenly slap an enormous tariff on Cuban sugar. The Spaniards consequently have an immediate surplus of sugar they can't sell, so they reduce sugar production drastically, putting a whole lot of Cubans out of work. The out-of-work Cubans revolt against Spain. We send Spain an ultimatum: 'Give our little brown brothers their independence or we'll have to help them out.' So here's your excuse to start a war, only much to President McKinley's surprise, the Spaniards agree to all our terms. He hadn't expected that. So what does he do? He doesn't *tell* anyone that the Spaniards have agreed. He just goes ahead and asks Congress for a declaration of war, which they are only too happy to give him. And all this stuff about our poor oppressed Latin brothers is just hogwash. Soon as the war's over, we take over Cuba. Make 'em agree to write into their constitution a little clause called the Platt Amendment that requires them to permit us to intervene in Cuba any time we think the domestic situation requires it—that is, whenever American business interests are threatened by the Cubans—requires them to get U.S. Senate approval for all foreign loans and business transactions, requires them to give us naval bases in Cuba. How do you think we got Guantanamo Naval Base? We still have a U.S. Navy base there fifteen years after Fidel Castro's Cuban revolution. And why did the Cubans agree to this? Because we still had all our troops there from the Spanish-American War, and we told the Cubans we wouldn't withdraw them until the Cubans agreed to the Platt Amendment. So much for Cuban freedom.''

I was up again and pacing, gesticulating as I spoke.

''Meanwhile, there's this little matter of Filipino independence. The Philippines was a Spanish colony too, and for years the Filipinos had been trying to gain their independence through a guerrilla insurrection. Even before war breaks out between Spain and the U.S., Admiral Dewey gets orders to head for Manila. He gets there all right, and blows the antiquated Spanish navy right out of the water in about two hours. But he's got no army, so he can't take the islands. So he talks to the Filipino guerrilla leader, a guy named Emilio Aguinaldo, and he says, 'Look, Emilio, you guys help me defeat the Spanish army and I'll see that the Philippines gets its independence.' But as soon as Spain's defeated, the U.S. claims the Philippines as a colony—we need it as a coaling station for U.S. naval vessels that have to protect American business interests in China and the Far East. Aguinaldo says, 'Wait a minute!' So we send an American army to the

Philippines, and it takes like four years—the Spanish-American War took eight weeks—but we finally crush the Philippine insurrection. And I mean we *crush* it. 'Oh, you'll get your independence, guys,' we tell 'em, 'but you're not ready yet; we have to civilize you first.' The Philippines remain a U.S. colony until 1946. And even now we still have two of the largest U.S. military bases in the world there, and American business comes and goes as it pleases, and the Filipinos live under martial law with a dictator who's declared himself president for life.''

I picked up my glass of wine and drained it before continuing.

''Shit, man, Vietnam's just the tip of the iceberg. The United States doesn't give a big rat's ass about freedom or justice or democracy for anybody, and we never have. What we want is freedom to do business on our own terms and as much of the damned pie as we can grab. It doesn't have a damned thing to do with communism or socialism or any other ism. This stuff's been going on since long before the Russians ever heard of Lenin or Trotsky. Was Geronimo a Communist? Emilio Aguinaldo? You ever heard of Queen Liliuokalani of Hawaii? She got booted out in 1894 by American pineapple growers. Look at what General Butler said. Even as he was *testifying,* for Chrissake, a creep named Somoza was taking over Nicaragua with an army trained, equipped, and paid for by the United States. And now his son's the dictator. A regular family affair. And American businesses get what they want, and Somoza gets what he wants, and the Nicaraguan people don't get squat. And it's the same thing in Honduras, in Guatemala, in Haiti, all over the Latin world. You think those people are going to put up with that forever? Look at Cuba, the Cuban revolution. Okay, maybe they *don't* have the kinds of liberties and freedom that we have. *But they never did.* And at least now they can all read and write, and they all have homes and shoes, and nobody roots around in garbage cans looking for lunch. But we won't deal with 'em because they're *Communists.* Why shouldn't they be Communists? What have they ever gotten from Western democracy and the free-enterprise system? A boot in the face, that's all. Look at South Korea. One of our staunchest allies. We've got enormous business interests in South Korea. They're our largest trading partner and our biggest recipient of military aid. And what do the South Korean people get? A martial law dictatorship. Sweatshop labor at fifty cents a day. Execution for treason for trying to organize labor unions. Half the Christian clergy are in prison just for asking for democratic elections, for Chrissake. How come American politicians aren't hopping up and down about oppression in South Korea? Look what happened in Chile last fall. For years, U.S. businesses had the run of the mill in Chile. Then Salvador Allende, a Marxist, gets legally elected president and nationalizes all foreign businesses. Next thing you know, he gets overthrown and murdered by a bunch of right-wing generals. They declare martial law, imprison thousands, summarily execute people for looking at 'em cross-eyed—and I mean hundreds of people, maybe thousands—and we support 'em lock, stock, and barrel. And when the dust settles, I'd be willing to bet that we'll find out the U.S. government had more than a little to do with Allende's overthrow. Free World, my ass. We'll support any little chickenshit tyrant that comes down the pike so long as he's willing to take his cut and let American businesses do what they want.''

I stopped talking abruptly, walked over to the desk, and sat down. Roger was looking at me the way an art critic might study a painting.

"Yeah, well, anyway," I said, refilling my wineglass and taking another drink.

"No, listen, this is interesting as hell," he said. "I'm not saying anything because I don't know what to say, that's all. You're a fucking walking encyclopedia. You learn all that stuff in college?"

"Hell, no. Most of it I learned on my own. Just reading. I read a lot," I replied, patting the three books lying on the desk between us and then gesturing to the row of books on the shelf. "I've been reading everything I could get my hands on for the last four years. Vietnam was just the beginning, man. I haven't stopped learning since."

"And you think Vietnam was all part of this business stuff, huh?"

"Pretty much," I replied. "I mean, Eisenhower came right out and said it back in the fifties, that we couldn't let Southeast Asia go communist because we needed their tin and tungsten and stuff. In a bizarre sort of way, all those guys really believed— still believe, I'm sure—that fucking domino theory. You know, 'If the Vietnamese can get out from under Western economic domination, maybe that'll put bad ideas in the heads of the Nicaraguans and the Jamaicans and the Angolans. And then where will we be? Oh, Lordy, we better put a stop to this right now.' Of course, they didn't say it *quite* that way, but what the hell's the fucking government supposed to say? 'Okay, folks, we're going to take your children and send them off to some godforsaken place you never heard of before to get their heads blown off for the benefit of United Fruit Company and RCA and Gulf Oil.' Hell, no. They say, 'Oh, mercy me, the Communists! It's the Communists again! If we don't stop them in Vietnam—or the Dominican Republic or Chile or Timbuktu—next thing you know, they'll be eating out of your refrigerator, and you'll be chained to the furnace in the basement.' And most Americans are dumb enough and brainwashed enough and happy enough to believe it because they can't even begin to imagine that the comfortable lives they live are had at the cost of taking what belongs to the rest of the world. Oh, it's a smart tactic, all right. The power brokers give most of the rest of us enough to think we're in Fat City—if you disregard a few niggers and redskins and welfare moochers who only want a free ride anyway—while they live like kings, and everything's hunky-dory, this'll last forever, folks, if we all just play ball, don't rock the boat. And if every now and then we lose a few of our children, well, they died for freedom and that's certainly worth dying for, isn't it? Meantime, nobody can figure out why half the world hates us, so it *must* be the Commies' fault, right?''

"What are ya lookin' at me for?" said Roger after a brief silence. "What am I supposed to say?"

"You don't *have* to say anything."

"Well, you *sound* convincing enough—but Jesus, Bill, if even half of what you're saying is true—man, that's really scary stuff.''

"You're damned right it's scary. What I'm talking about is ugly. Hideous. Most Americans can't even *begin* to cope with it. It's a fuck of a lot easier just to stick your head in the refrigerator and have another hard-boiled egg and come out once every four years to vote for Tweedledum or Tweedledee. That's the real irony of our so-called democratic system, Roger. In a perverse sort of way, most Americans get exactly the kind of leaders and leadership they deserve. The Vietnamese didn't deserve what happened to them—what's happening to them—but we sure as hell did. We let it happen. It never even occurred to most people that the power brokers might be wrong. Hell, most people don't even think of them as power brokers; they call 'em names like president and secretary of state, and they really believe they're looking out for the people. And it certainly never occurred to the power brokers that they might be wrong. They've had it their way for so long that having it any other way isn't even within the realm of their imagination. Americans have always taken what we wanted. Who would ever have thought that a rinky-dink little third-rate nation of rice farmers could stop the most powerful nation on earth cold in its tracks? Nobody in this country, that's for sure. Certainly not the folks who run the show. Look at that horse's ass Nixon. How many times have you heard him say, 'I am not going to be the first American president to lose a war'? Americans never lose wars. Nixon can't imagine it. None of 'em can. None of 'em ever could. And as for the people—the People,'' I said with mock solemnity—''most of 'em still don't believe that the war was wrong. The only reason so many of that vast Silent Majority finally stopped supporting the war was that they couldn't take getting their faces rubbed in it anymore. They couldn't understand why we weren't winning, and they wanted it to just go away and leave them to their little fantasy world again. The whole thing was coming too damned close to prying open the door to everything I've been talking about. Hell, even most of the people that were openly antiwar—where the hell are they now? The war's still going on. The Vietnamese are still dying by the thousands. The war would be over tomorrow if we cut off American aid to that creep in Saigon. But as long as it's not Americans dying anymore, well, who the hell cares what the government does with a few tax dollars? Christ, no wonder the government gets away with all the bullshit it gets away with. You watch, pal, in another few years, the government'll have its nose up somebody else's asshole somewhere, and the fucking people won't remember a goddamned thing about a place called Vietnam. It'll be like it never happened. Either that or they'll rewrite the history books and make it all seem like a noble cause after all.'' I lit a cigarette and sat back in the chair. I took a drag and exhaled slowly. ''Well, Roger, does that answer your question?''

''Geez, Bill,'' he replied, ''I don't know. I never heard anyone talk like you before.''

''Sounds crazy, doesn't it? Sometimes I wonder if I really am crazy. Most people I've dealt with in the last seven years have certainly seemed to think so.''

''Well, I don't think you're crazy,'' said Roger.

''Yeah?''

''Yeah. I don't know if I buy it all or not, but you certainly seem to know what you're talking about—''

"I know what I'm talking about."

"I just never heard any of this stuff before, that's all. You really got me thinkin', I'll tell ya. You think maybe I could borrow a couple of your books?"

"You serious?"

"Yeah, I'm serious. I'd like to know more about this stuff."

"Sure," I said. "But I gotta warn you, there's nothing in any of these books about reduction gears or electric generators."

"Well, maybe it's about time I learned something about something besides reduction gears and generators anyway. What should I start with?"

"Take these two," I said, picking up the copy of *Bury My Heart at Wounded Knee* and pulling off the shelf a copy of Bernard Fall's *Street Without Joy: Insurgency in Indochina 1946–1963*. "They oughta keep you busy for a while."

"It really matters to you, doesn't it?" said Roger.

"Come on, let's finish this game. I gotta go to work at eight, and so do you. What time is it, anyway? Must be after two."

Chapter 39

"Hi, guys!" Gerry grinned, poking his head into the bunker.

"Gerry!" I shouted. "What are you doin' here? Get your ass in here before you get it blown off." We slapped each other heartily. Gerry Griffith was my best friend, but I hadn't seen him in two weeks because he'd stayed with battalion rear when most of us had been sent up to this utterly miserable mudhole of a place on the demilitarized zone called Con Thien. "Good to see ya, buddy," I said. "What are you doin' here?"

"You said you were gonna send me a postcard of Mickey Mouse from Disneyland," he grinned. Disneyland was what the troops called Con Thien. "I got tired of waiting for it, so I came up to get it. So where is it? Let's have it."

Morgan tore the lid off a box of C rations and handed it to Gerry. "Here," he said. "We been meanin' to send it, but we didn't have a stamp."

"This ain't Mickey Mouse," said Gerry, studying the cardboard lid intently.

"The hell it ain't," said Morgan. "What's in that box?"

Gerry lifted the long box he'd brought in with him. It was shaped like a flower box, only larger. "Dunno," he said. "It's for you." He held it out to me.

"A care package from your mom!" shouted Haller, who had moved into the bunker with us after Seagrave and Walters had been evacuated. "Food! Open it." I took out my bayonet, cut the string and tape, and opened the box. Inside was the top of a pine tree, about two feet long, with all the branches carefully folded up along the trunk and held securely with a ribbon wrapped around the bundle like a barber pole.

"A real live Pennsylvania pine tree," I said slowly.

"It's a Christmas tree!" said Haller. "Incredible!"

"I don't believe it," I said.

"Your mother's amazing, Ehrhart," said Gerry.

"Will you look at that," I said, lifting the tree out of the box and cradling it like a baby. It was embarrassing. My eyes were getting watery. I blinked hard a few times. "I don't believe it," I said.

"There it is," Gerry beamed.

"Thanks for bringin' it, Gerry," I said.

"Let's put it up!" said Haller, who immediately began clearing a space in the corner among the pile of C-ration cartons. I emptied out the rest of the box, which contained a little homemade stand for the tree, and a smaller box of ornaments and tinsel. In ten minutes, we had the whole tree decorated.

"What do we put on top?" asked Haller.

"I got just the thing," I said. I rooted around in the ammo box that served as my footlocker and came up with a six-inch high paper angel with a paper base that just fit over the top branch of the tree.

"Hey! Where'd ya get that?" asked Haller.

"Friend of mine sent it to me last week," I said. "Sadie Thompson. She's a Quaker."

"Perfect," said Haller, straightening the angel unnecessarily. "Good old Sadie. Thanks a lot. Fuck all those guys with their tinfoil trees; we got a *real* tree!"

"We oughta sing a Christmas carol or something," said Gerry as we all sat there in the dingy bunker admiring our tree. He started to sing "Silent Night," and the rest of us sheepishly joined in, but we hadn't gotten two lines into the song when voices began cracking, and everybody looked away from each other and began to laugh with embarrassment.

"You know what Sadie said to me before I came over here?" I said, touching the angel lightly. " 'Try not to kill anyone.' "

"Merry Christmas," said Haller.

"Yeah," I said. We all sat back again, nobody saying anything, just looking at the tree. Incoming artillery exploded over on the other side of the perimeter, sounding very far away. Then a salvo shrieked in and went off down in the valley below us. We all ducked involuntarily, but none of the ornaments fell off.

"Welcome to Disneyland," I said to Gerry. "How long you stayin'?"

"Just overnight," Gerry replied. "I hadda bring some papers up for Colonel Glass to see. Gotta catch a chopper out in the morning. How much of that stuff you guys been getting?"

"Anywhere from twenty-five to two hundred and fifty rounds a day. Just goes on all the fuckin' time," I said. "NVA gunners got this place pegged cold. Like sittin' at the wrong end of a shooting gallery."

"Ain't you guys supposed to be controlling NVA infiltration through the DMZ?" said Gerry.

"Fuck," I said.

"Yeah, well," he replied, shrugging his shoulders.

"Man, those guys could be driving around out there in Greyhound buses and we wouldn't know the difference. We can't even get outside the perimeter without getting our asses kicked. Last week, me and Morgan went out with Charlie Company on a sweep—Christ, we didn't get a thousand meters beyond the wire before they jumped all over us with mortars. That was the last time we tried that. Now all we do is sit in here all day long and get shelled."

"And we kill rats," added Morgan. "We got twenty-three so far." He pointed to the makeshift scoreboard carved into one of the roof beams.

"That's all we do," I said. "That's it. You know we lost Frenchy and Ski, and Wally and Gravey got hit—"

"Yeah, I heard," said Gerry.

"—and we ain't so much as seen a gook since we got here,

let alone shot at one. It's the same old shit, man, only there ain't no civilians up here, and instead of mines and snipers, it's artillery and mortars. I got eighty-two days left, man. Eighty-two fuckin' days.'' I knocked on the wooden duckboards.

The next morning, Gerry headed down to the landing zone to wait for a chopper out. "See ya in a couple of weeks," he said, putting the palm of his outstretched hand over my ear and giving my head a shake.

"Next time you write your wife, tell 'er I said hello, will ya?'' I hollered after him as he shuffle-trotted down the muddy hill into the valley. He threw his hand up in the air in a gesture of acknowledgment, but didn't turn around, intent upon keeping his footing.

About an hour later, a medical corpsman crawled into the bunker. "Which one of you guys is Ehrhart?'' he asked.

"Yo,'' I said.

"One of the casualties gave me this," he said, holding out a mud-caked wristwatch. "Said I was supposed to give it to ya— said it was real important—you lost yours or somethin'?''

"Gerry?'' I said, my stomach wrenching so heavily that I nearly doubled over. "Gerry? What happened? What happened? Where is he, Doc?''

"Gone. We just put him on a chopper. Don't worry; he's okay. He's gonna make it.''

I slumped back against the sandbagged wall, rested my head against it, and took a few deep breaths. "What happened?'' I asked.

"Shrapnel in the knee," said the corpsman. "Looks like a million-dollar job; free ticket home. He got caught by incoming down at the landing zone. Might lose his leg—I don't know—but he's gonna make it. He was right near the battalion aid station when he got hit, so he didn't lose much blood. Nice Christmas tree ya got there, guys.''

I thought of Bobby Rowe. They'd said he was going to make it too, but he hadn't. And Ski had died on the chopper before they'd ever gotten him to the hospital.

"Listen, I gotta get back,'' said the corpsman.

"What? Oh, yeah, sure.''

"I just brought this up because the guy said it was real important; he made me promise.''

"Yeah. Yeah, it's important,'' I said. The corpsman turned to leave. "Hey, Doc, thanks for comin' all the way up here.''

"Yeah, sure."

"Keep your ass down," I shouted after him as he disappeared out the entrance. I looked at the watch in my hand. I'd lost mine on an operation a month earlier. Almost absentmindedly, I started to clean the mud off Gerry's watch. "Guy's all busted up like that," I said, not really talking to Haller or Morgan, "remembers I lost my watch." Gerry's watch was still running. I put it on. Then I crawled into the top bunk and lay down, turning my face toward the damp sandbagged wall.

Chapter 40

"So why the hell didn't you write to me?" I said. "I didn't know *what* the hell happened to you."

"I *did* write," said Gerry. We both started laughing again. The waitress in the all-night diner in Roseburg, Oregon, glanced at us nervously, as though she were trying determine if we were about to rob the place.

"Really?" I said.

"Yeah, really. I been wondering why you never wrote back."

"I never got your letter. It never got to me. When did you write?"

"January or February, I guess," said Gerry. "A couple of months after I got hit. I don't remember exactly—what's it been, three and a half years? I know it was while I was still in Oakland naval hospital."

"Well, that explains it," I said. "Things got real fucked up after you got evacuated. Your letter musta gotten lost somewhere along the way."

"What happened after I left?" asked Gerry. "I see you made it back in one piece."

"Yeah, but it was touch and go for a while there. We left Con Thien the day before Christmas and got sent down south of Quang

Tri for a month. Then we were supposed to go down to Phu Bai for a month of rest and refitting—I figured I was home free because I only had a month to go by then—only a couple days after we got there, the Tet offensive started and we ended up in Hue City.''

"Hue?" Gerry asked.

"Yeh, Hue. Christ, it was a hell of a swan song, I'll tell ya."

"I thought I read somewhere that Fifth Marines got stuck with Hue," said Gerry.

"They were there too—a couple of companies, at least. I know Fox and Golf companies were there, or maybe Hotel Company, I don't remember. But we were there first—not that that's anything to brag about. I'd have been happy if they'd gotten there first instead of us. We walked right into the biggest damn ambush of the whole fucking war. Those asshole Army MACV guys in Hue radio down one morning that they're takin' sniper fire and light mortars. 'Nothin' serious,' they say, 'but can ya send up a relief column to check it out?' So we put Alpha and Bravo companies and a command group onto trucks and head on up the road to Hue. This is like four o'clock in the morning. Nobody's ever heard of the Tet offensive yet. Christ, the NVA nailed us the minute we hit the city limits. They had machine guns and recoilless rifles dug in on either side of the road—just opened up at point-blank range with everything all at once. There it was, man. I spend twelve months runnin' around tryin' to find Charlie and comin' up with squat, and then one morning—zappo! They're crawlin' all over the place. Every fuckin' NVA in the world musta been there.''

"Bad, huh?"

"Like number-fucking-ten. They really unloaded on us. They literally had us outnumbered by about ten to one for the first week or so. You know, man, here I am with less than a month to go, and all of a sudden I'm in the middle of a *war*. The only thing good about it was that for once Charlie stood his ground and fought. At least we finally had something to shoot at besides old ladies and water bo. We lost a lot of guys, though."

"Anybody I knew?" asked Gerry.

"Major Miles, the operations officer, remember him? He got killed loading bodies onto the trucks the very first day—"

"What was he doing on body detail?" Gerry interrupted incredulously.

"Body detail? You're not listening, man. There wasn't any

body detail; there was just a hell of a lot of dead and wounded
Marines lying around, and *somebody* hadda try and pick 'em up.
Christ, Gerry, we took about fifty percent casualties just on the
first day, before we could get dug in. Gunny Krebs got killed the
first day. Captain Braithwaite got both legs broken by a fifty-
caliber machine-gun slug. You didn't know Bannerman and
Davis, did you?''

"No,'' said Gerry, shaking his head slowly as if trying to
recall.

"They were the guys that replaced Frenchy and Ski in December, while we were still up at Disneyland. Anyway, they both
got it. Thurston?''

"Yeah.''

"He got killed. Amagasu, remember him?''

"Kenny? Yeh.''

"Got his arm blown off. Same rocket that got me.''

"You got hit?'' asked Gerry.

"Yeah, but it wasn't bad. Shrapnel from a B-40 rocket. Kenny
got the worst of it. My flak jacket and helmet took a lot of the
blast. I got cut up a little bit, but the only really bad thing was
that I was stone deaf for about two weeks.''

"You get evacked?''

"Hell, no,'' I replied. "Listen, we really had our backs to the
wall. Anybody that could walk, see, and hold a rifle stayed. So
I'm runnin' around in the middle of the biggest battle of the war
stone deaf. Couldn't hear a thing.'' I started chuckling. "You
shoulda seen it, Gerry. Gravey or Mogerty or somebody would
have to be giving me hand signals all the time—get up, get down,
go this way, go that way, duck. Seems kind of comical now, but
at the time, it was really hairy. It was *strange.* ''

"Your ears okay now?'' Gerry asked.

"Pretty much. I've still got a partial hearing loss, and my ears
ring all the time. I tried to get some disability pay from the VA,
but they wouldn't give me a dime. Said it didn't impair my ability
to make a living. Shit,'' I scoffed, "maybe not, but you think
they'd give you something to compensate for having to listen to
your ears ringin' twenty-four hours a day for the next fifty years.''
I leaned over the table and began speaking in a deliberately con-
spiratorial too-loud whisper: "Look at that waitress over there.
She knows. She knows we've got grenades under our shirts. She
knows we're about to flip out at any moment.'' I suddenly looked
up at her, smiling broadly. She turned away quickly, embarrassed

to be caught eavesdropping on us. I started laughing. "So, I see you still got your leg. The corpsman that brought me your watch said maybe they'd have to cut it off." I held up my wrist and showed Gerry his watch.

"You still got that thing?"

"Sure do," I said. "You want it back?"

"Get outa here," he laughed.

"You know, Gerry, that was the nicest present anybody ever gave me. I, uh—" My voice cracked, and I looked away in embarrassment, composing myself before continuing. "It meant a lot to me, pal. Sure got lonely after you left."

"It was lonely all the time anyway," Gerry shrugged, trying to make light of the affection between us. I didn't press it. "So what happened to everybody else?" Gerry continued. "You didn't finish telling me."

"I don't know, really. When I got my orders, we were still in Hue. Who was left by then? Gravey, Wally, Hoffy, Mogerty, Morgan. I guess they're the only guys you'd know—"

"What about Randy Haller?"

"He didn't go into the city with us," I replied. "He stayed back at Battalion Rear. In fact, he was on R and R when I got pulled out of the city, so the last I saw of him was the day before we went up to Hue. The rest of 'em were still alive when I left. Mogerty and Morgan had both been hit, but they weren't evacuated either. I don't know how many of 'em made it. Never heard from any of 'em again. Strange, ain't it? You spend all that time with people, really feel like you're pretty tight—then all of a sudden it's all over, just like that, like they never even existed except in your own head. You know the way I left? We were in the middle of a firefight and some fuckin' young lieutenant wheels up in a jeep and hollers, 'Ehrhart, your orders are in,' and I just stripped off half my gear and passed it around, jumped into the jeep, waved good-bye, and that was that. Last I saw of 'em, they were all hunched over their rifles laying down covering fire for us. One minute I'm lyin' there firing away at the NVA; ten minutes later, I'm on a chopper three thousand feet up. Just like that. I don't suppose I'll ever know what happened to any of 'em."

"Well, I'm glad you found *me* at least," said Gerry.

"So am I," I said. "It's good to see you again."

"How did you find me, anyway?"

"Remember the time you lent me money to go to Hong Kong?"

"Yeah."

"And my parents were supposed to send the money to your wife? Well, my mom never throws away anything, and she still had your wife's parents' address. So I just called directory assistance and got your father-in-law's phone number. I didn't know you were gonna be in Roseburg too, but I figured he'd know where you were. What are you doin' in Roseburg, anyway? I thought you were gonna go to college and all."

"Oh, I tried to go to school," he explained. "Jan and I were both enrolled at Fresno State for a while, but we just couldn't make it on that measly GI Bill we get, so Jan insisted that I stay in school while she worked. Then she got pregnant, and that was that. We came back here because her dad said he could get me a job in one of the lumber mills. So here I am, workin' the four-to-midnight shift six days a week."

"Do you like what you're doin'?"

"I don't have much choice about it," he laughed. "At least I got a job." I thought I could detect an edge of bitter resignation in his voice. "Anyway, it's nice country around here. I get to go fishin' a lot. It's not a bad life. Hey, you wanna go fishin' tomorrow?"

"Sure, I guess so, but I'm not very good at it," I said.

"You don't have to be good," said Gerry. "Around here, the fish swim around just looking for hooks to jump onto. We can drive up the Upper Umqua a ways to a real nice spot I know and camp overnight. You wanna do that?"

"Overnight? Camping? You haven't had enough camping out for one lifetime?"

"Come on. This is all different, Bill; this is fun. I haven't been mortared yet."

"Shit, man, the only time I've been camping since I left Vietnam, I wished I had been mortared."

"Well," said Gerry, looking disappointed, "we don't have to stay overnight."

"No, listen, don't let me rain on your parade, my man. Why not? But the first fuckin' incoming we take, we pack it in, right?"

"Absolutely," Gerry said solemnly, holding up his right hand. Then he broke into a broad grin.

"Are you sure Jan's not gonna mind you goin' away overnight?" I asked.

"She'll get over it," said Gerry.

"I don't want her to have to get over anything," I said. "Listen, I don't mean to pry, but is that why she seemed a little cold tonight?'' I'd reached Gerry's house before he'd returned home from work; their two boys were already in bed, and I'd had to spend several hours alone with Jan. She'd been polite but distant. I'd felt very uncomfortable.

"What did she do?" Gerry asked.

"It wasn't that she did anything, really. Just a feeling, you know? Are you sure it's okay for me to be here? I don't have to stay if it's a problem.''

"Of course it's okay for you to be here,'' Gerry insisted. "It isn't that. I think she's, well, just a little jealous of you. She knows how close we were, you know? Part of her is really grateful to you that you were, well, you know, that you helped to keep my head together and all. But at the same time, Vietnam's a whole part of my life that she wasn't a part of and can't ever be a part of. I think she sort of resents that, that's all, that you understand it and she doesn't. It's nothing personal, believe me. Don't worry about it. She's a good woman really. One thing you gotta do, though,'' he added. "Watch your language around the house—''

"Oh, yeah, with the kids, sure.''

"It's not just the kids,'' said Gerry, smiling awkwardly. "Jan's pretty religious these days. I guess I've gotten a little religion, too, since I saw you last.''

"Yeah?''

"Well, yeah, kind of,'' he explained. He seemed uncomfortable. "I don't know if that's Jan's doing or mine, but well, it gives me something to believe in.''

"Geez, and I been sittin' here talkin' like a truck driver.''

"I'm not *that* religious,'' Gerry laughed. "Besides, I know where you're comin' from. Just be careful around the house, okay?''

It was nearly three A.M. by the time we got back to Gerry's house, but I couldn't sleep. Had coming here been a mistake, I wondered—like my visits with Smitty in Yuma and Charlie Quinlon at OSU? But Gerry was different, wasn't he? We hadn't been just buddies; we'd been real friends. How many times had he concocted excuses to visit me in the field, the way he'd done when he'd abruptly appeared at Con Thien? Surely I could still talk to Gerry.

I'd begun thinking about trying to find Gerry on the night I'd rolled into Medicine Hat, Alberta, only to discover that yet another Canadian town couldn't live up to its name. Then in Sacramento, I'd learned that Max Harris, my boyhood friend and fellow Marine from Perkasie, had died in a motorcycle accident, plastering himself all over a telephone pole. He'd been riding through town at night at high speed with no lights and no helmet. I didn't know if they'd ruled it a suicide or not, but I didn't need a coroner to tell me what had happened. The war had claimed another casualty.

It frightened me. Max had seemed to be doing all right when I'd seen him in the spring. What had gone wrong? Or was it only that once you got burned, you never healed again? Was the empty aching pain inside really never going to get any better? I'd certainly thought often enough about how easy it would be just to bail out. Could I really do it? Would I? Or would I one day just go crazy, shooting up a schoolyard full of children or a bunch of senators before the cops finally blew me away?

God, I wanted to *talk* to someone. But now that I was here, I didn't know what to say.

Chapter 41

"I got one! I got one!" I shouted, the fishing rod in my hands suddenly bending sharply, the reel humming as the line played out rapidly. The rushing tumble of the river among the rocks was so loud that Gerry, thirty yards downstream, didn't hear me at first, but I kept hollering until he did. He dropped his own rod and began scrambling over the rocks toward me. God, I didn't want to lose this fish! I'd already had three others jump off the delicate unbarbed fly hook.

"Don't jerk the line!" he shouted. "Hold it steady! Don't slack off!" The fish jumped: man, it was *big*.

By the time Gerry reached me, he was panting for breath. "Okay," he gasped, "set your drag." He pointed to a switch on the rod. "Don't jerk the line and don't let it slacken." He took several deep breaths before continuing. "Reel it in steady. When you feel the line slacken, reel in; when the line goes tight, just let it out slowly. You wanna tire him out." I held on to the rod as though my life depended on it, not talking at all. Suddenly the fish jumped again. "Geez, Bill, you got a beauty there! Must be sixteen inches at least. Maybe a foot and a half."

For nearly half an hour the fish fought me: darting back and forth, leaping, resting, bolting again. Gerry kept shouting instructions and encouragement in my ear: "Reel in a little more! You've got him! He's getting tired now. Don't lose your concentration." Finally the fish was right in the rushing water below me. Gerry grabbed the net and got ready to scoop the fish out of the river. I was sweating, and the muscles in my arms and upper back were tight and aching.

"Hold it, hold it steady. Got him!" he shouted, netting the fish in one smooth swift motion. "Ehrhart, that sucker's eighteen inches long." It was still twisting and fighting against the net.

"Wow," I said quietly, staring at it. "What kind is it?"

"It's a rainbow trout," said Gerry, pointing to the colored stripes on its flanks that shimmered almost iridescent in the sunlight. I put the rod down and reached into the net, grabbing the fish with both hands, holding it steady while Gerry removed the hook from its mouth.

"That's supper for both of us!" he exclaimed, his face beaming. "Nice work!"

I just stood there beside the river looking down at the fish in my hands. It was clearly exhausted, its sides pumping in and out, its gills working rapidly. It had fought hard—one could almost say bravely, I thought. Now it stared at me defiantly, or seemed to. You can catch me, it seemed to be saying, but you can't break me. That's silly, I thought, it's just a fish. But the feeling persisted. I looked from the fish to Gerry and back to the fish. "It's a beautiful fish, isn't it?"

"Yeah, it is," said Gerry, touching its flank. It whipped its tail as he touched it. My throat was tight. I couldn't have explained why, but I felt like crying. It was embarrassing.

"If I throw it back, will it live?" I asked without looking at Gerry.

"Yeah, probably."

I dropped my hands toward the water and released my grip: splash. I stared at the spot where the fish had just entered the river, but already there was nothing there. The fish was gone. Gerry put his arm around my shoulders gently, and we both stood there watching the river slice among the rocks beneath the Douglas firs.

"We got enough food to eat, anyway," Gerry said finally. "I brought some canned stuff. Come on, let's go set up the tent." We gathered up the fishing gear and put it in Gerry's car. Then we took out the camping equipment and hiked up into the ravine of one of the feeder streams to a small clearing by a waterfall. "Nice place, huh?" said Gerry.

"It's really beautiful here," I replied. "What's the name of this river?"

"The Umqua," said Gerry. "The Upper Umqua, actually. The two branches come together just west of Roseburg, right where we crossed that bridge."

"Strange name," I said as we began putting the campsite in order. "Indian?"

"Yeah, I guess so. Klamath probably. They used to be all over this part of the Cascades."

"Well, it figures," I said. "First we take their land and kill 'em all off, then we name everything after 'em."

"There's a Klamath reservation down south of here," Gerry replied. "Don't hit my fingers," he laughed, holding a tent peg in place for me to hammer.

"Still don't trust me, huh?"

"I've still got scars on my knuckles from the last time we tried this."

"You ever been there?" I asked.

"Where?"

"That Klamath reservation."

"No."

"Check it out sometime," I said. "Last month I went through a reservation in Minnesota, way up near Canada, out in the middle of nowhere. It was really sad. They were livin' in cardboard and tarpaper shacks. Looked like those ramshackle hooches the Vietnamese used to build out of American garbage. No electricity. Probably no running water or plumbing. Must be unbelievable in the winter. Here we are 'roughing it' in the middle of the summer, and we think it's fun. Those people live like that all the time."

"Let's collect some wood," said Gerry without responding to my remarks. Had I offended him, I wondered, baffled him? Did he have nothing to say about Native Americans? What could I talk about that would be safe? Four years ago, I would almost have been able to guess what he was thinking just by looking at his face. But now? I began gathering dead branches. The forest was full of them. We soon had a large pile of wood, and a small fire burned in the center of the stone circle we'd built.

"What do ya want to eat?" he asked.

"Whaddaya got?"

"Campbell's pork and beans," he replied, beginning to rummage through his pack, "beef stew, corned beef, hot dogs—"

"Corned beef," I said. "Hey, the trucks are gone. You notice that?" All day the only interruption to the stillness of the forest and the rushing river had been the constant noisy passing of big logging trucks loaded with massive tree trunks racing along the narrow winding highway beside the river toward the mills in Roseburg.

"They're pretty much done for the day," Gerry replied. "It'll be dark soon."

"Peaceful out here," I said, adjusting the can of corned beef in the fire. Gerry was heating a can of beef stew. "You come here a lot?"

"Whenever I can get away. I can't wait till the boys are old enough to come along."

"They're nice kids. How old are they?"

"Michael's two and a half. Timmy's almost one and a half."

"You got a nice family, Gerry."

"Yeah, I do. I'm glad you think so. Bill, what ever happened to Jenny?"

"Jenny?" I snorted. "Nothin'. Nothin' at all. She wouldn't even go out with me when I got back. I never saw her again."

"Heck of a time to send you a Dear John, wasn't it?"

"The way it goes, I guess. It wasn't her fault, I suppose. Wasn't anybody's fault. We were just kids. Remember the time her roommate from nursing school wrote and asked me if I wanted to be her pen pal?"

"Do I? I hadda tie you down to keep you from doing bodily injury to yourself."

"Well, anyway, Jenny's long gone by now," I said. "Good luck to 'er."

"You ever hear from that woman you met in Hong Kong? Dorrit?"

"Yeah, Dorrit. You got a good memory. No, she's dead now. Got killed about a month after you left."

"Oh, no. Really? What happened?"

"She got raped and murdered," I replied. "It was in *Stars 'n' Stripes* because they thought it was an American serviceman that did it, but then I read later that they arrested some Chinese guy."

"Geez, that's too bad."

"Yeah."

We ate slowly, talking as we ate. It was getting dark rapidly now, and the firelight flickered among the trees.

"I think about her sometimes," I said. "I wonder if she really loved me, or if she just felt sorry for me. She told me she was twenty, but the newspapers said she was twenty-three. Maybe they got it wrong—they spelled her name wrong—or maybe she just told me that to make me feel more comfortable; I was just barely nineteen then. She was kind enough to have thought of something like that. Did I ever tell you about the brass cannon I bought her?"

"I don't think so. Anyway, I don't remember it."

"Well, I bought her this handmade ornamental cannon for a going-away present—all inlaid with gold and silver—but she wouldn't take it. Said she didn't want to remember me that way, like associated with guns and military stuff. She made me buy her a silk flower instead. You know, I don't even know her parents' address in Denmark. She's just gone. Like some kind of dream."

"You got any girlfriends now?" Gerry asked.

"No. Heck, Gerry, any woman crazy enough to fall in love with me is too crazy for me to deal with." I tried to laugh, but it came out sounding more like a croak.

"Yeah, I know what ya mean," he said. "I'm lucky Jan stuck with me. I was pretty wired up when I got back, and she couldn't understand it. If we hadn't been married already, we might not have made it." He didn't elaborate further, and I didn't elaborate further, and I didn't want to press him. We both stared into the fire for a while. "How's school going?" he asked.

"Oh, it's okay. Some of my courses have been pretty interesting. I took a great course this year in political theory—Plato, Aristotle, Locke, Hobbes, guys like that. Had a good poetry workshop with a man named Dan Hoffman. Ever heard of him?"

"No, should I have?"

"No, I guess not. I never heard of him either till I took the course, but he's a darned good poet."

"Workshop, huh?" said Gerry. "You writing poetry these days?"

"Yeah, some."

"You bring any with you?"

"No."

"Well, send me some of it, will you? I'd like to read it."

"Yeah, okay," I said, "but don't hold your breath. I ain't exactly William Blake."

"How are your grades?"

"Pretty good. I guess I'm doin' all right. Strange place, though."

"How so?"

"Well, nobody there has the foggiest notion where I'm comin' from. I'm the only Vietnam veteran in the whole school."

"You been gettin' hassled?"

"Well, not exactly," I said. "That's what I was afraid of when I first got there, but I've gotten more hassles from rednecks in bars than I have from the people at Swarthmore. Funny, you know, they're all against the war and everything, but they're as fascinated by war as I was before I knew any better. I been there two years, and I still got total strangers comin' up to me out of the blue, asking me what it was like, did I ever kill anybody, stuff like that. It's like I'm not a real person, you know? Like I'm some kind of cross between John Wayne and Godzilla. It's hard to deal with sometimes."

"I got that at Fresno for a while," Gerry replied. "There were a few other vets there, but not many. Up here, nobody bothers me. Pretty much live and let live, so long as you mind your own business. I like it that way. You think you'll finish?"

"I don't know. I'd pretty much made up my mind not to go back this year, but maybe I will. Don't know what else I'd do. What do I know how to do except fill sandbags and dig fox-holes?"

"Isn't there anybody there you're friends with?"

"Oh, yeah," I said. "It's not *that* bad. There's a few people there I can deal with. I guess there's bound to be a few good people in any batch of assholes."

"You do any sports or anything like that?" Gerry asked.

"I been on the water ballet team the past two years—"

"Water ballet?" Gerry roared.

"Yeah, water ballet. Imagine that. I didn't believe it either when a buddy of mine first suggested it, but it's kind of fun actually. I been on the swimming team, too."

It was completely dark now, the fire crackling and popping between us, illuminating our faces. I almost began to tell Gerry about being a proctor, but I hadn't been renewed for the coming year and it still rankled me. I decided not to get into it. We both sat quietly for a while.

"Gerry, does it ever bother you?" I asked.

"What?"

"The war. What we did over there?"

"Yeah, sometimes. Mostly I try not to think about it. What's the point?" Gerry replied. "What's done is done. I got other things to think about."

"You ever dream about it?"

"Yeah, sometimes," he said. "I dream about being interrogated by those national police dudes. And about getting caught in the artillery barrage, only I can see the gunners firing, and they're always pointing at me and laughing. 'You got yours, buddy. How do you like it?' "

"It does bother you, doesn't it?"

"Of course it does. But what am I supposed to do about it? That was four years ago. I can't take it back, you know? It happened. But I got a wife and two kids to deal with now. They depend on me. Somewhere along the line, you just gotta let go and get on with it."

"I *know* that, man. I'd *like* to let go, Gerry, but it's stuck to me like flypaper. You can't pick up a newspaper. You can't turn on the TV. We *did* all that stuff, Gerry. And it's *still* goin' on. It didn't just happen; it's happening right now! Remember the talks we used to have? We *knew*, Gerry. We knew it then—even if we couldn't face up to it. Remember Sergeant Trinh? All the stuff he told me about rigged elections and how stupid and arrogant we were? Why the heck does a guy who's spent six and a half years fighting the Vietcong suddenly just quit like that? Remember what he said?"

"Yeh, I remember," said Gerry. " 'You Americans are worse than the VC.' "

"He was *right*, Gerry. He was right."

"You really think so?"

"Don't you?"

"Geez, Bill, I don't know," Gerry replied.

"Well, you ought to!" I could tell that Gerry was very uncomfortable. I should back off, I told myself, but I couldn't. "Have you read *The Pentagon Papers?*"

"Just a little bit in the newspapers. I haven't paid much attention—"

"Well, read the damned thing, man! We were on the wrong side, Gerry! We were the Redcoats."

Gerry didn't reply. He picked up a stick and began poking the fire.

"I could almost deal with it if it had been for something worthwhile," I continued in a quieter voice, "if we'd really been doing what they told us we were doing. But it wasn't like that at all, and you and I know it. Gerry, if guys like you and me don't speak out now, where's it gonna stop? Those lunatics in Washington are out of their minds, man. Somebody's gotta stop 'em."

"How do you propose to do it?" Gerry asked.

"I don't know," I replied. "But if enough guys like you and me refused to keep our mouths shut, maybe *somebody* would start listening. Look at how far we've strayed from our roots, Gerry. Think about guys like Thomas Paine and Patrick Henry. They'd be rolling over in their graves if they could see what we've done to Vietnam in the name of life, liberty, and the pursuit of happiness. What we've done to our own country. We've got to find a way to get back to what this country's supposed to be, Gerry. That's the one good thing that just might come out of all this insanity. Maybe if guys like us can manage to turn this country around, maybe it just might turn out to have been worth it after all. If we can't do that, Gerry, then it really will have been for nothing. And I don't want it to have been for nothing. We paid too high a price."

"You really think you can turn this country around?" Gerry asked, scratching his chin and peering across the fire at me.

"Not if I have to do it alone, I can't."

"I don't know, Bill," said Gerry, pausing for a long moment before continuing. "I wouldn't even know where to begin. I'd get fired in ten minutes if I started talking like you around the mill. These people are real down-homers, man. I gotta—listen, Bill, you wanna know something? I'll tell ya something straight, buddy; listen to this. I can't even talk to Jan about any of this stuff. One time when I was still in the hospital in Oakland, I started tryin' to tell her about Vietnam, about what was really happening, and she started crying and told me to stop talking about it. Same thing happened two or three more times. I finally quit trying.''

"You can't even talk to your *wife?*''

"No. I don't understand it. I don't understand at all, but she just doesn't want to hear a word about it. That's why she's so uncomfortable around you—you were right; I noticed it this morning. I'm really sorry she's acting that way—''

"It's okay,'' I interrupted. "You don't have to apologize. I guess I'm kind of like some kind of ghost, huh?''

"She's not like that usually,'' he continued. "I don't know. Seems like she's angrier about the war than I am, but I don't know why because she won't talk about it. I don't know if she thinks we shoulda nuked Hanoi or never gotten into it in the first place. Bill, I understand what you're saying. You're right, and I know it. It's been bothering me ever since I left Vietnam. Some nights, I can't even sleep at all. But I gotta deal with things the way they are, Bill. Jan's not perfect by a long shot, but she's a good woman and a good wife and I love her very much. I'm lucky to have her, Bill. I can't afford to lose her. She's all I've got—her and the boys. I *need* them. And I need my job. Can you understand that?''

"Yeah, I guess so,'' I said.

"You think I'm a coward?'' he asked.

"Come on. You know I know better than that. You got a lot to lose, that's all. I envy you.'' I reached for another log and placed it on the fire. "What'll ya do when the government orders *your* boys off to some jerkwater fiasco like Vietnam?''

"I don't know,'' he replied. "I guess I'll just have to deal with that when I get there.''

Neither of us spoke for a long time. I leaned back against a rock and stretched my legs out. The air was comfortably cool, and the smell of pine was sweet and refreshing.

"Is that why you threw that fish back today?'' Gerry asked.

"Remember the day I killed that snake out in front of my hooch?''

"Yeah, I remember.''

"Pointless,'' I said. "No reason for it. They turned us into killers, Gerry. We were just supposed to do it, and not ask questions. And now they wanna disown us. You know, Gerry, I'd have a hard time trying to pass myself off as a pacifist after all the crap I've done. But I'll tell you one thing: The next time I kill anything, I'm gonna know damned good and well why I'm doin' it. And I'm gonna do it for my own reasons, not somebody else's.''

"Amen to that," said Gerry. H reached into his pack again. "I got some marshmallows. You wanna toast 'em?"

"Yeah, sure. I haven't had toasted marshmallows in years."

"Wonder what ever happened to Trinh," he said.

"Beats me," I replied. "They probably shipped him off to an ARVN suicide battalion. Maybe he defected. Who knows? Up in Hue City, one night we caught a bunch of ARVN soldiers looting our supplies, and I shot two of 'em. I was really outraged because, you know, here we were trying to take back *their* city from the NVA, and the first time I saw any ARVN anywhere in the whole city, they were tryin' to steal our chow. That coulda been Trinh, for all I knew. I didn't even care by then. But you know what we'd been doin' when we caught 'em? We were comin' back from gang-bangin' some starving Vietnamese refugee who'd agreed to screw us for food. Turned her into a whore for a half a case of C rations. And we used to sit around wondering why the heck the ARVN wouldn't fight."

"Well," said Gerry, "that chickenscratch excuse for a government in Saigon didn't help any. Remember that district chief in Dien Ban that used to sell USAID rice to the highest bidder?"

"And them national policemen?" I added. "I wonder how much *they* made selling M-16s to the VC. Geez, between us and our Saigon stooges, it's no wonder Trinh quit. *I* wonder why it took 'im six and a half years to get around to it."

"You know who else I wonder about?" said Gerry. "Co Chi. Remember her?"

"Sure I remember her. The one down at Hieu Nhon that always wore a white *ao dai.*"

"Remember the day we came back from China Beach and spent the night sitting in the outhouse while the VC overran Hieu Nhon?"

"God, that was the worst case of the trots I ever had," I said.

"You think she was there that night?"

"I doubt it. She only worked at Hieu Nhon. Lived somewhere in Hoi An, I think. Anyway, for all we know, she was probably a VC agent."

"You think so?"

"Heck, I don't know. It wouldn't surprise me."

Gerry put another log on the fire and handed me the bag of marshmallows. There were no clouds in the sky, and here and there you could see patches of stars among the branches overhead.

"I like it here," I said. "This is a nice place."

I tried to think of something else to say, but there was nothing between us but the fire and the marshmallows and the war.

Chapter 42

It was a routine patrol, like most patrols, the tension so low-key you were hardly aware of it. The heat rose out of the earth with the same dull intensity that made each motionless day a mirror image of the ones on either side of it. It was easily 120 degrees.

We were about three miles north of battalion, moving slowly through ricefields between two small hamlets on the back side of the loop formed by our circular patrol route. We'd been out nearly three hours. Aside from a few water buffalo standing around asleep on their feet, we hadn't seen much of anything. Everyone but us obviously had enough sense not to be out in heat like this.

And then I spotted the figure in black pajamas running along a paddy dike about three hundred meters ahead and to the left. "Got one!" I hollered. "Ten o'clock. He's mine."

The muttered warning to halt—regulations: "Dung lai!" Drop to one knee. Safety off. Sight in. Squeeze. *Crack!* The figure in black went flying like a piece of paper in a gust of wind.

"Get some!" Morgan shouted.

"Nice shot," said Mogerty.

When we reached the body, it was sprawled in one of those impossibly awkward postures only people who die violently while in motion are capable of assuming. I nudged the corpse faceup with my boot. It was a woman of indeterminate age, perhaps fifty-five or sixty.

"Stupid gook," said Wally. "What'd she run for?" Vietna-

mese from the nearby hamlets were beginning to gather in clus-
ters nearby, afraid to approach the old woman while we were still
there, some of them keening softly as Wally radioed in to battalion:

"Annunciate, Annunciate; Annunciate Two Sierra."

"Annunciate; go ahead, Two."

"We got one Victor Charlie Kilo India Alpha; Bravo Tango
two-niner-two three-six-zero; negative weapons."

"That's a roger, Two. Do you require assistance?"

"Negative assist, Annunciate. Everything's cool here. We're
proceeding in. Over."

And then we moved on through the silent steel heat.

Chapter 43

I felt like I was suffocating. Trapped. In prison for life with
no parole. In a lifetime that had seemed to have reduced itself to
little more than a continuous succession of bummers, this one
was the ultimate. My uniform clung to my body like a rusty suit
of armor, too small to fit and impossible to shed. How in God's
name had I *ever* allowed myself to get into this predicament?
What terminal disease possessed me? What crippled, twisted part
of my soul had ever imagined I could get away with this? I
wanted to bolt and run. What would they do to me if I did? Court-
martial me? Send me to Portsmouth naval prison? I fought desperately to control myself as the executive officer introduced me
to the roomful of officers and staff noncommissioned officers.

"I want to welcome aboard Staff Sergeant Ehrhart here, the
newest member of our unit," said the major, gesturing toward
me as I stood before the group. I tried to smile. I felt like my
skin was shrinking, stretching dangerously taut across my bones,
ready to split and dump my guts all over the floor. "He's just
begun his third year at Swarthmore College. He's also a Vietnam

veteran with a very distinguished combat record. He'll be working in our intelligence section. Please make him welcome, gentlemen.''

There was a brief round of applause, and then I sat back down and the meeting went on. Christ almighty, I thought frantically, what have I done? What in the hell have I done?

It had all started simply enough. After quitting my job building swimming pools, I'd spent the summer criss-crossing the continent, driving thirteen thousand miles in eleven weeks, hitting seventeen states and four provinces of Canada.

Then I'd arrived back in Perkasie in late August to discover a couple of economic setbacks I hadn't anticipated. For one thing, my parents' 1964 Studebaker Lark had unexpectedly given up the ghost, requiring them to shell out for a new car. It made me feel guilty that I'd spent the summer carousing around the country instead of working, only to get home and find them strapped for cash. To make matters worse, the state of Pennsylvania, which had paid me a bonus of several hundred dollars two years earlier for having served in Vietnam, was now claiming two years later that I'd been overpaid and that I owed *them* several hundred dollars.

All of which was made more difficult by the fact that I had not been renewed as a proctor for my junior year, which meant that I would have to come up with five hundred dollars to pay for my room at school. That one really rankled. Having been probably the first sophomore proctor in Swarthmore's history, I now had the added distinction of being the first proctor in anyone's memory not to be renewed. It had been embarrassing—humiliating, really.

Well, all right, so there'd been the president's tea. And the trash can of water in Frazer's room the night we'd started and finished the Third-Floor Dana Beer Cartel. And the dozen or so doors we'd smashed, and the sixty or so heart attacks we'd nearly caused, during our raid on Willets Dorm. And the Great Fire Extinguisher Fight. And the time I'd mooned Kathleen the cafeteria supervisor in the small dining room in Sharples, a feat that had earned me the coveted Swarthmore Delta Upsilon Order of the Harvest Moon. And—

Well, what the hell, so I'd kicked up a little dust. Didn't I deserve it? I'd had my youth stolen from me at eighteen; at nineteen I'd been an old man. If I'd managed to steal back a small part of those lost years and youthful spirits, should I be punished for it? Especially by a bunch of kids on some student committee who didn't know jack squat about real responsibility?

Maybe I hadn't been the world's greatest proctor—but I hadn't done that badly either. I had dutifully let people who lost their keys into their rooms at two A.M. I'd kept an eye on the freshmen as the year progressed, stopping by to talk with them from time to time, making sure they weren't being overwhelmed by homesickness or academic pressure. I'd spent a whole night sitting up with Alex Walters when he'd learned that his father had died of a heart attack, driving him to the airport in the morning.

Why, I'd asked Dean Bradley, why hadn't I been renewed? "You haven't done anything wrong," he insisted, smiling uncomfortably and lighting his pipe repeatedly. "The committee just thought that other candidates were more attractive."

"That's no reason to fire me! What have I done *wrong?*"

"It was the committee's decision," he'd replied. "It's out of my hands."

Fucking shitheads, I'd thought. There it was. In their minds, in less than a year, I'd gone from guru to goat—and most of them knew nothing more about *me* than they'd known when I'd first set foot on campus. Was I going to have to spend the rest of my life failing to live up to other people's pipe dreams and fantasies of what I was supposed to be? I'd been gnawing on that one all summer. It seemed as though I couldn't influence the outcome of anything: not Didi's decision to leave school nor the police riot in Washington the previous spring nor the death of Max Harris nor the ignorance of the hard hats and rednecks nor the course of the needless insane war in Vietnam. I hated the feeling of helplessness. Along with the loneliness, it had become a chronic condition of my life.

And then at the end of August, with school only a few weeks away, I'd found myself saddled with a serious financial crisis. Maybe I could get a job on campus, lifeguarding at the pool or something. There had to be a way I could scrape up a few bucks.

In the meantime, while I'd been away, a letter had arrived for me and was waiting for my return. It was from the Marine Corps Reserve Records Center in St. Louis. Though I'd been released from active duty in June 1969, I was still technically an inactive reserve until April 1972, seven months away. The letter informed me that I had been promoted to staff sergeant in the Marine reserves, effective as of the previous May. Right about the time the pigs had tried to split my head open, I'd thought. I could pick up my warrant for promotion, the letter said, at Willow Grove Naval Air Station, where the nearest active Marine reserve unit was located.

"Hey, get a load of this, Mom," I'd said waving the letter. "I've just been promoted to staff sergeant. Who are they trying to kid?" I grabbed my hair with both hands, pulling it away from my head to show how long it was. "Maybe they promoted me in recognition of my distinguished service against the pigs in Washington last spring. Combat in the streets of America! Conspicuous bravery in the face of hostile forces. Gung ho!"

"I wish you wouldn't call them pigs," my mother had replied, making a sour face.

"Well, you know what they say, Mom. A rose by any other name. Listen, Mom, you wanna have some fun? I'm gonna go down there and make 'em give me this thing. That oughta lock their jaws up tight. You wanna come along?"

"Bill, honestly, why do you want to start trouble? Can't you just live and let live?"

"Aw, Mom, I won't start any trouble. I just wanna see their faces when they have to promote a hippie to staff sergeant. Come on with me. It'll give you something to do. Besides, they won't dare bust my skull with you there."

She'd reluctantly agreed on the condition that I promise to behave myself, and the next day off we'd gone—me in sport coat and tie, brightly colored headband and sandals. A major and a first sergeant, both in dress uniforms, had greeted us and ushered us into the major's office. To judge by their outward reaction, I might have been a Wall Street stockbroker in a pin-striped suit; they never batted an eyelash at my appearance, maintaining an air of professional courtesy. Good old Marine Corps discipline, I'd mused, a little startled and more impressed than I cared to be. After some preliminary chitchat, the two men had come to attention while the major read the warrant:

"To all who shall see these presents, greeting," the major had begun, as though addressing a formal gathering instead of the four of us standing in his office. "Know ye that reposing special trust and confidence in the fidelity and abilities of William D. Ehrhart, 2279361, I do appoint him a staff sergeant in the reserve of the United States Marine Corps, to rank as such from the first day of May, nineteen hundred and seventy-one."

I'd made an attempt to stand at attention while the major read, but I'd hardly been able to keep from laughing. Special trust and confidence, I'd thought, fidelity and abilities? Christ, I hadn't even been in a uniform for more than two years. How could the guy keep a straight face? But he'd continued on bravely to the end of the warrant, which had been signed, the major informed us, by the commandant of the Marine Corps himself. It had been all I could do to keep from whistling, "Well, la-di-da."

Then the major had handed me the warrant. "Congratulations, Marine," he'd said, smiling and shaking my hand, "you're a credit to the Corps." That one had sent my teeth right through my tongue. Then the first sergeant had shook hands and added his congratulations. I'd been all set to bolt for the door—this hadn't been nearly as much fun as I'd anticipated—but the major had gestured toward the chairs and asked us to sit down again.

"I took the liberty of having the records center forward your service record book to us," the major had said. "I wanted to see who it was I'd be promoting. I must say, I'm impressed."

"Thank you, sir," I'd replied, wondering where he was going.

"I see you've never been active in the reserve, have you?"

"No, sir. When I was released from active duty, they told me I didn't have to do any reserve duty because I'd been in Vietnam." I'd let it go at that, not adding that I'd been ecstatic to discover that my active reserve obligation had been canceled, and that I'd never once considered uncanceling it.

"Well, Sergeant, we could use a good man like you around here. Have you ever thought about going active?"

"Not really, sir," I'd replied, beginning to feel more than a little nervous. "I started college right after I got out, and with studying and all, I just don't see how I'd have the time for it."

"Oh, it really doesn't take that much time, son," the major had replied. "Just one Saturday and one Sunday each month—sixteen hours a month—and two weeks in the summer. Surely you can spare that small amount."

"Well, gee, sir, I don't know—"

"And you get *four* days' pay for two days' work," the first sergeant had interjected. "Four days at staff sergeant's pay isn't chicken feed, you know."

"I'm sure you could use the extra money," the major had added. "Can't we all? But especially with you being in college— I know that GI Bill you boys are getting is a pitiful disgrace." Well, the major and I agree on one thing at least, I'd thought.

"Gosh, Major, I really don't know," I'd replied, feeling *really* uneasy by this point. "I'll have to think about it."

"Well, you do that, and give us a call if you decide you want to join. We'd sure be pleased to have you. I think you'd be a real asset to our unit. And there isn't an easier way to make a little extra money."

"Just in case you're interested," the first sergeant had added, "these are to get you started." He'd handed me a pair of staff sergeant's stripes. "Maybe you can get your mother here to sew them on for you—try 'em out and see how they feel." He'd smiled almost warmly.

A staff sergeant, I'd thought bitterly as we'd driven home. Man, if someone had told me back in boot camp that one day I'd be a staff sergeant, I'd have shouted for joy. Hell, my senior drill instructor had only been a staff sergeant, and he'd been *God!* Sergeant Wilson, the man I'd admired most in Vietnam, hadn't made staff sergeant until he'd been in the Corps thirteen years. Even my all-time favorite comic-book hero, Sergeant Rock, had only been a buck sergeant, the same rank I'd made on active duty.

Yes, there'd been a time when I would have been proud of this day. But now? What did it mean now? What was left to be proud of? A war that should never have been fought? A government full of vain, arrogant liars willing to go on killing indefinitely rather than admit the obvious? A country full of Mayflower Bars? The man who'd ordered me to fire on the old farmer with his hands tied behind his back down on Barrier Island had been a staff sergeant. One more time, I'd been cheated.

My mother was speaking to me.

"Huh?" I'd said. "I'm sorry, I was just thinking."

"I said that reserve program sounds attractive," she'd repeated. I'd just shrugged my shoulders and grunted softly, lightly fingering the staff sergeant's strips I'd been given: three stripes up, a rocker stripe below, with crossed rifles in the middle. "What *are* you going to do about money, Bill?"

"I don't know yet. I don't know. I'll figure something out."

Late that night, after my parents and younger brother had gone to bed, I'd gone to the attic and hauled out my old seabag, rooting around in it until I'd managed to piece together a complete summer dress uniform. Feeling strange and confused, I'd put it on, pleased to discover that it still fit. Needs a little pressing, I'd thought. I'd pulled my hair back and held it behind my head with one hand, trying to imagine what I'd look like with a regulation haircut. With the other hand, I'd held one of the staff sergeant's stripes against the sleeve, covering the buck sergeant's stripes. Staff Sergeant Ehrhart.

What the hell, I'd thought, the Marine Corps hadn't started the Vietnam War. They'd only tried to do what the government had ordered them to do. Was it our fault that we'd failed at an impossible task? Hell, I owed my life to the Marines. They'd had eight weeks to take a seventeen-year-old kid who'd been hell-bent on going to Vietnam and teach him enough to stay alive. And they'd done a pretty good job of it, too—long after my private life had come completely unglued over there, after Jenny had stopped writing and Trinh had refused to fight for the Americans anymore and the questions had gotten too ugly even to ask, let alone try to answer, I'd still been able to function well enough to keep from ending up in a box.

When it came right down to it, I hadn't had such a bad time in the Marines. I'd been treated fairly. I'd risen through the ranks quickly. Hell, if it hadn't been for that fucking war, maybe I'd even have made a career of it. More than once, my superiors had offered to get me an appointment to Annapolis. Marine reserves. Eighty bucks a month for two eight-hour days, huh? Well, I could sure use the money. I had to come up with it *somehow*.

Two weeks later, I found myself in uniform, with short hair and a neatly trimmed regulation mustache, gleaming shoes and polished brass, standing before the officers and staff NCOs of Marine Attack Squadron 131, being introduced by the same major who'd given me my promotion. I couldn't *believe* what an incredible fool I'd been. What in the *world* had gotten into my head? Had I been in a *coma* for the past two weeks? Hadn't I learned *anything* in the past four and a half years? The tattoo had been bad enough. But this. This! Oh, you're in a *world* of shit now, you flaming asshole.

Sitting back down, I gazed around me furtively. The old woman in the ricefield, the young mother in the sixty-millimeter gun pit in Hue, the Vietnamese national police, the My Lai massacre, the invasion of Cambodia, Kent State, the Mayflower Bar, the pigs in Washington, *The Pentagon Papers*. The people around me were sworn to support and defend all that. *All of it!* Richard Nixon and Spiro Agnew and John Mitchell and Henry Kissinger, for Chrissake. What bizarre comic-book mentality had locked onto my soul in the murky depths of my childhood and refused, absolutely refused in the face of all reason to let go?

I was frantic. Panic-stricken. Sweating profusely. Barely able to keep my body from visibly shaking. Oh, you've really done it this time, you worthless piece of shit. You *knew* better, and you went right out and screwed yourself right to the wall. Staff Sergeant W. D. Ehrhart. God, oh, God, what terminal sickness possessed me? I wanted to die.

Back at college that night—school had started the week before—I sneaked into my room in Wharton Dorm, afraid that someone might see me in uniform. How in the hell would I ever be able to explain it? The outspoken opponent of the war, and of everyone and everything that had caused it and now perpetuated it, an active part of it again. I couldn't even explain it to myself. I began drinking immediately, but five hours later, by midnight, I still hadn't managed to drink myself to sleep. I had to go back the next day. I was trapped! There was no way out of this. I'd committed myself for at least a year—that's what the personnel officer had told me, at least a year if I wanted to go active reserve.

Would the fall from my third-floor window be enough to kill me, or would I botch that up, too, and end up a cripple for the rest of my life? Could I make it to the Canadian border before they caught up with me? About two-thirty A.M., I went across the hall and woke up Sam Kaufman, Daniel's brother. He and his girlfriend Jan had been sound asleep, but they let me in. By then I was completely distraught, crying, virtually incoherent. They couldn't figure out what I was ranting about. "What's the matter with me, Sam?" I shouted. "What kind of crazy man am I? How in the world did I let this happen?" Sam didn't know. Neither did Jan.

Finally, it must have been around four A.M., I went back to my room. The next thing I knew, someone was knocking on my door. "There's a phone call for you, Bill." I woke up and looked at the clock. Eight-thirty! Oh, Jesus Christ! I was supposed to be at Willow Grove by eight!

"Find out who it is!" I shouted through the door as I hurriedly pulled on my uniform.

"It's a Captain Thomas from Willow Grove, Bill," came the reply a few moments later.

My stomach wrenched violently. I wanted to throw up, but there was nothing to heave but bile. "Tell 'im I'm not here!" I shouted through the door. "Tell 'im I left a little while ago—you think I was having car trouble." Oh, Christ, oh, Christ, now I was *really* screwed! My second day, and already I'm absent without leave. And they come looking for me that fast! Half an hour late, and they come looking for me! I'd *never* make it to Canada.

By the time I got to Willow Grove, between the lack of sleep, the hangover, the hasty way I'd dressed and shaved, the harrowing high-speed fifty-mile drive, and fully twenty-four hours of fever-pitch panic, I must have looked like the living dead. I certainly felt that way.

"This isn't a very good way to get things started, Sergeant," said the personnel officer sternly.

"I know, sir. I'm very sorry. My car wouldn't start. I hadda call Triple A and get a tow truck to come and give me a jump. It won't happen again, sir."

I spent the rest of the morning fighting to maintain some semblance of composure, but I knew I couldn't go on like this. There *had* to be a way out, even if it meant the firing squad—and I was serious. But they wouldn't shoot me, I realized with a sickening feeling, they'd put me in prison. I wondered if prison was really as bad as I'd heard. Undoubtedly it was, I thought, the sickening feeling wrapping itself around my ribs and constricting. But I *couldn't* go on with this. God, it was just like Vietnam: stuck in a horrible, hideous place with no way out. There *had* to be a way out. But how? How?

The day before, I'd met an old warrant officer who had seemed like a nice guy. What made me think so? I didn't really know, but I knew I had to talk to someone, and given what I had to choose from, there was no one else around who even came close. I decided I would have to trust him. What did I have to lose, really?

"Gunner, can I talk to you?" I said, stepping into his office just before lunch. Gunner was an appropriate way to address a warrant officer, a rank between the highest noncommissioned officers and the lowest commissioned officers.

"Sure," he smiled, looking up from his desk. "Come on in. Ehrhart, isn't it? What can I do for you?" He pointed to a chair and gestured for me to sit down.

"Sir, I, uh, don't know how to explain this. Well, uh, listen, can I level with you? Strictly in confidence?"

"Fire away," he replied.

"Well, sir, I don't know how the hell I ended up here, but I don't belong in the Marine reserve. I shouldn't be here. Until three days ago, I had hair half-way down my back. I've spent the past two years protesting the war in Vietnam. I've demonstrated in the streets. I don't—I don't even know if I love my country anymore." I stopped abruptly, afraid I'd said too much already.

"You volunteered for reserve duty, didn't you?" he asked.

"Yessir, I did."

"Why? I mean, we didn't come looking for you. You didn't have to join up. Under the circumstances," he said, lifting both hands and tilting his head in a gesture of bewilderment, "why did you do it?"

"Christ, I don't know. I needed the money—or thought I did." I explained the financial bind I'd found myself in. "I figured it would be easy money, but it's all—I don't know—like Flashback City. Like bein' back in Vietnam. I feel like I'm suffocating, Gunner. It just isn't right. I don't belong here. I don't know what the hell got into my head."

"Well," said the gunner, "I'm not sure I agree with you about the war. Then again, I'm not sure I disagree with you either. In any case, that's neither here nor there. Right now, you've got a problem, don't you?"

"Yessir, I sure do."

"You were a class three reserve before you went active, weren't you?"

"Yessir."

"And you served in Vietnam."

"Yessir. Thirteen months."

"Well," he said, chuckling softly and tugging on his chin, "I don't suppose the folks over at personnel told you this, but you're free to go any time you want."

"What?"

"There it is. A class three reserve going class two is strictly voluntary. You can walk out of this office right now and drive away and never come back."

"But they told me I'd have to do at least a year's duty. They told me I'd even have to extend my discharge date for five months."

"Yeah, well, the military's not too popular these days. I guess *you* understand that," he laughed. "It isn't easy to get new reserve members. I guess they're runnin' a little short in the ethics department over in personnel."

"Je-sus Christ. Jesus Christ!"

"When you get home," the gunner continued, "just write the personnel officer a letter telling him you wanna be dropped from the active roster. That's all there is to it.'' I just sat there, my whole body feeling like I'd just been removed from the rack. ''Well? What are you waiting for?''

Chapter 44

''Hey, Bill, break time,'' said Mike Morris, walking into my room and sitting down heavily on the bed.

''Yeah, I guess so,'' I replied, pushing my chair away from the desk, leaning back and rubbing my eyes hard. ''Man, I can't even see straight anymore. What time is it?''

''Half past midnight. How's it comin'?''

''Slow. I won't be ready to start typing for another hour yet. I'm gonna be up all night.''

''Me, too.''

''JC gave me a couple hits of speed a little while ago. You want one?''

''I'll pass,'' Mike replied. ''I take any of that stuff, I won't be able to sleep tomorrow. I got another paper due on Thursday. I'm gonna have to get some sleep somewhere along the way before I tackle that one. I'll take a beer, though. You got any beer?''

''In the fridge. Get one for me, too.''

Mike reached into the tiny refrigerator beside my bed and pulled out two beers, opening both and passing one to me. It was January 1972. The first semester of my junior year was coming to a close. I was trying to finish a paper on Coleridge's ''The Rime of the Ancient Mariner,'' due at nine A.M. Mike, who lived directly above me in Wharton Dorm that year, was working on a paper, too.

''Hard to believe I got through my first year and a half here without pulling an all-nighter,'' I said. ''Man, I used to start papers two weeks in advance. Used to turn 'em in *early* my freshman year. Then I discovered that I wouldn't get thrown into the brig for turning a paper in late. Every semester it gets worse and worse. One of these days, I ain't gonna make it.''

"So what if you don't?'' said Mike.

"You should talk. What are you doin' up tonight?''

"I just wanna get the damned semester over with so I can get the hell out of this place,'' Mike replied.

"You and Archie really gonna bike all the way to California in the winter?'' I asked. Mike and Archie Davison were planning to take the spring semester off to do some traveling.

"We're going the southern route,'' Mike replied. "It won't be so bad.''

"Well, I think you're crazy to go anywhere on a motorcycle. A good friend of mine was just killed this summer on a cycle. Those things are suicide machines.''

"We'll be careful. They're only dangerous if you get reckless with 'em.''

"That's what Max Harris used to say,'' I said. "Listen, I want you back here in one piece next fall. I got too many dead friends already.''

"Don't worry,'' said Mike, "I'll be careful.''

"I'm gonna miss you, Mike. Real people are hard to come by around here.''

"I'll miss you, too, buddy.'' He took a drink of his beer. "You remember the time Daniel Kaufman introduced us in the library your freshman year?''

"Yeah, I remember.''

"You know why Daniel brought me over there?''

"I don't know,'' I replied, shrugging my shoulders. "You wanted a date with me?''

"He never told you?''

"No. What's the big secret? Oh, you know, now that you mention it, one time he told me I should ask you about that. I think it was when we went to California last Christmas. Some time or other last year. Anyway, I completely forgot about it. So what gives?''

"Well,'' Mike said, "I'll tell you how it happened. We were at a DU meeting that night, talking about who we wanted to invite to join, and your name came up. I think Bart Lewis recommended you. Anyway—Christ, this is really embarrassing.''

"What? What?''

"Well, when your name came up, I said something like, 'Hell,

I don't want some fucking Marine sergeant in my fraternity.' I don't remember what I said exactly, but it was something like that. And Daniel turned to me right there in the meeting and asked me if I'd ever even talked to you. Well, I hadn't, so he just said, 'Let's go.' I thought he was kidding, but he got really mad. 'Come on, asshole,' he said. 'The least you can do is talk to the guy, you dumb shit.' And he dragged me right out of the meeting to find you.''

"No kidding?" I said. I took a swig of beer and laughed.

"Yeah, no kidding. Now you know why I never told you before. I was too embarrassed. Man, by the time I left the library that night, I felt about small enough to hide in my left shoe.''

"No kidding? You certainly had me snowed. I had no idea you were feelin' like that. What a way to start a friendship.''

"Hey, I'm serious, you really blew me away that night. I expected you to be some fucking gung-ho nail-eating maniac.''

"Well, it ain't the first time somebody's pigeonholed me,'' I said, "and it sure as hell hasn't been the last time. At least you were willing to change your mind. Most people just ask the same stupid Audie Murphy questions—if they bother to ask at all—and then they slip back into the fog.''

"That's what really gets me, Bill. If it hadn't been for Daniel, I wouldn't have bothered either.''

"Well, good for Daniel,'' I said. Then I burst out laughing.

"What's the joke?'' asked Mike.

"I was just thinking about last week. Daniel and me were eating lunch in Sharples, and sure as hell, some kid that I don't know from Bossie the Cow comes up to me and says, 'You're Bill Ehrhart, aren't you? Do you mind if I ask you a few questions about Vietnam?' And Daniel takes a glass of milk and throws it at the kid. Just throws it at him. 'Beat it, asshole!' he roars. Milk all over the kid. It was great. God, I've wanted to do something like that for two and a half years. I get so damned tired of bein' a fuckin' curiosity around here.''

"Do I ask you too many questions?'' asked Mike.

"Naw, I don't mean you, man. See, the thing is, you don't ask *stupid* questions. 'Gee whiz, you were in Vietnam? Oh, gosh, what was it like? Tell me a war story.' Christ. No, Mike you've always asked me intelligent questions—believe it or not. That was something that impressed me the very first night I met you. And you *listen*, you know. You've always tried to *understand* what I'm saying. That means a lot to me, Mike. I haven't run into too many people that are really willing to listen.''

''Well, I haven't run into too many people like you either, so I guess that makes us even,'' he said. We both sucked on our beers for a few minutes, not talking.

''What did you think of those guys that took over the Statue of Liberty last month?'' Mike asked, breaking the silence. He was referring to a group from Vietnam Veterans Against the War that had barricaded themselves inside the statue, flying an American flag upside down from Lady Liberty's crown. The photos on television and in the papers had been very dramatic.

''I think it's great,'' I said. ''I wish I'd been with 'em. If we're ever gonna turn this country around, it's gonna be guys like that that do it.''

''You think we're ever gonna turn this country around?''

''I don't know,'' I replied, ''but I'm not ready to give up yet. And I'll tell you this: The government really fucked up this time. They got a whole generation of veterans who are pissed as hell, and they can't shut us up. They're gonna have to deal with us, or they're gonna have revolution in the streets. We *believed* in this country, and we were betrayed. We aren't going to forget that. I sure as hell never will.''

''I don't know that I ever believed in it,'' said Mike. ''I knew right from the start that *I* wasn't going to Vietnam, no way, no how.''

''Yeah, and you're two years younger than me. By the time you graduated from high school, the Tet offensive had happened, Johnson announced that he wasn't going to run for reelection, and a lot of people were starting to question the whole damned shooting match. Man, *nobody* in Perkasie ever questioned *anything* in the spring of 1966. Ever read this shit?'' I said, reaching for a copy of *Bury My Heart at Wounded Knee* and sending it flying across the room toward Mike. ''I didn't learn *anything* like this in high school history. I didn't know jack squat about my own country when I went to Vietnam. And I sure as hell didn't know anything about Vietnam. Oh, boy, here we go,'' I said, grabbing my head with both hands. ''I can feel the speed kickin' into gear.''

''How much longer you think it can last?'' Mike asked.

''Oh, about twelve hours or so.''

''Not the speed, dufus, the war.''

''Hell, I don't know. Forever.''

Chapter 45

"NIXON ON THE WALL," screamed the headline. Right beneath it was a photograph of the president, standing on the Great Wall of China, grinning like a mad fool and shaking hands with Chou En-lai, premier of the People's Republic of China.

Hadn't I gone to Vietnam to help stop Communist Chinese and Soviet expansionism in Asia through their surrogates and puppets, the Vietnamese? That's what we'd been told in no uncertain terms. The domino theory, they'd called it. Jack Webb of *Dragnet* fame had told us all about it in a training film we'd seen in boot camp.

And now? Christ almighty, to look at that photograph, any sane person would have thought that old Tricky Dick and Comrade Chou had been lifelong buddies. News commentators were calling it the diplomatic triumph of the century. Yet even as King Richard the Milhous stood there on that wall in February 1972, American GIs were still fighting and dying in Vietnam.

What the hell for? Certainly not to stop the Chinese. We were great pals with the Chinese. Hell, Nixon said so. And certainly not to stop the Russians. They were our pals, too. Kissinger had already gone to Moscow to hobnob with Leonid Brezhnev, and Nixon was scheduled to visit there in the spring. Henry the K, in fact, had recently declared a new era of détente between the two great superpowers.

So what for? Now it was for Peace with Honor, upholding our commitments to our allies, giving the Saigon government a fair chance to defend itself, and the release of American prisoners of war being held by the North Vietnamese. And when those excuses fell through, what would they invent next?

The Chameleon War, I thought as I stared at the newspaper, unable to make up my mind whether to tear the paper to shreds or scream bloody murder; the war that changes colors with the seasons. Billions of dollars, hundreds of thousands of broken shattered lives, a generation of war—and no one could explain why. No one but the politicians and the generals, and they were proven liars. Yet the war raged on. How fucking stupid can the American people be, I wondered.

"Hey, Bill, you going to swimming practice?" Dave asked.

I looked at the clock. "What's your hurry?" I replied. "We got plenty of time. Relax." He disappeared back into his room.

Dave Carter was my new roommate. He was a freshman. I'd gotten to know him because he was on the swimming team. When he'd first come to Swarthmore, he'd ended up with a computer-matched roommate who had proven beyond a doubt the fallibility of computers. By January, he'd been ready to commit unspeakable atrocities against his roommate, a fellow who couldn't study with the windows open because the chirping of the birds in the trees disturbed him, but who played Rod McKuen records loudly while writing love letters to his girlfriend back in Bumfart, Iowa.

I'd rescued Dave from an all-but-inevitable prison sentence by talking Dean Bradley into letting Dave and me move in together into a two-room suite in Wharton that had come vacant at the end of first semester. With a two-room double, I still had the privacy of a single room, and Dave was saved from the ruin that would have befallen him for murdering his roommate. It was a nice arrangement, and I felt very noble about it.

Living with Dave, in fact, was turning out to be fun. Eighteen and just out of Cherry Hill East High School in New Jersey, he was energetic, exuberant, and optimistic as a babe in the woods. Over six feet tall, lean and athletic, he didn't smoke, drink, or take drugs. He played the violin and the trombone. It was refreshing. He almost made me believe that I wasn't as old as I felt. God knows what he thought of me. He probably ranked me right up there somewhere between King Tut and the Hunchback of Notre Dame. But he was clearly grateful to me for rescuing him from his disastrous rooming situation, and we got along pretty well. I liked him.

"You see this crap?" I hollered. Dave reappeared in the doorway between the two rooms. I held up the newspaper. "We were supposed to be fighting the Chinese in Vietnam, you know? Them and the Rooskies. The Vietnamese really didn't have much to do with it. They were just puppets, you know? So what are they now? Can you tell me that?'' Dave gave me a blank look and shrugged his shoulders. "Yeah, me, too," I said. "Come on. Let's go swimming.''

Chapter 46

The temperature was well above a hundred. The heat pressed down from a cloudless sky and rose out of the ground in visible waves that distorted vision at less than two hundred meters. Progress was slow. Now and then, sporadic gunfire would erupt from the lead elements ahead of us, but it never lasted long. As the hours ticked by we picked our way down the flat sandy expanse of Barrier Island, occasionally passing an isolated thatch-roofed hut in the middle of bone-dry ricefields waiting for the heat to pass and the autumn planting to begin.

We detained every male Vietnamese we encountered. None of them were armed, but they would be questioned later about Vietcong activity on the island. By late afternoon, I found myself in charge of a straggly group of six older men, their dirty pajamas hanging from bony bodies, their gray wispy chin-beards dangling long strands of thin hair in the hot breeze, their hands tied behind their backs. We were moving across an open sandy area with tree lines on all four sides when suddenly the crack of incoming sniper fire erupted.

I hit the deck immediately as bullets zipped around me, thwacking into the earth nearby. Though there were no visible targets, Marines began returning fire in the general direction of the incoming, the intensity quickly rising to a sharp firefight. Suddenly I realized that most of the detainees were still on their feet, confused and frightened by the gunfire. I knocked a couple of them down with my rifle—those I could reach without standing up—wielding it like a club, but four of them took off running toward a tree line off to my left.

"Dung lai! Dung lai!" I hollered several times, but they kept running. Staff Sergeant Taggart and Staff Sergeant Trinh were shouting at them, too.

"Waste 'em!" Taggart shouted at me. "Shoot, goddamn it!" I picked out the one farthest away, sighted in, and fired one round. The man went down like he'd been hit on the back of the head with a brick. The others stopped instantly. Then one of the others suddenly snapped up straight and twisted sharply to the ground, caught by someone in the crossfire. The other two dropped to their bellies.

In a few minutes the shooting stopped, trickling off like an engine sputtering out of gas. Marines all over the ground began to rise warily. I helped the two prisoners near me to their feet, then headed toward the other four. Two of them were dead. Taggart came over and began kicking the other two to their feet, shouting obscenities at them. Trinh glared at Taggart but said nothing.

We camped for the night where we were. Nearby was a dry ricefield surrounded by a dike that formed a natural defensive perimeter. I herded the prisoners into a corner of the field, sat them down and tied their feet, then sat down myself and opened a can of beef stew. I hadn't eaten all day, but after two or three mouthfuls, I realized that I wasn't hungry at all. It was nearly dark. I threw the unfinished can over the paddy dike, laid my poncho out for a ground cloth, and stretched out. It felt good to lie down, but I couldn't sleep.

One of the prisoners moaned loudly. Lying there in the sticky darkness, I thought of the day on frozen Lake Lenape in Perkasie when I was about nine years old and for no reason I could understand, Jerry Dougherty had begun punching me in the face over and over again, taunting me to fight, and I didn't know how and was too frightened even to try to defend myself, and so I'd just stood there crying while the other boys stood around us laughing. And the time in the boys' room on the second floor of the junior high school when Lloyd Drescher started pushing me around and I'd been saved only by my tough pal, Larry Carroll, and Larry and I went off to lunch with me telling him what I had been about to do to Lloyd and knowing it was all lies and still shaking so hard inside I could barely control my voice. And the time, only a year before I'd enlisted, when Jimmy Whitson had spit in my face at a party and said he was going to kill me for messing with his girl, and I'd left by the back door at the first opportunity, and after that "his girl" had never treated me the same again.

"Ask a Marine," the recruiting posters had said. "Tell it to the Marines." I thought of the old man lying a few hundred meters away, his hands still tied behind his back, the small hole in the back of his head, and half his face blown off. I thought of the old woman in the ricefield back in June, and the young girl with the AK-47 Russian assault rifle and the smile of grim determination in the photograph I'd taken off the corpse of a young Vietcong guerrilla. I thought of Sadie Thompson, my Quaker friend from high school, whose parting words before I'd left for Vietnam had been, "Please try not to kill anyone."

Chapter 47

"Hi, Bill," said Dave. "You have a good time?" I just grunted. I'd gone home to Perkasie for the weekend. I went over to the refrigerator and took out a beer. "I've got some bad news, I'm afraid," said Dave.

"What is it?" I asked, taking a long pull on the beer. "Nixon invaded Cleveland?"

"Jamie McAdams had a heart attack," he said.

"What? What happened? Where is he? He's not dead, is he?"

"No," said Dave. "He's in the hospital. He keeled over at work Friday night."

"Jesus Christ," I said, sitting down on the bed. "How serious is it?"

"Apparently, it's not too bad. He's okay now. But he's probably going to be out for two or three weeks."

"That's the whole rest of the season," I said.

"Well, he might make it back for the championships."

"Damn. That's just what I needed. What's the point of swimmin' without Jamie? Can we call him?"

"Barney said not yet. Maybe sometime this week."

"Damn," I said. "What a pisser."

"That's not all," said Dave. "Remember when the FBI office over in Media got broken into the other week?"

"Yeah."

"Well, some antiwar magazine named *Win* just published all of the stolen records, and it turns out that the head of our campus security and at least one of our switchboard operators are FBI informants."

"Oh, Je-sus fuckin'-A Christ!" I shouted, my jaw and neck tightening with anger. "The fuckin' creeps are *everywhere*. Fuckin' J. Edgar Hoover! There it is, man. If you're against the war, you gotta be a Communist. If you exercise your right to free speech, you must be a subversive. If you expect the fuckin' country to act like a civilized nation, you're a radical. God damn."

"I don't know, Bill," Dave said. "It really frightens me sometimes."

"Well, it *pisses me off,* that's what it does to me," I replied. "This goddamned country's turnin' into a goddamned Nazi Gestapo stronghold. There's fuckin' Nixon tryin' to dress up the White House guards in Prussian military uniforms. You know who's on the FBI's Ten Most Wanted Criminals list? Antiwar people. All ten of 'em! Oh, yeah, they're wanted for violent crimes, all right—like us 'violent' demonstrators down at the Justice Department last spring. Christ, ya got murderers out there, rapists, child molesters. How come the pigs didn't arrest any of them fuckin' hard hats in New York last spring? The ones that beat up all those antiwar people on Wall Street? Did you see the newsreels? The pigs were standing right there—didn't lift a goddamned finger. They were cheerin' 'em *on,* for Chrissake. Like the brownshirts in Berlin in the 1930s. And down there in Washington last May Day? Pigs locked up five thousand legal demonstrators without any charges at all. Like detainees in Vietnam. Didn't file a single charge—'cuz there was nothin' to charge 'em with!—just hauled 'em all off the street and locked 'em up. And to hell with the fuckin' Constitution, anyway. Who needs a constitution? Not Tricky Dick. Not John Mitchell. They locked up so many people, they hadda use RFK Stadium for a jail! Oh, yeah, the bad-ass peaceniks. We're dangerous, man. We're *un-American!*"

Dave sat on the corner of my desk, not saying anything. He looked troubled. Was it what I said or the way I said it that bothered him, I wondered. I finished my beer.

"It frightens me, too, Dave," I continued more quietly. "The freakin' switchboard lady. And Potter. Good old Quakerly Swarthmore. You know, Dave, the more I learn about this country, the more I'm beginning to believe that people who believe in liberty and justice for all really *are* un-American. Ah, well, fuck it. So listen, what are we gonna do without Jamie?''

"I talked to Barney about that today. He and Colin are going to run practices and do the lineups for the meets. We all know pretty much what to do, anyway. And Don Parsons is going to help out." Don was a biology professor and faculty adviser for the team. He'd been one of Jamie's swimmers back in the late 1940s.

"That sounds okay, I guess," I said, walking over to the refrigerator and taking out another beer. "You want one?"

Dave shook his head no. "I've got an eight o'clock class tomorrow morning," he said.

"So what? You know what your problem is? You're too damned conscientious. You let these ivory-tower types con you into thinkin' all of this crap is important. I had an eight o'clock class first semester last year. Went to it six times all term—and I'd been up all night and drunk on my ass when I got to class three of those times. I got a B for the course."

"I guess I haven't learned the shortcuts yet," Dave replied.

"Yeah, well, with any luck at all, maybe you never will. I don't suppose you wanna get stoned either, do you?"

"I don't think I'm ready for that stuff."

"I didn't think so," I replied, loading my hash pipe and lighting it.

Chapter 48

"Readin' again, huh?" asked Roger as he walked into my cabin.

"Rereading," I replied, looking up from my desk. I put the

book down and reached for a deck of cards. "You ready to get your ass kicked again?"

"Sure, sure. *Winning Hearts and Minds: War Poems by Vietnam Veterans*," he said, picking up the book and reading the cover. "Is it any good?"

"Well, *I* think so. But I guess I'm biased; there's a few of my poems in there."

"Really?" said Roger. "You didn't tell me you were a published author."

"It's just a handful of poems."

"Lemme see it." He picked up the book as he sat down and began flipping through it. "Where's one of yours? Here's one. 'Hunting.' "

"You wanna play casino or not?" I said, feeling embarrassed and pleased at the same time.

"In a minute, in a minute; lemme read this. 'Sighting down the long black barrel,' " he said, reading aloud, " 'I wait till front and rear sights form a perfect line on his body, then slowly squeeze the trigger. The thought occurs that I have never hunted anything in my whole life except other men. But I have learned by now where such thoughts lead, and soon pass on to chow and sleep and how much longer till I change my socks.' Wow."

"The way it was," I replied. "I was even a little kinder on myself than I shoulda been. Most of the time, all we hunted was old ladies and kids."

Roger flipped the book over and began reading the jacket blurbs. *"New York Times Book Review, Newsweek, Chicago Sun-Times, St. Louis Post-Dispatch.* Geez, this is really big time."

"Yeah, sort of. I'll tell ya the truth, Roger, I was really proud of that book. I was really makin' a statement, you know? We all were. I never met any of the other guys in there except the three editors, but I kinda feel like—well, like we're brothers."

"How'd you manage to get your stuff in here? How'd you hear about it?"

"Well, what happened was, when I was a sophomore in college, one of my professors saw a notice in the *New York Times* asking for poetry about Vietnam for an anthology, and he cut the notice out and gave it to me. I sent some poems off, and got a letter back saying they liked them and wanted to publish them."

"Who was 'they'?"

"Turns out it was a couple of guys from Vietnam Veterans Against the War. That made me real nervous." I laughed. "Even at that point, I still didn't want to be associated with 'radicals.' This was before *The Pentagon Papers,* before I went to that demonstration in Washington I told you about. So I wrote back and said, 'Hey, gee, guys, you're not gonna make me look like a Commie crazy, are you?' Man, I can't believe how long it took me to understand what the hell Vietnam really meant. Anyway, I finally agreed to let them use my poems. Then it took 'em about a year to get the book published. At first, none of the commercial presses would touch it with a meathook. So they borrowed some money, formed their own publishing company, and published the book themselves. Called themselves First Casualty Press."

"Is that supposed to mean something?" asked Roger.

"Yeah. A Greek playwright named Aeschylus once said that in war, truth is the first casualty. They took the name from that. Anyway, they printed ten thousand copies in a cheap paperback edition. No money for advertising. Book's available only by direct mail. But it got reviewed everywhere. Really good reviews, too. The damn book took off like a rocket. So *then* all these commercial publishers start comin' out of the woodwork: 'Say, fellas, about that book you've got . . . ' The great American way. Suddenly these assholes are seein' dollar signs all over the place, so *now* they want a piece of the action. Stupid creeps coulda had the whole project for a hundred and fifty bucks six months earlier. The editors finally negotiated a deal with McGraw-Hill for onetime reprint rights. Made 'em pay through the nose for it, too."

"You make any money on it?" asked Roger.

"*We* didn't. I mean, the book made money, but the writers didn't. We all agreed to put the money from the First Casualty edition back into the press, and the money we made from the McGraw-Hill edition we gave to some Quaker relief fund for Vietnamese civilian casualties of the war. Anyway, within six months after the book was first published, there were about thirty-five thousand copies in print. For a book of poetry, that's a runaway best-seller. And to think I was almost too scared to get involved with it. I don't think I've ever been prouder of anything in my whole life."

"Well, I think it's neat that you've had stuff published," said Roger. "I never met a published author before."

"The only problem was that it didn't change a goddamned thing. The war just went right on like before, like the book never existed. I don't know why I thought it would make any difference, but I guess I did. Apparently, King Richard the Milhous doesn't read poetry."

"It really matters to you, doesn't it?" he said. I shrugged my shoulders. "I'd like to read the book. Can I borrow it?"

"Sure, help yourself."

"Okay, shuffle the cards," he said, laying the book aside. "Let's get down to business. You got any wine? Where's your tapes?"

"Where they always are," I said, shuffling the cards and beginning to deal. "Have you heard anything about how much longer we're gonna be in dry dock?"

"Another day or two," said Roger as he rooted through the pile of tapes on top of my bunk. "Where's your Allman Brothers tape?"

"It's up there somewhere. You know, it's really awesome to see this ship completely out of the water. I was walking around underneath the hull this morning. Man, imagine the stress on those shoring timbers. I didn't realize dry docks still used wood to hold the ship in place."

"It's the best thing to use. Gives more than steel; bends and compresses instead of breaking. I like these guys," he said, turning on the tape player. He sat back down and picked up his cards.

"I heard them play back in the spring of 1970," I said. "Back before anybody ever heard of them. Swarthmore got 'em to come and play for like five hundred bucks. They put on a hell of a show, too. Played till four in the morning."

"You wanna go up and eat dinner tonight in the Space Needle?" asked Roger. The towering silver needle had been built for the Seattle World's Fair. "The whole top of the needle rotates. They got a restaurant up there."

"Sure, why not?" I replied. "Hey, you can't build sixes. You're already building nines."

"Oh, yeah," said Roger. "I forgot."

"Right, you forgot."

"I *did*," he said, picking up the nines. I took the six he'd been trying to build on.

"You got the ten of diamonds, don't you?" I just grinned. "You bastard," he said.

By the end of the first hand, I had all eleven points. A skunk.

My game. "Damn it!" Roger shouted. He grabbed a fistful of cards and bolted for the porthole.

"There's workmen out there!" I said, bolting after him. I reached Roger's side just in time to see a shower of cards descending into the dry-dock well beneath us. "Those were my cards, bozo," I said.

Chapter 49

The night Nixon mined the harbors of North Vietnam, I ruined a perfectly good color television set. It was a useless gesture, but what else could I do?

A month earlier, back in April 1972, the North Vietnamese and the southern National Liberation Front—by then called the Provisional Revolutionary Government—had launched a new offensive, the biggest since Tet 1968. The offensive had quickly and rudely put the world on notice that "Vietnamization" remained a failure. I had watched with numb fascination as the NVA/VC forces bulldozed south from the DMZ, taking control of many of the very places I had slept in, patrolled through, and fought over—places in which friends like Mike Stemkowski, Greg Aymes, and Frenchy Falcone had died nearly five years earlier: Con Thien, Dong Ha, Ai Tu.

Powerless to give the Saigon armies the will and tenacity they had always lacked, in retaliation Nixon had unleashed the bombers once again against the cities of Hanoi and Haiphong. But the bombing had had no effect on the offensive. The major provincial capital of Quang Tri had fallen by early May. For a few days, I'd even thought that perhaps this would be the final offensive, that perhaps the endless war might finally really be nearing an end. The thought made me giddy.

But in my more rational moments, I knew that Nixon would never allow the end to come with a hundred thousand U.S. troops still in Vietnam. Imagine the spectacle: American GIs scrambling aboard helicopters and troop transports, the NVA guns zeroing in, pandemonium, retreat in the face of hostile fire. No, I knew that Richard Nixon would never sit idly by while Walter Cronkite and John Chancellor narrated the visible collapse of American might in Vietnam. No way. The only question was: What would he do to prevent it? Would he send in more U.S. troops? Would he bomb the dikes on the Red River Valley? All it would take was one air strike, and half of North Vietnam would be underwater. Was he crazy enough to use nukes?

That's why I'd borrowed a television set that warm spring night in May. Nixon was going to address the nation. Undoubtedly, he would use the speech to try to justify whatever it was he was planning to do to stop the offensive. Dave Carter was off somewhere or other, and I was alone in my room in Wharton when Nixon appeared.

"Hey, you, Ehrhart," he sneered, his jowls shaking, "I just mined Haiphong. This time I'm going to make those gook fuckers squeal like stuck pigs, and you can't stop me. Put that in your little hash pipe and get high on it, you bleeding-heart pinko Commie creep. Why don't you move to Russia? Who needs you, anyway?"

He prattled on and on in the euphemistic language of politicians and diplomats, alternately smiling or shaking his finger, as if on cue. But the gist of what he said was that he had tried everything he could think of to get the North Vietnamese to do exactly what he wanted them to do so that the United States wouldn't appear so much like the colossal helpless fool it was, but since the North Vietnamese wouldn't play ball by his rules, he had been forced to take his ball and blow them up with it. There it was. Maybe most other people watching the speech that night didn't realize what was happening, but I did.

In Vietnam, I'd read the same newspapers and magazines filled with official statements and explanations that people back in the States were reading. The difference was that I had had something against which to evaluate what I was reading—395 days of somethings, actually.

We'd all read about McNamara's Wall, the series of outposts along the DMZ designed to stop North Vietnamese infiltration into the south. But I'd spent thirty-three days at Con Thien, and we had not even been able to step outside our own perimeter wire without getting our backsides kicked; the DMZ belonged to the

NVA. We'd all read about the thousands of Vietnamese civilians who fled from Vietcong-controlled territory to the safety and protection of Saigon-controlled "safe hamlets." But I had witnessed the forced relocations—people herded at gunpoint or driven out of their sacred ancestral homelands by saturation bombing—and I'd seen their jam-packed cardboard shantytowns where men had no work and women rooted through American garbage looking for food for their children. We'd all read the weekly box scores from the war zone: so many Vietcong killed in action. But I'd done the killing, and I knew that vast numbers of these so-called VC were unarmed civilians of indeterminate political persuasion. We'd all read about the free elections of September 1967 when General Nguyen Van Thieu had been democratically elected president of South Vietnam. But I had seen the ARVN soldiers marching voters to the polls at gunpoint. We'd all read about VC strong points neutralized. But I'd seen whole hamlets fried in jellied gasoline because a lone sniper had fired a single shot at a Marine patrol.

And the pattern of half-truths, misinformation, and lies had continued in the years since: the headlines versus the truth. We all read about those violent subversives known as the Chicago Seven who looked like bums and behaved like gorillas, the ones who'd been charged with conspiring to blow up the Democratic National Convention in the summer of 1968. The headlines had been lurid, the trial spectacular. Most Americans remembered the terrifying sight of Abbie Hoffman wrapped in an American flag and Huey Newton chained to his chair. What most Americans didn't remember was the verdict, rendered by a jury of twelve American citizens: not guilty.

We all read about the Camden Twenty-eight, a group of anti-war activists charged with trespassing on government property, breaking and entering, and destroying federal records in the form of the files of the Camden draft board. That made the headlines. But how many people knew that, months after the original indictments had captured the headlines, the presiding judge had thrown the case out of court on the grounds of entrapment by federal law enforcement officials? That the prosecutions's star witness, a paid informant, testified that he'd infiltrated the group on orders from the FBI? That he had had to argue long and hard for the break-in plan which he himself had suggested? That after people had reluctantly agreed to the plan, he'd had to procure the necessary equipment and tools, and train the others in their use?

And that he'd admitted that the Camden Twenty-eight were the most peaceful, nonviolent, law-abiding people he'd ever met?

Month after month and year after year, we'd read about the violent demonstrations. But I'd been a part of one of those so-called violent demonstrations, and even though the next day's newspaper had stated that we'd been throwing rocks and bottles and behaving in a generally disreputable manner, I knew perfectly well that the only violence that day had been instigated and carried out by the police.

We all read about Pennsylvania Senator Hugh Scott's evaluation of the men of Vietnam Veterans Against the War who went to Washington in April 1971 to return their medals to Congress. "These protesters are a minority of one-tenth of one percent," the good senator had stated. "I'm probably doing more to get us out of the war than these marchers." But I knew Scott's voting record: from the Gulf of Tonkin resolution to the latest emergency military aid bill, Scott had consistently voted the administration line on the war.

Month after month and year after year, we all read the exhortations of politicians and generals not to let down our boys serving in Vietnam who deserved our support and backing and respect. But where were the politicians and the generals when the veterans' interests were at stake rather than their own?

So when Nixon announced that he'd mined the harbors, I figured there was probably a lot more to it than we were being told, or ever would be told. Even as he spoke, the bombing of Hanoi and Haiphong continued. And to what end? Given the agrarian nature of the Vietnamese economy, and the proven fact that the North Vietnamese could wage war effectively without the massive industrial base so necessary for this country's war machine, there could be no military value to the bombing. I knew that, and so did Nixon. As far back as 1963, *The Pentagon Papers* had revealed, American analysts had come to that conclusion. Thus, Nixon's decision to bomb was nothing but vindictive reflex—deliberate punishment inflicted upon the people of North Vietnam in retaliation for their refusal to bow to the will of the American government.

And now the mining. Christ, I thought, mines! Soviet ships go in and out of those ports all the time. What if a Russian ship hit a mine? What if Soviet citizens were killed? Would the Russians just sit back in silence and let it happen? Was Nixon willing to risk nuclear confrontation with the Soviet Union? Hell, yes, or he wouldn't be doing it. Nuclear war over a morass of rice-fields and mangrove swamps on the far side of the world. God help us. What else was he willing to risk? What else was he capable of, rather than admitting defeat?

Nixon, the man who had been elected to Congress as a strident anti-Communist and Red-baiter, the man who had stood at the right hand of Joseph McCarthy, the man who had used a dog and a wife to cover his own improprieties, the man who had lashed out at the California press like a spoiled child, had finally overcome all obstacles and setbacks and risen to the most powerful seat in all the world. And he was not about to be thwarted or humiliated by anyone ever again. That's what Peace with Honor meant to Richard Nixon.

As I sat there alone in my room, listening to the president of the United States of America, I found it hard to believe that there had ever been a time when Lyndon Johnson had been the arch-villain of villains, and Richard Nixon had only been the guy with the five o'clock shadow that the press wouldn't have to kick around anymore. Even harder to believe that I had ever believed that Nixon would end the war. In the three and a half years since Nixon had come to power, he'd intensified the war beyond anything imaginable in Johnson's time.

Oh, he was bringing the troops home. But he hadn't had much choice about that. Morale among the GIs in Vietnam had long since gone all to hell in a handbasket; it had begun to break down in the wake of the Tet offensive of 1968. A large portion of the ground troops were now no longer eager volunteers as I had been, but rather unwilling conscripts who had accepted the draft because they didn't know how to beat it, and reluctantly chose to take their chances on a year in Vietnam rather than going to prison for three to five or Canada for life.

They knew, as almost everyone but the most narrow-minded of hawks knew by mid-1968, that the war in Vietnam was a lost cause, that the patient was terminally ill, and that it was only a question of time. They were cynical, bitter, pragmatic, and unwilling in the extreme to die for the delusions of Bob Hope, John Wayne, and Martha Raye. People I knew who'd come back from Vietnam after 1968 reported that drug use among GIs in Vietnam was rampant, unlike anything I had seen when I was there. Desertions, AWOLs, and "bad paper" discharges—discharges less than honorable or general—were skyrocketing. Hundreds of active duty soldiers were requesting discharges as conscientious objectors.

And that wasn't all. American units in Vietnam had begun to effect unwritten truces with their VC and NVA counterparts, both sides realizing it was senseless to go on killing each other when all they had to do was wait it out. Junior enlisted men were regularly "fragging" officers and senior noncommissioned officers who tried to make them fight aggressively. Whole units up to company and even battalion size were disobeying the orders of their superiors and refusing to take the field. Career officers and senior NCOs were resigning from the service in alarming numbers.

No, it was not Richard Nixon's decision to bring the troops home from Vietnam. The armed forces of the United States of America were breaking apart on the rocks of Vietnam. He had to get them out while he still had an army at all.

Yet even that setback Nixon had turned to his advantage: "Look, everybody, I'm winding down the war. See, the boys are coming home." But even as the boys came home, the fury of the war increased. In any ninety-day period of Nixon's term, more bombs fell on Indochina than in the entire five-and-a-half year reign of Lyndon Johnson. Though the ARVN remained as incompetent and dispirited as ever, by that spring of 1972, the ARVN generals found themselves in possession of one of the most modern and extensive arsenals on earth. And under the euphemism of Vietnamization, casualties among the Vietnamese civilian and military population, north and south—not to mention Cambodians and Laotians—climbed almost vertically even as American casualties dropped to almost zero.

It was the most vicious kind of war. War by proxy. A war fought by the American government with the lives of Asians. It was a racist war. Americans didn't like to see their sons and husbands and fathers and friends and neighbors coming home in body bags for no discernible reason. Such had been the undoing of Lyndon Johnson. But Asian bodies didn't get shipped home to American families for burial in American cemeteries.

Thus, well before that spring of 1972, Nixon had discovered that he could convince a significant portion of the American public that he was putting an end to the Vietnam War while successfully prosecuting and prolonging the war almost indefinitely. He could point to the reduction of U.S. ground troop levels and U.S. casualties. He could point to the ongoing peace negotiations in Paris. He could play upon American sympathies by using American prisoners of war as a pretext for not disengaging immediately. And by harnessing the all-too-willing services of U.S. law enforcement agencies and manipulating an all-too-gullible press, he could suppress the antiwar movement while making it appear to be no more than a collection of radicals, violent criminals, Communists, cowards, and traitors.

I knew, of course, that Richard Nixon wasn't solely responsible for all of this. I knew that Nixon was getting lots of help from guys like Hugh Scott and Senator John Stennis and FBI Director J. Edgar Hoover and Attorney General John Mitchell and National Security Chief Henry Kissinger and the Reverend Carl McIntyre. And from the thousands of anonymous advisers and analysts and bureaucrats and war contractors whose vested interests and combined energies acted with the inertial force of a runaway diesel locomotive of cosmic proportions.

And he was getting lots of help, too, from those millions of ordinary Americans who still lived the glory days of World War Two, when good was good and Hitler and Tojo and Mussolini were bad and mothers planted Victory Gardens and Boy Scouts collected old newspapers. Those millions of ignorant people who in ten years had never bothered to learn a thing about Vietnam or America, who could not believe that America could be fundamentally wrong in Indochina or anywhere else, or that American leaders could commit so grandiose an error, much less deliberately act out of greed, pride, malice, or pure emotional reflex. That vast Silent Majority who refused even to consider that an entire generation of young Americans who dressed funny and smoked pot and played loud music could possibly be right about anything, incredibly finding it easier to believe that somehow, mysteriously, the children they had raised had turned into a generation of misfits, drug addicts, malcontents, traitors, cowards, and Commies.

No, Nixon wasn't alone. But he alone bore a special and paramount responsibility. Because back in 1969, when he'd first taken office, he could have chosen to end the war swiftly. He had promised to do so. He had been elected with that mandate. In the wake of the Tet offensive, when the light at the end of the tunnel had finally gone out forever, only the most rabid of hawks would have opposed him. But instead he had chosen not to become "the first American president to lose a war." He had chosen instead to shatter the fragile national consensus on the futility of the war that had been achieved by the spring of 1968, in the process dividing the nation as it had not been divided since the Civil War, and spreading still more fire—year after year of fire—over the lands and peoples of Indochina.

Fighting in Vietnam had been easy compared to the years since, I thought as Nixon droned on. It had taken me more than two agonizing years to come to terms with the war, to be willing to admit that the war had been a mistake, and to begin speaking out against it. They had been two hard lonely years, but even then, I had been able to continue believing.

If I could use my experience to convince others that the war had to end, if I could make people understand that further continuation of the war was senseless, a waste of lives and money and time all around, if I could keep others from having their lives shipwrecked and their dreams and bodies and minds broken, if I could help my country regain its moral balance, its perspective on itself and Vietnam and the world—then, perhaps, in some small but real way, my own experience might gain some positive meaning after all.

But no one had listened, and the war had gone on like a ball-peen hammer in the hand of a steady workman, and the years had worn me down, and the truth had become harder and harder to run from. And finally, on that warm spring night as Richard Nixon leered at me with all the arrogance and malice of a Machiavellian megalomaniac and the mines splashed into the harbors and the bombers screamed north, seeking no end but pure punishment and human misery, I knew the chase was over. There was nowhere else to run. Trapped like a cornered rat, I knew at last that nothing I had ever done in Vietnam would ever carry with it anything but shame and disgrace and dishonor; that I would never be able to recall Vietnam with anything but pain and anger and bitterness; that I would never again be able to take pride in being an American. And the rage and sorrow and tragedy of it all was overwhelming.

In one swift unthinking reflex instant, I pulled off my boot and hurled it at the face of Richard Milhous Nixon. The boot hit him right square flush on the face.

The television exploded.

The screen tinkled to the floor in little pieces, the electronic guts spluttering and crackling. Nixon vanished, the room descending into an eerie silence filled with the mildly pungent odor of burning electrical circuitry.

And then I just sat there, hunched over on my bed, staring at that blind smoking Cyclops. Ten minutes? Thirty minutes? Christ, I thought finally, how am I gonna pay for this television set?

And then I was laughing hysterically.

And then I was crying.

Chapter 50

We're out in the boondocks—me and the rest of the scouts. It's night, and we've set up in a tight perimeter with a mangrove swamp to our backs and an open sandy area in front of us broken by a series of hedgerows beginning about one hundred meters out. Everyone's asleep but me and Morgan; it's our turn on watch. There's no moon. It's very quiet except for the usual night sounds of Vietnam: artillery booming from the battalion compound several miles away; distant small-arms fire; the shrill whine of jet fighters high overhead—sounds you hardly even notice anymore.

"Hey, Bill," Morgan suddenly whispers, "there's movement out there."

"Where? I don't see anything."

"Down on the deck, just in front of those trees sticking up out of the hedgerow, about one o'clock," he says, pointing ahead and slightly to the right.

"Are you sure? I can't—yeah, yeah! There *is* something out there—I can't tell—looks like three or four—Jesus! Rolly, ten o'clock!"

"Fuckin' A! Look at 'em—must be thirty or forty— Hey! Pssst! Get up," Morgan growls in a hoarse whisper. "Get up, wake the fuck up. Hey, you guys, we're gonna get hit!"

They're creeping across the sand now, down on their bellies, using scrubby bushes and the soft curves of the land for cover— hollows you'd never even notice in daylight. They obviously know where we are, but they don't seem aware that we've spotted them. Sergeant Seagrave, the chief scout, quietly takes charge. Everybody's awake now, sliding into firing positions, checking ammo and grenades, waiting.

"Hold your fire," Seagrave whispers. "Hold your fire. Let 'em get in good and close."

Jesus, they don't know we're wise to 'em. They don't fire. They don't get up and charge. They just keep inching forward like snails. They think they're going to jump us, but they're walking—no, crawling—right into a reverse ambush. I'm shaking inside—the kind of feeling I used to get just before a race when I was a kid, standing on the starting blocks at a swimming meet all crouched down and ready to spring, just waiting for the starter's pistol.

There must be at least forty of them—little dark figures creeping across the pale sand. There's only nine of us, but we've got the advantage: we're concealed and we're ready, and they're out in the open and they *think* they're ready but they aren't *even* ready for what we're about to do to them.

"Hold your fire," Seagrave keeps whispering over and over again, softly, almost gently, like a lullaby or a steadying hand stroking a nervous horse. "Wait till they charge. Hold your fire. Hold your fire."

One of them jumps up and shouts and waves his rifle over his head, and they all leap up shouting and open fire, but just in that moment the starter's pistol goes off, Seagrave hollers "Fire!" The swimmers spring from their blocks, we all open up full automatic, catching them totally off guard, the air filled instantly with noise and tracer rounds and powder smoke and shrieks and screams and shouts, and they start dropping like rocks, we're hardly taking any return fire at all—it's a goddamned shooting gallery—we cut 'em to pieces, and it's all over in a few minutes.

Absolute silence. After a while, we move out onto the sand and begin checking bodies—we've radioed in and we've got illumination rounds popping overhead now from the eighty-one-millimeter mortar battery at battalion, lighting up the whole area, and—my God! Oh, my God! They're all children! They're goddamned kids—little girls and boys—nine, ten years old. Just kids! And they're all armed with twenty-two-caliber single-shot rifles. And they're all dead. Every last one of them. And I'm crying. And Dave Carter is standing in the doorway of the darkened room: "Hey, Bill! Hey, Bill! Wake up. You're having a nightmare. It's all right."

* * *

Only it wasn't all right. For weeks I'd been having the same dream. At first it was only every other week or so, but as the spring had progressed, the dream had become ever more frequent. Now it was coming every couple of nights, sometimes two or three nights in a row. I was a nervous wreck. I'd always had nightmares—ever since I'd left Vietnam—but nothing like this. This was surreal. It was always the children. Always children. Spring term of my junior year was almost over, and final exams were rapidly approaching, but I couldn't work, I couldn't sleep, I could barely function anymore. I'd taken to eating speed to stay awake during the day, then smoking enormous amounts of marijuana or hash to try to drug myself to sleep at night. The cycle was becoming increasingly vicious.

Chapter 51

"I *hadda* break the contract," I said. "There was no way I could take that job. The nightmares were driving me crazy, man—and it's still another three weeks before the job even begins."

Back in late March, I'd applied for a job as a counselor at a summer camp in the Poconos. It had sounded like fun—eight weeks in the mountains, no telephones, no newspapers, just lots of good country and energetic kids. I liked kids. The only position they'd had available by the time I'd applied had been for riflery instructor. I'd been a rifle expert in the Marines. Hell, I'd thought, I can teach riflery. So I'd signed the contract. That's when the nightmares had begun.

"What'd the camp director say when you told him?" asked Allen.

"Well, he didn't like it very much. I don't think he had the foggiest notion what I was talking about. But I didn't leave him much choice. I just couldn't go through with it, that's all. See, the thing is, I never got around to thinking about it until I actually took the job, you know? To make the connection between Vietnam and—" I paused, still trying to find a way to explain what I felt intuitively. "Well, between Vietnam and stuff like teaching kids how to shoot. You know what I mean? Our whole cultural fascination with guns and violence and martial glory. Like when I enlisted: I didn't know squat about war, but I had all kinds of false notions about it, and mostly I thought what I'd be doing was a good thing. Oh, sure, a few people might get killed, but that's the way it goes in a war, right? And anyway, I'd never seen a dead person in my life, so what the hell did that mean? Where'd I get those ideas? Where'd they come from? I didn't invent 'em. They got taught to me somehow. Look at the cartoons kids grow up watching. Popeye's always punching Bluto's lights out. Roadrunner's always blowing up Wile E. Coyote with dynamite. Sylvester's always gettin' torn to shreds by some dog. I mean, horrible things, and you just sit there and laugh at it. Oh, well, they're just cartoons, right? You tell me it doesn't have any impact. Who are the great legends of American history? Wyatt Earp. Davy Crocket. George Armstrong Custer—Christ, the guy was a mass murderer, and he's practically been canonized."

Allen just nodded his head, listening. I took a drink of beer. Except for Jamie McAdams, Allen Williams was the only non-student adult type at Swarthmore that I could relate to. I couldn't figure out what he was doing at a place like Swarthmore, but he was one of the deans. I'd first met him two years earlier in Tarbles Student Center during the furor in the wake of the Cambodian invasion, and since then we'd occasionally gone drinking together. Mostly I ranted and raved while he listened. He was a good listener. On this particular occasion, I'd asked him to celebrate my decision not to take the camp counselor's job. It was early June 1972, and we were sitting in Green's Bar in Morton, the town next to Swarthmore.

"You know, Allen, I can still remember the Christmas I got a toy forty-five-caliber automatic pistol. Had a leather military-style holster with USMC embossed on the flap. I was so proud of it, I ran right out to show it off first chance I got. I musta been about eight or nine. And the super-neatest Christmas present I *ever* got was a genuine plastic thirty-caliber machine gun. A machine gun! Had a tripod, a battery-powered noisemaker, flashing red barrel—the works. A Christmas present, for Chrissake. The

birthday of the Prince of Peace. And my father's a minister! It
never occurred to my parents that there was anything incongruous
about it. And they're good people, too. It's not like they're war-
mongers or fascists or something. Man, it's so damned pervasive
nobody even realizes it.''

"What do you propose to do about it?" asked Allen.

"I don't know. It's depressing." I took another swallow of
beer. "One thing I'm gonna *not* do is teach ten-year-olds how to
shoot rifles. Man, I'm glad I'm out from under *that* one. I can't
believe how fuckin' stupid I can be. Terminal idiocy. Sometimes
it seems like my whole life is nothin' but a matter of scrambling
out from under my own stupid mistakes."

"A little hard on yourself, aren't you?"

"Not hardly," I replied. "You ready for another beer?" He
drained his mug and I held up two fingers to the bartender.

"So what are you going to do this summer?" Allen asked.

"Find a job for a few weeks, I guess, then head west again.
Did you know Bart Lewis?" I asked.

"The name sounds familiar," he replied.

"Graduated in 1970. He's in med school now. Anyway, he's
gonna be spending the summer at some clinic in Denver. Wants
me to come out and do a little camping in the Rockies. I guess I
will. Travel around a little. Just hang out, you know?"

"You planning to come back next fall?"

"Yeah, I guess so," I said. "I made it this far. Might as well
finish. At least it'll give me another year to figure out what to do
next."

"What are your options?" he asked.

"Hell, I don't know. I'd get the hell out of the country if I
could figure out where else to go. I thought about going to Swe-
den or Denmark, but I don't speak the language. And what would
I do there, anyway? Fill sandbags? Clean rifles? That's the problem with Australia, too. I even wrote to the Australian embassy.
If you got some kind of special skill—engineer, doctor, pipe fit-
ter, almost anything useful—they're glad to have you. But me?
A B.A. in English literature from Swarthmore College and three
years in the military? I could be a kangaroo hunter, I suppose.
Read Shakespeare to the wallabies. That's about it. I don't know
what the hell I'm gonna do. Mostly, I just wish the next forty or
fifty years would hurry up and go away."

"Well, maybe it's not as bad as all that," he said. "You'll
think of something."

"That's what I keep telling myself, but I really don't *see* myself doing anything. I try to imagine the future, but there's nothing there. Just a black hole with nothin' in it but me."

"Well, then, you probably have time for another beer, don't you?" he said.

"Might as well. I can't sing, and the dance floor's closed." The bartender brought two more mugs of beer. "Allen, why the hell didn't the college fire those creeps that were finkin' to the FBI? That's outrageous what they've been doing. And for the school to keep them on—Christ, what the hell, man?"

"Oh, they were just doing their civic duty, Bill. You can't fire people for doing their duty, can you?"

"What?"

"Hey, that's not my opinion. You asked me why the school didn't fire them."

"Jesus Christ."

"Oh, that's nothing," he continued. "You remember after Kent State when all those colleges and universities were shutting down in protest? You ever wonder why Swarthmore didn't close?"

"Yeah. Why not?"

"Because the board gave Rich Cramer explicit orders: Under no circumstances will this school shut down."

"But why?"

"Image, you know. You know that the year before you got here, the black students association took over the admissions building."

"Yeah."

"And right in the middle of the protest, the guy who was president before Cramer—"

"Yeah, yeah," I said, "I know all that. He died of a heart attack. So what?"

"So the whole thing was *very* embarrassing to the board of managers," said Allen. "They felt like the school was out of control, like the place was falling apart. You know, Swarthmore's supposed to be this dignified, respectable ivory tower, and here's the headlines in every newspaper in the country: 'Swarthmore President Dies of Heart Failure As Black Students Take Over.' The board members were shitting bricks. There was no way they were ever gonna let that happen again. When they hired Cramer, they put him on the carpet and laid it right out."

"Are you kidding me?"

"Nope. Oh, when the Cambodian business blew up, there were a lot of other reasons given for public consumption, but that's what it came down to."

"Jesus fucking-A Christ! You got U.S. troops invading a neutral country, you got American soldiers shooting down American kids in the streets of America, and all they're worried about is their *image?* And this is supposed to be a *Quaker* school, for Chrissake."

"A Quaker institution, Bill," Allen replied. "And the controlling word there is institution. Institutions have a way of existing for their own sakes, regardless of the circumstances. They do whatever's necessary to survive, the same way people do. Look where the U.S. government started and where it's ended up. Swarthmore's no different. There's a lot of wealthy alumni that don't see the world the way you do, you know. Hell, Bill, Senator Scott doesn't make a move without checking with Terry Maxwell first. Peter Hollister made his fortune filling Pentagon contracts. Guys like that have a lot of influence around here, and they've been climbing the walls lately. They don't like ending parietal rules. They don't like coed dorms. And if they had their way about it, they'd call in the National Guard and make everybody get haircuts and join ROTC."

"I just don't believe this fuckin' country. It's everywhere, isn't it?" I said.

" 'Course, I can't *prove* any of this," he added, grinning and raising his eyebrows. "Anyway, I didn't say it."

"Cover your ass, huh?"

"Listen, I don't see myself spending the rest of my life at Swarthmore College, but I'm not ready to leave yet. One more round for the road?"

"What the hell," I said, draining my mug.

Chapter 52

"Level with me, Paul, I gotta know," I said. "What's goin' on?"

"Bill, I'm telling you, you know as much about it as I do," Paul replied. "The first I knew about *any* of this shit was when the federal marshals handed me the indictment and took me away in handcuffs. I've never even *met* four of the guys I'm supposed to have conspired with."

"Look what their case is based on, Bill," Jim added. "One lousy FBI informer with a history of psychiatric disorders. They don't have a damned thing, and they know it."

"There's nothing they *could* have," said Paul. "We didn't *do* anything."

"They don't *need* anything," said Jim. "They've already got what they want. Front-page headlines in every paper in the country: 'Crazed Vietnam Veterans Indicted.' They don't have to *prove* anything."

"No, there's even more to it than that," added Paul. "Look when the indictments came down: two weeks after the Watergate burglary hit the news. Nixon's trying to divert attention from his own criminal conspiracy by lockin' in on us."

"Yeah, yeah, okay," I said, putting up both hands. "I knew it. I fuckin' *knew* it. I just hadda hear it from you, that's all. Christ."

We were sitting around the table in Jim Best's kitchen in Brooklyn. It was September 1972. Jim, whom I'd gotten to know over the previous year through various antiwar activities, was one of the original founders of Vietnam Veterans Against the War. I'd stopped in to visit him before returning to Swarthmore to begin my senior year, and we'd been talking about the Gainesville Eight conspiracy trial. "Wait a minute," Jim had said. "You can hear the story firsthand.'' He'd made a quick phone call, and fifteen minutes later, Paul had joined us.

A former Army lieutenant who'd earned a Bronze Star and the Vietnamese Cross of Gallantry, Paul Mason was one of the eight members of VVAW indicted two months earlier for ''conspiring to cause riots during the Republican National Convention with firebombs, automatic weapons, and slingshot-propelled fireworks.'' He'd been arrested and jailed, but was free on bail pending trial. Six of the other seven men indicated were also Vietnam veterans; all of them had been honorably discharged, and all were members of VVAW. Between them, they had earned another Bronze Star and Cross of Gallantry, in addition to Paul's, four Purple Hearts, a Distinguished Flying Cross, and three Air Medals in the service of their country. Now each stood in jeopardy of five years in federal prison and a ten-thousand-dollar fine.

''You know whose case this is, don't you?'' asked Jim. I shook my head. ''Guy Goodwin's,'' he explained. ''The same jackass that brought charges against Phil Berrigan and the Harrisburg Seven. And it was the same kind of case: testimony from one FBI informant; that's all the government had for evidence in that trial, too.'' The case of the Harrisburg Seven had involved an alleged conspiracy to kidnap Henry Kissinger. The verdict had been ten to two for acquittal.

''He loses one case and then goes right on to the next one without even breaking stride,'' said Paul.

''That's the point,'' added Jim. ''He doesn't have to win. All he has to do is get the headlines. It's the same pattern that's been going on since the Chicago Seven trial—ever since Nixon's been president. It's all part of Nixon's strategy. Discredit the antiwar movement. Keep us off balance. Keep the headlines lurid and fresh. Put dissenters on notice that *anyone* who speaks out could be next. Force the movement to spend hundreds of thousands of dollars trying to keep innocent people out of prison, instead of using that money and energy on stopping the war.''

''And who knows?'' said Paul. ''Maybe they'll even win one if they keep trying long enough. All it would take is the right jury. A few of those redneck flag-wavers, and there you are.''

''There's just no bottom to it, is there?'' I said. It wasn't really a question. ''Man, when I think where my head was when I enlisted. You know what I had written on my notebook cover in high school? 'Ask not what your country can do for you . . . ' John Fitzgerald Kennedy.''

"Yeah, don't ask," Paul scoffed. "You don't wanna know. *This* is what your fuckin' country can do for you—try to stick you in prison for exercising your constitutional right to free speech."

"Jesus Christ. Jesus *fucking* Christ!" I shouted, banging the table hard with my fist. "I hate this fucking country!"

"Better watch what you say," Paul whispered, picking up a flowerpot as though checking it for an electronic eavesdropping device.

"That's not funny," said Jim.

"No, sir, it is not funny," Paul replied.

"What now?" I asked.

"I'm not sure," said Paul. "Our lawyers are trying to get a delay in the trial until after the November elections."

"You think it'll matter?" I said. "McGovern hasn't got a snowball's chance in hell of winning."

"I know," Paul replied. "But maybe some of the political dust'll settle after the election. I don't know. My lawyer says it's just good strategy to delay as long as possible."

"Who's payin' your legal fees?" I asked.

"*And* my living expenses, since I got fired from my job after the indictment hit the news, and no one'll hire me. Good question."

"VVAW's trying to raise money for a legal defense fund," said Jim.

"Christ almighty," I said. "First they make you fight their dirty little war for 'em. Then they try to throw you into prison. It's *scary,* man. It's really scary."

"You think *you're* scared," said Paul.

Chapter 53

"What are ya doin'?" asked Roger.

"Oh, hi, Roger," I said without looking up. "Sit down. I'm almost finished."

"Writing a poem?"

"Not hardly. I'm writing a letter to my congressman."

"Oh, yeah? What about?"

"I think Congress should impeach Nixon, that's what about," I replied.

"No kidding?"

"No kidding. There!" I said, signing the letter with a flourish. "I'll mail it when we get to Long Beach. You wanna play some cards?"

"No," Roger replied. "It's a nice night out. Not too cold. Let's take some wine and sit up on the stack deck for a while. I need some fresh air."

"Okay," I said, grabbing a coat. "Wine's in the locker."

Outside, it was cool and breezy, but much milder than it had been only a few days earlier and farther north. Sailing the coast run in winter was schizophrenic. One day you'd be pounding through a snowstorm off Washington; five days later you could sunbathe on the boat deck while the ship slid gently through the Santa Barbara Channel. The seasons changed almost weekly.

In a few minutes we were nestled beside the smokestack, out of the wind and with our backs to the warm stack housing. The only sounds were the wind, the groaning of steel as the ship plowed through easy swells, and the steady powerful throb of the engines far below us. I leaned back and lifted my face to the dark sky. There were no clouds, and the stars sparkled everywhere. Only in the high desert had I seen so spectacular a sky as one could see on a clear night at sea. There were millions of stars. Billions even. The Milky Way was so bright it appeared as if someone had unfurled a broad satin ribbon right across the sky. Because of the rolling of the ship, if you looked straight up and focused on a point just above the stack, it looked and felt as though the ship were steady and level while the whole cosmos rotated in a slow figure eight above the ship.

"No wonder the ancients made up stories about the stars," I said. "I never used to be able to understand how they saw things up there like bears and hunters and crabs. But what do most people ever see these days, with all the surface light and smog and pollution? A few little white dots, that's all. A sky like this— you can find almost anything in it."

"Could you see this many stars in Vietnam?" asked Roger.

"Not very often," I replied, shaking my head to dispel the illusion that the heavens were rolling instead of the ship. "There were always flares going off somewhere or other. Even a little sixty-millimeter mortar flare a mile away would generate enough light to take out half of what you're looking at up there. They had these big magnesium flares they used to drop on parachutes from C-130s, five or six of 'em at a time. You get a string of those things burning, and they'd literally turn night into day. We didn't like nighttime very much. Nighttime was Charlie's time."

"Charlie?" asked Roger.

"The Vietcong."

"You ready for some more wine?"

"Yeh," I replied. "Hey, look! Here comes the moon." As we watched, the tip of the moon peeked up over the dark rim of the ocean. In a few minutes, it rose above the horizon and began to spread a sparkling river of light over the moving water. "Moon river," I said.

"Beautiful, ain't it?"

"You ever notice how it always comes straight to wherever you are?" I asked. "No matter where you stand, the path of the light always comes right to you. Like you could just step out onto the water and walk all the way to the edge of the world."

"I never thought of it like that," said Roger. "But yeah, I guess that's what it feels like."

"I like it out here, Roger. It's a world all to itself. Sometimes I wish we could make the run to Kharg Island sometime—sixty days at sea, instead of two days here and four days there."

"You'd get bored with it pretty quick, believe me," said Roger.

"I don't think so. I like it out here. No hassles. I could stay out here forever, you know? Maybe I will."

The river of light from the moon began to narrow as the moon rose higher into the sky, blotting out the stars around it.

"You really gonna send that letter?" asked Roger.

"Sure. Why not?"

"I never wrote a letter to a congressman," he said. "You think they'll really impeach him?"

"Hell, I don't know. I don't know how the guy's managed to survive this long. I can hope, can't I? It's funny, you know? All the shit that peckerhead's pulled in the past five years, and if they ever do get him it'll be for some chickenshit little bugging operation he didn't even need to get reelected anyway."

"You don't think Watergate's really all that important?"

"Oh, it's important. Here's the president of the United States tryin' to bug the Democratic National Headquarters like some kind of common criminal. And then he spends two years lyin' through his teeth about it to the whole world. Throwing his loyal lieutenants to the dogs one by one, tryin' to save his own ass. Deliberately obstructing justice, withholding evidence, tryin' to use the CIA to squash the FBI's investigation, erasing tapes—I mean, it's just sordid and vulgar and slimy. The whole filthy thing. Stuff you'd expect from a third-rate ward heeler in South Philadelphia. And here it is, the president of the United States of America. Sure it's important. What I mean is that he's done so many other things that are far worse than any of this Watergate crap. Christ, it's so damned ironic, I don't know whether to laugh or cry."

"Take your pick," said Roger.

"Well, I'll take what I can get. At this point, I don't much care what they get him on, just so long as they nail him. I'd give my left nut to see that son of a bitch impeached. Hell, I'd give both nuts to see him behind bars. That's where he belongs. That's where they all belong. His vice president turns out to be an extortionist. His attorney general's a perjurer. His secretary of state has the audacity to accept the Nobel Peace Prize in the middle of a war."

"Kissinger?"

"Yeah. You didn't know that?"

"No."

"Yeah, last year after they signed those bogus Paris peace accords, the Nobel committee awarded the peace prize to Kissinger and Le Duc Tho, the North Vietnamese negotiator. And Kissinger actually had the nerve to accept it."

"The other guy didn't?" asked Roger.

"Nope. All he said was, 'Hey, you guys are crazy. This war ain't over yet.' That's class, man. There it is in a nutshell: The United States of America has got no class. None at all. It makes me sick to my stomach."

"You really care, don't you?" asked Roger.

"About what?"

"About America."

"Not anymore, I don't. It ain't my country anymore. Never was—it just took me a while to realize it, that's all."

''Then why are you bothering to write to your congressman?'' he asked.

''Gimme some more wine, will ya?''

Chapter 54

The day Henry Kissinger announced that peace was at hand, I was getting ready to give a poetry reading in the Rathskellar of Tarbles Student Center. I was one of five or six students who had been invited to read. I'd only read in public once before, and I was very nervous. I was sitting in my room in Wharton that afternoon in October of 1972, trying to decide what to read, when Dave Carter stuck his head in the door.

''You heard the news?'' he asked.

''No. What's up?''

''The war's almost over,'' he said.

''Huh?''

''Kissinger announced it this afternoon. They're about to sign an agreement in Paris.''

''Think so?'' I replied. ''I'll believe it when I see it. Talk's cheap.''

''Well, at least it's something.''

''We'll see.''

I was sorry that Dave and I were no longer roommates. In spite of the fact that he and I were very different—I was five years older, and aside from swimming and a love of poetry and literature, we didn't really have that much in common—I liked him and had enjoyed sharing a suite with him. But the rules of room choosing were such that we would have ended up in a one-room double, and I wasn't going to live in a one-room double for anyone or anything; three years in the Marines had given me my fill of lack of privacy. So, for my senior year, I'd taken a single in a coed section of Wharton, and Dave was in a one-room double with another sophomore swimmer over in Hallowell.

For Dave's sake at least, it was probably just as well. The only time he'd gotten stoned with me the previous spring, he'd ended up passing out in the bathroom. I'd found him sprawled out on the floor mumbling something about the Philadelphia airport, and he had a large knot on his forehead where he'd hit something solid on the way down. Probably the urinal. Neither the urinal nor Dave's head had sustained any permanent damage, but it had given us both a scare.

"You're reading tonight over in the Ratt, aren't you?" he asked.

"Yeah. You gonna be there?"

"Wouldn't miss it. See you there." He disappeared again as abruptly as he'd appeared, and I went back to my manuscripts for a while. Then I went to supper. Then I went by Denise Sawyer's room in Parrish, and the two of us headed off to the poetry reading.

I wondered if it was true that the war might really be over soon. Some part of me had always wanted to believe that it couldn't last forever, that it *had* to end eventually. But the war had been going on for so long by now that the part of me that wanted to believe it could ever end had shrunk to little more than some sort of useless atrophied organ like an appendix. It was hard to imagine a world without the Vietnam War in it.

By the time the reading began, the dark basement room was nearly full. I listened as several other people read, trying not to think about how nervous I was. Then it was my turn. I began with a poem about geese and autumn, read a couple of love poems and a poem about friendship, then finished up with this poem, which I'd written only a week earlier:

A Relative Thing

We are the ones you sent to fight a war
you didn't know a thing about.

It didn't take us long to realize
the only land that we controlled
was covered by the bottoms of our boots.

When the newsmen said that naval ships
had shelled a VC staging point,

we saw a breastless woman
and her stillborn child.

We laughed at old men stumbling
in the dust in frenzied terror
to avoid our three-ton trucks.

We fought outnumbered in Hue City
while the ARVN soldiers looted bodies
in the safety of the rear;
the cookies from the wives of Local 104
did not soften our awareness.

We have seen the pacified supporters
of the Saigon government
sitting in their jam-packed cardboard towns,
their wasted hands placed limply in their laps,
their empty bellies waiting for the rice
some district chief has sold
for profit to the Vietcong.

We have been democracy on Zippo raids,
burning houses to the ground,
driving eager amtracs through new-sown fields.

We are the ones who have to live
with the memory that we were the instruments
of your pigeon-breasted fantasies.
We are inextricable accomplices
in this travesty of dreams:

but we are not alone.

We are the ones you sent to fight a war
you did not know a thing about.
Those of us who lived
have tried to tell you what went wrong.
Now you think you do not have to listen.

Just because we will not fit
into the uniforms of photographs
of you at twenty-one
does not mean you can disown us.

We are your sons, America,
and you cannot change that.

When you awake,
we will still be here.

I got through the whole poem, though my voice almost frac-
tured with emotion several times. I'd had no idea that would
happen, and it surprised and embarrassed me. There was a brief
silence as I gathered up my poems. I was shaking, and it wasn't
from nervousness. I wanted off that stage as quickly as possible.
Suddenly a wild burst of applause and loud cheering erupted from
the audience.

"Don't applaud, goddamn you!" I lashed out without thinking. Just as suddenly as the outburst had begun, it stopped. "What
are you cheering about!" I shouted. "This isn't some fucking
party! It's 1972, and people are still dying, and you ought to be
crying, not cheering. What the hell's the matter with you? You
think this is some kind of football game or what? We're talking
about human beings here—millions of them—and I'm sick to
death of it, and I just want it to end."

I stalked off the low stage and over to the corner booth where
Denise sat waiting for me. Dave Carter came over, and I think
he was saying something about the poetry I'd read, but I couldn't
hear him. I couldn't hear anything. I just sat there staring at
nothing and thinking of things far away from Tarbles Student
Center. And then I was sobbing softly, and Dave was gone, and
Denise had her arms around me and was cradling my head between her breasts.

Which turned out to be not such a good thing.

Less than a month before, I'd begun dating a woman named
Karen Dolan, who was a sophomore at a nearby college. I'd met
her through her sister Martha who, like me, was a senior at
Swarthmore, and whom I'd known since our freshman year. I'd
even dated Martha a few times early in my sophomore year, and
though nothing had come of it, we'd remained friends. During
my junior year, much to Martha's delight and relief, I'd persuaded her boyfriend Chuck not to enter a Marine officers' training program, and after that, the two of them had occasionally
invited me to spend time with them. So in late September, when
Martha had suggested that I spend a weekend at Princeton, where
Chuck was a senior, I'd readily agreed. That's where I'd met
Karen, whom, as it turned out, Martha had also invited.

It had been a very pleasant weekend. We'd all gone to the
Rutgers-Princeton football game, and then to a party in New

Brunswick. And by the end of the weekend, I'd made a date with Karen for the following weekend. I hadn't been so excited about anything in a long time. I couldn't make the week pass quickly enough. I'd even persuaded Fred Charles to throw a party. Fast Freddie was famous for his parties, and I wanted Karen to have so much fun that she'd fall in love with me forever.

I'd picked her up that Saturday night, and everything seemed just fine for a while, but the closer we'd gotten to Swarthmore, the quieter she'd become. It was obvious that something was wrong, but I couldn't figure out what. Finally, I'd asked her what was bothering her.

"Can you take me back to Immaculata?" she'd asked.

"Of course I'll take you back," I'd replied.

"I mean right now."

What the hell's going on here, I'd thought. "Why?" I'd asked. "What's the matter? Have I done something wrong?"

"You haven't done anything wrong," she'd replied. "It's just that—well, I don't know any of these people. I don't think I want to go to the party."

"Hey, you'll like them," I'd said. "They're really nice people. You'll see." Jesus Christ, they're throwing the damned party for you, I'd thought, but I hadn't said it.

"I'm sure they are," she'd replied, "but—but, well, I just don't feel comfortable, that's all."

"Why not? I don't understand."

"Bill, I'm just not sure I'm ready for you."

"What's that supposed to mean?" I'd asked.

"I'm only nineteen years old, Bill. You're twenty-four. You've been in the Marines. You're—well, you're experienced. I don't know if I'm in your league."

"Oh, come on, Karen. Not that. Bad-ass ex-Marine too crazy for civilized girl. Tries to rape and kill on first date."

"Bill," she'd said.

"Well? How am I supposed to feel? Guilt by stereotype. You haven't even given me a chance."

"I'm sorry. I really am. I don't want to go to the party. Please take me back to school."

"Yeah, sure, whatever you want," I'd said. I was crushed. It suddenly dawned on me that in one short week I'd constructed a whole fairy tale with me and this woman I hardly knew falling in love and living happily ever after. It was embarrassing to realize how rapidly my mind had moved, and painful to see it all collapse. Mister Sucker one more time. Just another pipe dream, like the elaborate fantasies I'd lived on day after day in Vietnam. Just another dead end to add to the lifetime of dead ends I'd already accumulated.

The drive back to her school had taken forever that night. Neither of us said a word. When we arrived, I'd walked her to the door of her dorm, said good night quickly and curtly, and turned to go.

"Bill," she'd called after me, "wait."

Now what, I'd thought. I was embarrassed and hurt and angry, and I just wanted to get the hell away from there as fast as I could.

"Do you want to come up to my room for a while?" she'd asked.

What the *hell's* going *on* here, I'd thought—but I'd been unable to suppress the sudden jolt of delight surging through me, like a condemned man who's just been granted a stay of execution.

"I'm not allowed up there, am I?" I'd replied as coolly as possible, trying not to sound too eager. Besides, I *wasn't* allowed up there. It was a Catholic women's college. Men weren't allowed in the dorms, women caught with men in their rooms could expect to be summarily expelled, and the security guards carried loaded revolvers.

"I can sneak you up the fire escape," she'd replied. Then she'd smiled and giggled, and my face involuntarily erupted into a grin from ear to ear.

Things had progressed rapidly after that. Twice the following week, I'd driven up to see her, and the next weekend she'd come down to Swarthmore. She'd arranged to stay with her sister Martha, but had ended up staying with me instead, offering me her virginity and shortly afterwards telling me about Tom.

"Who the hell's Tom?" I'd asked as we lay together in bed.

"He's my boyfriend," she'd replied. "Well, he *was* my boyfriend." Then she'd giggled and kissed my cheek. Tom and Karen had gone to high school together, she'd explained, and had been dating for four years. He was now a sophomore at the University of Virginia.

"No wonder you didn't want to go to the party with me," I'd said.

"That was part of it," she'd replied. "I wasn't lying about

the other things, though. I *didn't* know any of your friends, and I *was* a little intimidated by you.''

"Me? Seriously,'' I'd said, lightly brushing one of her nipples with my lips.

"Well, I was!''

"Why did you change your mind?''

"Because I liked you. And I was afraid I'd never see you again.''

"You probably wouldn't have,'' I'd replied. "I probably woulda wrapped myself around a telephone pole or something.''

"Bill!''

"Well, I felt *awful,* I'll tell ya. I couldn't figure out what the hell you were tryin' to do to my head. 'Yes, I'll go out with you. No, I won't go out with you. Take me home—' ''

"Hush up!'' she'd said, putting her hand over my mouth. "I love you.''

"What are you gonna do about Tom?'' I'd asked.

"I'm supposed to go down there at the end of this month for his homecoming weekend,'' she'd replied. "I'd still like to go, if you don't mind. I'd like to tell him in person what's happened. I *did* date him for four years. I owe him at least that much. Remember how you felt when you got that letter from that girl while you were in Vietnam?''

"Remember?! Yeah, I remember,'' I'd said. "But he ain't exactly in a war zone.''

"Bill, I owe it to him. Please don't worry. Nothing's going to happen between us. I've said no to him for four years; I'm certainly not going to give in now. Not when I don't even love him anymore.''

So a few weeks later, Karen had gone to Charlottesville to tell Tom he was an ex-boyfriend, and I'd gone to the poetry reading in the Rathskellar with Denise Sawyer. There was no harm in it. We were just friends.

Denise was a freshman at Swarthmore. I'd noticed her from the first day of school because she was impossible not to notice. She had olive brown skin as though she was suntanned except that it was her natural skin color, soft dark eyes, and thick chestnut hair that tumbled halfway down her back. And she always wore long dresses like the ones Didi Barnesly had worn. If Karen was pretty, and she was, Denise's beauty was awesome.

Most remarkable of all, Denise was a nice person. Intense beauty, the kind that leaves men speechless and groveling, is frequently accompanied by a personality convinced of its own royalty. But Denise seemed completely oblivious to the intimidating power she possessed. From the first time I'd spoken with her, I'd been charmed as much by her quiet gentleness and self-deprecating manner as by her physical attractiveness.

I'd also quickly discovered that she already had a boyfriend – some guy named Tippy who was a crewman on some millionaire's oceangoing yacht. The discovery had scotched my brief hopes for bigger things, but I liked Denise anyway, and continued to spend time with her. We'd become good friends even before I'd begun dating Karen. So with Karen gone for the weekend and unable to come hear me read, I'd asked Denise to accompany me instead.

And everything would have been fine if I hadn't broken down that night, transmitting need so desperately that Denise just couldn't refuse me. Not that I asked, because I didn't. She didn't really offer, either. It just sort of happened. And by morning I found myself in one hell of a mess.

The next few weeks were insane. Though Denise and I spent most of our time together suffering severe guilt feelings over cheating on our respective lovers, we just couldn't stay away from each other, and I was juggling time and women like a circus performer. It was all so intense that I hardly had time to lament the crushing defeat handed to George McGovern by Richard Nixon in the November election. I couldn't say I was surprised by the outcome of the election. Nor was I surprised that the Paris peace talks had collapsed again. I'd told Dave Carter I'd believe it when I saw it. And just as I'd suspected, Kissinger's bold statement that peace was at hand had turned out to be nothing more than a grandstand ploy to give Nixon's campaign one last shot in the arm before election day. Fucking assholes, I thought, when I had time to think about it at all.

Which I didn't most of the time. Here I was, after years of one-night stands or no stands at all, suddenly having to choose between two of the most beautiful and kindest women I'd ever met. It never rains but it pours, I thought, banging my head against the wall. I had to figure a way out of my bind before the whole thing blew up in my face. And I knew it *would* blow up sooner or later. With Karen's sister at Swarthmore, and a close friend of Karen's sister living just down the hall from Denise, it was just a matter of time before the rumors started to fly.

And they did. One weekend in mid-November, Karen asked me straight out: "Who's Denise?"

Oh, Jesus Christ almighty, I thought. "She's just a friend," I said. "That's all. Can't I have any female friends? You've got male friends, don't you?"

"Amy Stanley told Martha you've been sleeping with her," said Karen.

"That's a lie," I said.

"You took her to that play, didn't you?"

"I'd already bought the tickets before I knew you were going to Virginia. What was I supposed to do, throw them away?"

"Did you buy her roses?" she asked.

"Well, yes, but it's not what it looks like. She proofread a paper for me that I needed to turn in quick. She wouldn't take any money, so I got her the flowers. That's all there was to it."

"That's not what Amy says," she replied.

"Oh, Christ, Amy Stanley has *never* liked me," I argued. "Damned if I know why, but it's true." It was, too. "She's just trying to screw us up. That's all." That was probably true, too. I strongly doubted that Amy gave a big rat's ass for Karen's welfare. She was a mean vicious person who had already told Denise enough lies about me to stuff a steamer trunk. The only problem was that, in this case at least, she was telling the truth—or at least enough truth to make it very hot for me. "Kitten, I love you," I said. "Who are you going to believe, me or Amy Stanley?"

That worked for a while, but things were getting too close and I knew it. Especially when Martha collared me one day and warned me that I'd better not hurt her sister. "I won't," I'd said, and I'd meant it. "I won't. Gimme a break, Martha, this is for real." Man, I had to get out *now*.

Then one night when Karen was staying over, Denise called. She was in tears, and insisted that she had to talk to me right away.

"Why tonight?" I asked. "Can't it wait? Karen's here. What's wrong?"

"Bill, please! I have to see you now."

So I told Karen that the Swarthmore KGB must be hassling Denise again—Amy and Martha had been pretty rude to Denise several times already—and I had to go see what the problem was, and I'd be right back.

I thought that's what the trouble really was. But it turned out that Denise was all upset because she'd decided that she couldn't go on two-timing Tippy anymore, and would have to stop seeing me. What could I say?

"Okay, Denise," I replied. "If that's the way you want it, I guess that's what you have to do." I knew it had to end one way or another. This was as good a way as any. I walked back to my room feeling almost buoyant, relieved that the impossible tangle was finally over, and that I'd gotten out of it without getting burned.

But when I got back to my room, Karen was gone. Oh, Jesus Christ, what now, I thought. It took me an hour to find her, and when I did, she was sitting in Denise's room talking to Denise. How in the hell did Karen get here, I thought, what the *hell's* going on? But I knew that my ticket had just been canceled. From the look on Karen's face, it was obvious that Denise had been very open and honest with Karen—not realizing that a nineteen-year-old Catholic ex-virgin wasn't prepared to deal with the truth, the whole truth, and nothing but the truth—especially after I'd spent two solid weeks lying to her. Karen looked totally wiped out. Her eyes were red, and her skin was a white pasty color. I felt like I'd just swallowed an anchor.

"I'd better leave you two alone for a while," said Denise, who got up and left.

God, don't leave me here alone with her, I wanted to scream. I had no idea what was going to happen, but I didn't want to find out. Karen just sat there for what seemed like forever. She was shaking like a leaf in a late-autumn wind. She wouldn't look at me. I knelt on the floor at her feet and tried to speak several times, but the words died on my tongue. Nothing came out but a croak. It was like I'd been without water for two or three days.

Finally, she got up slowly. She walked over to the door like a zombie and opened it. Then, with one hand on the doorknob, she turned back to me. Her eyes burned. They were the same eyes I'd seen the day I'd tried to knock Pam Casey's head off, the same eyes I'd seen on the faces of the Vietnamese peasants whose lives I'd routinely made so miserable. I could hardly believe what I was seeing, or the pain that I had inflicted. Was there no end to what I was capable of?

"You are the cruelest, most coldhearted bastard I've ever known," she said in a voice that seemed detached from anything living. "I wish you were dead." Then she walked out.

Chapter 55

A week before swimming season began, and only about a week after Karen and Denise both bailed out on me, the college athletic director called me and told me he wanted to see me. I looked at myself in the mirror. Christ, I look like hell, I thought. I hadn't washed, shaved, or combed my hair since the big night up in Parrish, and I'd been living mostly on canned hard pretzels and cheap wine. I got cleaned up and walked down to the field house.

"What's up, Mr. Stevens?" I asked when I got to the director's office.

"Sit down, Bill," he replied, gesturing toward a chair across from his desk.

"So?" I said, sitting down.

"Jamie McAdams won't be back this year," he said.

"What? What are you talking about?"

"Jamie's not going to be coaching this year."

"What? Why not?" I asked. "What the heck are you talking about?"

"His health just won't permit it," said Stevens. "It's just too taxing for him to keep up with it any longer."

"Says who?" I replied. Yes, Jamie had had a mild heart attack the previous winter, forcing him to miss several weeks of the season. But he'd returned before the season ended, and had never given any indication since then that he had anything in mind except returning. "Who says his health won't permit it?" I asked again. "Did Jamie say that?"

"Let's just say it was a mutual decision."

"Whadda ya mean, 'Let's just say'?"

"We all thought it would be in Jamie's best interest—"

"Who's 'we all'? What are you tryin' to pull here?"

"We're not trying to *pull* anything, Bill. Jamie's not a young man anymore—"

"You mean you're puttin' him out to pasture—"

"Now, Bill, that's not—"

"The guy gives you thirty-six years of his life, and then when he gets too old to suit you, you just shuffle him out the door!"

"Bill, that's not it at all," Stevens replied. "Be reasonable—"

"Be reasonable?" I almost shouted. "I'm not interested in bein' reasonable. I wanna know what the hell's going on here. Whose decision was it, why was it made, and how come you wait until a week before practice starts to tell me?"

"Here's your new coach," said Stevens, ignoring my questions as he handed me a résumé. His bald scalp was glistening with sweat. I quickly glanced through the résumé.

"What the hell, Mr. Stevens, this guy's just a *kid*. He's never even coached anything before but summer age group. You gotta be kidding me!"

"We've checked him out," said Stevens, "and we think he'll work out just fine—"

"Checked him out, huh? With the same thoroughness that you've dispatched Jamie, I suppose. You're not telling me the truth, Mr. Stevens."

"This is the way it's going to be, Bill," said Stevens. He was clearly laboring to sound firm. "You might as well accept it. I'm counting on you, as team captain, to help the new coach adjust— and to help the team adjust to *him*. That's part of your responsibility."

"You're outa your fucking mind, man," I said, tossing the résumé down and standing up. Stevens stared at me with a surprised look on his face. I thought hard about reaching across the desk and trying to strangle some straight answers out of him, decided against it finally, and turned for the door.

"Now just wait a minute, Bill—"

I walked out. What the hell was the point of swimming without Jamie? They fire the good ones, I thought, and keep the FBI informers.

A week later, Denise showed up at my room. I hadn't seen her since the big night in Parrish. As soon as she got inside, she broke down in tears. "I just can't stay away," she cried. "I can't live like this."

I couldn't help myself. I'd called Karen repeatedly, but she had refused even to come to the phone. The photos I'd given her of myself had come back in the mail a few days earlier; there was no note and no return address. I folded Denise into my arms, and held on tight. "What are you going to do about Tippy?" I asked.

"I don't know," she said, "I don't know."

During Christmas break, I gave Fast Freddie a ride to his home in Miami, then spent a few days with an old high school friend in Fort Lauderdale. I liked Florida. I liked being warm. I'd gone down the previous Christmas break, too. This year, however, the Florida excursion was mostly an excuse to spend a few days with Denise at her home in Charleston, South Carolina.

As I drove north from Fort Lauderdale, I heard on the radio for the first time that Nixon had unleashed the big B-52 Strategic Air Command bombers against Hanoi. So the bastards are finally going to do it, I thought angrily, thinking back to General Curtis LeMay's advice during the Johnson years that the U.S. ought to bomb the North Vietnamese back to the Stone Age. Peace is at hand, I thought, my ass. "You fucking assholes!" I hollered out the window as I drove along through the warm afternoon. "You're all fucking crazy! You're insane!"

I reached Denise's house by late afternoon. The first thing she said to me was: "Tippy's coming."

"What?" I said.

"He called this morning," she explained. "He's bringing the boat into Charleston tonight. He'll be here about two A.M. I tried to call you in Fort Lauderdale, but you'd already left."

"Oh, what the fuck, Denise?"

"I didn't know, Bill. Honestly, I didn't know he was going to be here."

"How long's he staying?"

"I don't know."

"So I have to leave, huh? Jesus Christ almighty."

"I'm sorry, Bill. Please don't be angry with me. I'll make it up to you when we get back to school. I promise."

It was hard to be angry with Denise—or at least to stay angry with her. She was small and delicate, like a faun, and she seemed so vulnerable. "When are you gonna decide, Denise?" I asked.

"I don't know, Bill," she replied, her voice nearly breaking.

"I don't know what to do. I love you." She put her arms around me and kissed my neck.

"I love you, too, kid," I said. "You just don't know. You really don't know."

By midnight, I was driving north again. I thought of the B-52s raining fire and destruction on North Vietnam. Once, up on the DMZ, I'd been awakened in the middle of the night by tremors that had shaken the ground violently. I'd thought it was an earthquake, but it was only the B-52s. They flew so high that you couldn't hear them, and the bombs fell without warning. What they left behind was a landscape that looked like the moon.

At the end of Christmas break, in early January 1973, I picked Denise up at Philadelphia Airport. She threw herself into my arms, nestling her face against my neck. She was radiant, chattering like a schoolgirl, almost jubilant. We spent nearly twelve solid hours in bed.

Denise flew home again for a few days during semester break near the end of January. I picked her up at Philadelphia Airport again. She was uneasy and distant. I sensed it immediately. What happened, I wondered.

"What's the matter?" I asked as we drove back to school.

"I can't sleep with you anymore," she said. "I can't do this to Tippy."

"What about me, for Chrissake?"

"I can't."

"They signed the Paris peace accords," said Mike Morris, stopping by my room one afternoon in late January. He'd ended up taking two semesters off, and had only just returned to school after a year's absence.

"Yeh, whoopee," I said. "The only reason the North Vietnamese signed it is because we bludgeoned them into it with the Christmas B-52s. Deck the halls with bombs and napalm. There's a Christmas carol for you."

"They were ringing church bells in town this afternoon," he said. "Can you believe it?"

"Church bells? What the hell for? Those people have been fighting for twenty-eight years, man. The independence movement holds seventy-five percent of all Vietnam—"

"I know, I know."

"They got rid of American military personnel in South Vietnam, that's all. But they still gotta get rid of Thieu. And you can bet your sweet ass Nixon and Kissinger ain't about to abandon him now."

Mike just looked at me and shrugged.

"I think I'm pregnant," said Denise.

"Pregnant?" I said.

"And I think it's yours." In spite of her resolve not to sleep with me again, we'd continued to see each other—and we'd ended up sleeping together several more times during the winter. I hated the thought of Tippy, and I hated my lack of self-control—but I hated my empty bed more than anything in all the world. Each time she said yes was a few more hours that I didn't have to be alone.

"What are you going to do about it?" I asked. She didn't answer. "Denise, marry me."

"I can't. I just can't."

"Do you want to abort it?"

"I can't do that, Bill."

"Well, what the hell are you going to do?"

"I'm going to tell Tippy it's his."

One afternoon a week later, in late March, I came back from class to find a telephone message taped to my door. It was from Denise. "The dam broke," it read.

In early April, Richard Nixon gave a dinner at the White House for the five hundred or so American prisoners of war just returned to the United States from North Vietnam. It was on the news. Look at those guys, I thought, lapping it up like dogs—like Nixon did 'em a favor or something. What do the other three million of us get? Why doesn't he give a dinner for all the guys rotting away in the VA hospitals? How come *we* don't get lifetime season tickets to the Redskins' football games?

By the time I got to Fast Freddie Charles's room in Dana, I was roaring drunk. He'd told me at supper that there'd be a party in his room that night, but the door was locked. I knocked loudly several times, but no one answered, so I took a running leap at the door and kicked it with both boots. The wood around the latch and locking mechanism splintered apart and the door flew open, banging against the wall loudly. It sounded like a cannon shot. I landed on my feet in the middle of the room. Fred and his girlfriend were lying in bed. They were both staring at me, their eyes wide with surprise and fright.

"Oops," I said.

"What the hell are you doing, Ehrhart?" Fred finally managed to ask. Julie pulled the sheet up around her shoulders.

"You said there was a party here tonight," I managed to reply.

"Jesus, are you crazy?"

"Didn't you tell me there was a party tonight?"

"Yeah, yeah, come back later," he said. "Jesus Christ, Bill, you broke down my door!"

"Damn, Freddie, I'm sorry. You said there was a party tonight. I'm sorry, man."

"Get out of here, will you?"

I beat a hasty retreat out of the room, stalked down the hall, and called Denise from the campus phone in the second-floor lounge. "I wanna sleep with you, Denise," I said.

"You're drunk, aren't you, Bill?" she said.

"So what if I am. I gotta see you. Please."

"Please don't come up here now, Bill," she said. "I can't deal with you when you're like this."

"Like what? What the hell's the matter with me?"

"Please don't come over tonight, Bill," she said. "Come see me in the morning."

"Goddamn it!" I shouted. "Why didn't you stay away from me in the first place? It wasn't me that started it all up again. I coulda stayed away from you. *You're* the one who came to me, remember? 'Oh, Bill, I can't stay away from you. I can't live like this.' "

"Bill, please!"

"What the fuck are you tryin' to *do* to me?"

"Come see me tomorrow, Bill. I've got to go now."

"Whadda you think I am, some kind of yo-yo or something?"

She hung up. I took the receiver away from my ear and stared at it. Then I pulled the whole telephone off the wall and threw it through the big picture window of the lounge. The glass exploded with a roar and crashed to the concrete below.

Chapter 56

"Look at that smog, man," I said.

"Pitiful, ain't it?" Roger replied, leaning on the railing.

We'd left Long Beach a few hours earlier and we were steaming northwest through the Santa Barbara Channel toward San Francisco. We were right in the heart of the Los Angeles Basin. Though the air in the immediate vicinity of the ship appeared to be clear, it was only an illusion. All around us, for 360 degrees, a thick soupy brown haze obliterated the horizons.

"Even animals know enough not to shit in their own nests," I said. "What a world we've made."

"You never heard from Karen again?" he asked after a long pause.

"What's that got to do with smog?" I asked.

"Nothing," he replied. "I was just thinking about what you were saying last night."

"No, I never heard from her again. She cut me out like a bad cancer. I've never seen anybody slam the door so fast or so hard. What the hell, man, can you blame her?"

"But you didn't *mean* to do all—"

"What I meant don't count for squat," I said. "It's what you do that counts. I never meant to kill all those people in Vietnam either, but they're dead, ain't they?"

"Well, that's not exactly—"

"The hell it ain't. What's different about it?"

"Will ya stop interrupting me?"

"Sorry," I said. Turning my back to the wind, I lit a cigarette.

"What about Denise?" he asked.

"What about her?"

"She never, uh—she decided to stay with Tippy, huh?"

277

"Well, here I am, pal."

"She sounds like a real bitch, if you ask me," said Roger.

"No, she wasn't a bitch. Oh, hell, I don't know what she was. I guess she didn't mean me any more harm than I meant Karen."

"Think so?" he said.

"I don't know what to think. Doesn't matter now, anyway. A wino of the heart, Roger, that's me."

"So you shipped out."

"That's only part of it, Roger. It's a lot of things. It's everything, I guess. Seven years ago, I went to fight a war in Vietnam, and I ended up at war with my own country and damned near everybody in it. And there ain't no way to win. You ever seen a photograph of a sculpture called *End of the Trail?*"

"I don't think so."

"It's a statue of an Indian warrior on a horse. They're both absolutely exhausted. The man's hunched forward, his head hanging down, his war lance pointing toward the ground. The horse's head's bowed down toward the ground, too. I don't remember who the artist is, but the original statue's somewhere in Oregon, I think, perched on a cliff overlooking the Pacific Ocean. Like the Indian and his horse have run from one end of the continent to the other, and there ain't no place left to run. It's the end of the trail."

"Only you found a ship and kept going," said Roger.

"That's about the size of it. I probably got another thirty or forty years to get rid of, and I just can't hack it on the beach anymore. But I gotta do *something* with all that time. So here I am. Ain't a bad life, either. I kinda like it."

"You ain't gonna stay out here the rest of your life," said Roger.

"You got any better ideas? Come on, let's go play some cards. I got half an hour before I gotta be down in the engineroom."

"You gotta repaint the starboard generator this trip, don't you?"

"Yeh. Man, I hate bein' anywhere near those damned generators. All that juice. One bad roll and it's fried Ehrhart."

Roger laughed. "Just stay away from the brushes," he said. "That's where all the juice is. Come on, let's play some cards."

Chapter 57

"You shoulda seen John Mitchell on television today, Mike," I said. "It was the scariest thing I've ever seen."

"Yeh?" said Mike.

"Yeh. Sittin' there puffing on his pipe with a shit-eating little smirk on his fat face the whole time, just lyin' through his teeth. The former attorney general of the United States. It was *scary.*"

"So what's new?" he replied. "They're all crooks and liars."

"I'm tellin' ya, you shoulda seen it. I don't even know why he was different. I've watched Haldeman, Ehrlichman—they're all creeps. But Mitchell—geez, it gave me the chills. The man just emanated evil."

"Are they gonna get Nixon?" Mike asked.

"Fuck if I know. I'll tell you this, though: John Dean's tellin' the truth. But those shitheads in Congress aren't gonna do anything about it unless somebody can come up with some corroborating evidence that they can't ignore—like if those tapes got anything on 'em—and if somebody can pry them loose from Tricky Dick. They're gonna have to be forced into it before they impeach the son of a bitch."

"You know why, don't you?" said Mike.

"Yeah, I know why."

"There ain't a *one* of 'em that's clean, that's why. It never woulda gotten this far if it hadn't been for Dean and Judge Sirica and those guys from the *Washington Post.*"

"You know," I said, "one time about three years ago, I got involved for a short while in a local political campaign for representative to the state assembly. There was some hack Republican that'd been in Harrisburg for about twenty years. The guy was practically comatose. All he did was get fishing licenses for his pals. And there was a pretty good Democrat running against him for a change, but Perkasie's overwhelmingly Republican, so the only way the Democrat could get elected was if he got a lot of Republican support. So me and another guy went to see one of the Republican committeemen to try to get his support?''

''Yeah?''

''And the committeeman tells us horror stories about this incumbent assemblyman for about half an hour. Says our man is far and away the better man. Then he says, 'I'd really like to help you fellas, but you know how it is around here. If I come out for a Democrat, I'd be risking my job at the bank. I've got a wife and two kids, fellas.' The guy comes right out and admits it. And this is a rinky-dink local committeeman, for Chrissake. They got that kind of pressure on 'em at *that* level, imagine what it's like the higher up you go. There ain't a person in politics with an ounce of morality. You gotta sell your soul just to be dogcatcher. It's sick, man. Just sick.''

''Dollar Democracy,'' Mike laughed. ''Land of the Big Buck.''

''It ain't funny.''

''I know.''

''All that civics-book crap we were taught,'' I said. ''That's just what it is: crap.''

''What can ya do about it?'' Mike shrugged.

''I'm gettin' out, that's what.''

''Have you heard from ARCO?'' he said, his face suddenly lighting up.

''No, not yet. I called 'em again today, but they still don't have anything.''

''Well, hang in there.''

''I'm gettin' pretty low on money, you know?'' I said. ''Another week or so, and I'm gonna have to find some kind of job to hold me over.''

I'd been trying to get a job on an oil tanker since before I'd graduated back in June. ARCO was one of the few companies that owned its own fleet, so I'd been particularly persistent with the ARCO marine personnel director. But no job had materialized by graduation, so after a restless two weeks at my parents' home in Perkasie, I'd taken a train to San Francisco. ARCO had four ships on the West Coast and only three ships in the east, so I'd figured that my chances were better out west.

I'd spent the first three weeks in San Francisco living with Jack Gold's girlfriend and her two roommates. I had no money to pay rent, and aside from watering the plants and washing dishes, I didn't do very much but watch the Ervin committee Watergate hearings all day long and sit around most evenings in morose silence. The situation had quickly gotten tense and uncomfortable. Nobody asked me to leave, but when Mike Morris got an apartment of his own on Rivoli Street and asked me to move in with him, I'd jumped at the chance.

"You wanna go have a few beers tonight?" Mike asked.

"What? Yeah, sure, I guess so."

"Look at all these women, Bill," said Mike, gesturing around the crowded bar a short while later. "You can't tell me there isn't some fox out there just waiting for you."

"Give it up, man," I said. "I've had my guts wrenched around enough. I got thirty or forty more years to burn, and I just wanna get it over with as quietly and painlessly as possible."

"Oh, bullshit!" said Mike.

"It ain't bullshit, man. How many times I gotta get kicked in the head before it sinks in? I just wanna be left alone, that's all. Denise was the last straw. She *loved* me, Mike. I've *gotta* believe that—"

"Maybe she did love you," said Mike, "and maybe she didn't. What difference does it make? She screwed you to the wall, just the same. For Chrissake, forget Denise."

"How? Tell me that, will ya?"

"Bill, you *gotta* snap out of this," Mike said with sudden and quiet vehemence.

"I don't gotta do *nothin'*! I've done enough for one lifetime!" Mike winced. "Look, I'm sorry, Mike," I said more quietly. "I didn't mean to yell at you. It's just—it's all such a waste, that's all. I never thought it would end up like this, that's all. Man, when I went to Vietnam—the plans I had. The *dreams*. And it was all over the day I got there. And I didn't even know it. I shoulda been killed, Mike—"

"Oh, come on, man."

"No, it's true. I shoulda been killed. It woulda saved everybody a lot of grief. I been a walking dead man ever since, anyway. It just took me all these years to realize it. They've taken my dignity. They've taken my self-respect. What they didn't take, Denise did. I got nothin' left but time."

"You really believe that?" said Mike.

"What else is there to believe?"

"Well, you've got friends like me," he said. "You can believe that."

"Yeah, I know, Mike, I know. And I appreciate it. I really
do. But it ain't the same. You understand that, don't you?"

"Yeah, I do."

"I mean, when I lie down at night, there ain't nobody there
but me and all those nightmares. All those years. All those broken dreams and broken lives and broken promises. And all for
nothing. For worse than nothing."

"Well, I got the job," I said to Mike when he came home
from work a week later.

"That's great!" he said. Then he paused. "You don't look
too happy about it."

"Should I be? The Bechtel Corporation? Coat and tie. Fifteenth floor of a high-rise office building in downtown San Francisco. Ride the streetcar twice a day at rush hour just like all the
rest of the rats in the race. It's *awful,* that's what it is. Christ,
why can't I get a ship? Is that so much to ask? Don't I deserve
at least *that* much?"

"Maybe something'll turn up yet," said Mike.

"God almighty, I hope so. I ain't gonna be able to hack this
Corporate America shit, I'll tell ya that."

"What do they have you doing?"

"They don't really know yet," I said. "Today they started
teaching me how to use a computer terminal, but they won't have
a permanent assignment for me for a few days yet."

Three days later, the Bechtel Corporation offered to make me
project safety analysis coordinator for a nuclear power plant they
were going to build in Massachusetts, and all I had to do was
promise to work for them for at least three years after they'd
trained me. Nuclear power plant, I thought; three *years!* And I
had to stand there in the supervisor's office and smile and say,
"Yes, sir, yes, sir, that sounds wonderful, thank you, sir," while
my insides were boiling like lava. The first break I got, I ran
down to the pay phone in the first-floor lobby and called the
ARCO marine personnel director in Philadelphia.

"You've *got* to give me a job, sir," I pleaded. "Please! I've
got to get out of here! They're going to make me a nuclear project
safety analysis *coordinator!* I don't even know what it *is!* Please,
you've got to have *something!* I'll take *anything!* I don't care."

"I'm afraid we just don't have anything open right now," he

said. "I'm really sorry. I'll let you know if something comes up."

I couldn't sleep that night. The next day, I would have to sign an agreement with Bechtel. I *couldn't* take the position Bechtel was offering me. But I was dead broke. All night long, it tore at my guts like hot steel twisting and scraping at the soft flesh.

The next morning before the alarm clock rang, the telephone did. It was the ARCO marine personnel director back in Philadelphia.

"We've had a personal emergency aboard one of our ships out there during the night," he explained. "One of the crew had to take an emergency leave. Do you want the job?"

I couldn't believe what I was hearing. My heartbeat shot up instantly. It was like a jolt of electricity. "Yeah, yeah!" I shouted into the receiver. "I'll take it!"

"Okay. The ship is the *Atlantic Endeavor*. It's tied up in Long Beach harbor right now, at the ARCO dock on the San Pedro River. If you can be there by one this afternoon, the job's yours."

"I'll be there! I'll be there!" I shouted. "Thank you! I can't tell you what this means to me. Thank you."

"Well, you'd better get moving," he said. "The ship sails at one-thirty."

"Right, right, thank you!" I hung up. "Mike, Mike! Wake up! You gotta take me to the airport! I've got a ship!"

Chapter 58

"What do you want to do?" asked Mike.

"Let's go eat at the Top of the Mark," I said.

"You serious?" he asked.

"Sure. Why the hell not? I just got paid. It's on me."

"Are you sure? That place costs money."

"Hey, I'm in oil these days," I said. "Didn't I tell you?

Anyway, after last summer, I owe you one. You won't take money because you're too damned stubborn—so let's eat. Eat, drink, and be merry, that's what I say.''

"For tomorrow we die?" he laughed.

"Maybe.''

"You don't owe me anything,'' said Mike. "You'd have done the same for me.''

"Suit yourself. Anyway, let's go. You ever eaten there?'' I asked.

"Not hardly,'' said Mike.

"So let's do it. I had drinks up there once, back when I was in the Marines, just before I went back overseas the second time. I couldn't afford a meal, though! Now I can. Comin' up in the world, you see?''

"So how the hell you been?'' he asked, slipping his car into gear and pulling away from the dock. I hadn't seen him in nearly three months. It was already March 1974.

"About the same,'' I replied.

"This the first time you've been to San Francisco since December?''

"Yeah. We been running between Long Beach and Bellingham a lot lately. We tied up at some offshore terminal in Monterey Bay last month, but we were only there overnight, and they didn't have launch service to bring us ashore. That's about as close as we've gotten. How *you* been?''

"Pretty good. I got into that graduate program at the University of Washington I told you about—''

"Oh, yeah?''

"Yeah,'' he said. "I just found out a couple weeks ago.''

"That's great. When do you start?''

"Not until the fall semester,'' he replied. "But I'm going up to Seattle in June to find a place to live, check out the area, maybe see if I can find a part-time job.''

"Well, that's good. We get into Seattle at least as much as we get in here. I'm glad you're not going to Idaho or something.''

"It's a little hard to study saltwater marine life in Idaho.''

A short while later, we were seated in the restaurant at the top of the Mark Hopkins Hotel in downtown San Francisco. It was early evening, and the lights from the cities and towns surrounding the bay sparkled on the dark water.

"Can you see the ship from here?'' Mike asked.

"No," I replied. "See the east end of the San Rafael Bridge? It's just south of that. Beautiful up here, ain't it?"

"Yeah, it is."

"You could almost believe that God's in his heaven and all's right with the world."

"Used to be even prettier," Mike added, "before they started building those monstrosities." He pointed toward the looming tower of the Transamerica Building that blocked out a large chunk of the view.

"Progress," I said. "Ain't nothin' in the world that can't be improved upon with a little American ingenuity. Listen, order anything you want. Really. I'm makin' good money, and there ain't much to spend it on these days."

"You hear any news from anybody?" Mike asked.

"Yeh, every once in a while," I replied. "Sam and Jan got married last spring—"

"Yeah, I knew that," he said.

"Sam just got some kind of job working for the Pennsylvania Crime Commission. Daniel's managing a do-it-yourself home improvement store. JC's working as a tennis instructor at some resort in Scottsdale, Arizona."

"I got a letter from JC this winter," said Mike.

"Well, it sounds like you know about as much as I know."

"Listen, Bill, I've been thinking," said Mike after a pause. "Before I go up to Seattle, I've been thinking about doing a little camping in the Sierras—before the summer crowd starts showing up. You think maybe you could get a few weeks off and come along? You must be due for a little vacation by now."

"Well, it would be nice to spend the time with you, Mike, but I don't *need* a vacation. I'm *on* vacation."

"Bill, how much longer are you gonna stay out there?"

"I just got there," I replied. "I've only been out eight months, man. I'm in no hurry to go anywhere. Where the hell am I gonna go?"

"That's what worries me," he said.

"What's that supposed to mean?"

"Look, Bill, I can see this job's been good for you," he said. "I've never seen you so relaxed—"

"Damned straight," I said.

"But sooner or later, you're gonna have to figure out where you go from here—"

"Why? What the hell for? I like it right where I am."

''Because you *can't* waste the rest of your life floating around on an oil tanker, that's why!''

''Sure I can! Why not? Beats hell out of what I been doing for the last eight years! Would you like to explain to me what I been doing for the last eight years? I'd like to know. I'd really like to know how any of this happened.''

''You got screwed, that's what happened,'' Mike said. ''You and a lot of other good people.''

''That much I know. Tell me something I don't know. Where the hell's the waitress? I want a drink. I know this much: For the first time since I went to Vietnam, I feel—well, comfortable. Content. Like I belong someplace. You know what my ambition is?''

''I didn't think you had any,'' said Mike, half laughing.

''I wanna be able to make those engines sing the way Roger does,'' I said.

''That's ambition?''

''Sure! What's wrong with it? Keeps me occupied. Pay's good. And I'm not hurtin' anybody. For the first time in years, I'm not *hurtin'* anybody, Mike. What else could a man ask for? A coat-and-tie job and a house in the suburbs with a tricycle on the front lawn?''

''But you aren't *happy* out there,'' he said.

''What's that got to do with anything? What—this American dream crap? Life, liberty, and the pursuit of happiness? Just another myth, man, just another pipe dream. I forfeited my right to happiness a long time ago. The only difference now is that I don't feel it so much out there, that's all. It makes *sense* to be lonely when you're out there. It's the first thing that's made sense in years.''

''Bill, I don't pretend to understand what you've been through,'' Mike replied, ''but I know you can do better than the engineroom of an oil tanker. Jesus Christ, Bill—''

''Jesus Christ, nothing. You know what's happened to Vietnam veterans? A hell of a lot of them—''

''Yeah, I know.''

''The jails are full of 'em. The morgues are full of them. Every week, you read about another one going off the deep end and killing everybody in the house. They're junkies, suicides, rummies. Nobody'll give 'em jobs. Nobody's ever given 'em anything but bad paper, a bad rap, and the back of a hand. Oh, I could be doin' a *lot* worse than I am, Mike. A hell of a lot worse.

All things considered, I'd say I'm not doing too badly. I got a steady job. I'm not gettin' in trouble. I've got time to read, time to write, nice scenery. Hell, man, you know what my problem's always been?"

"I have a feeling I'm about to find out," he said.

"No, I'm serious. Every time I got a good thing goin', I always blow it. Well, not this time, buddy. This is one good deal I *ain't* gonna blow."

"Would you like anything from the bar?" asked a waitress.

"Ah, my dear, I thought you'd never ask," I said. "I'll have a gin gimlet on the rocks."

"Make that two," said Mike.

"Look, don't worry about me," I said, turning back to Mike. "I'm doin' a hell of a lot better than I got any right to expect. I'm doin' just fine."

"Yeah, well, I don't know about that."

"Well, I do," I replied. "Whaddaya want to eat? Don't spare the horses, either. I'm havin' surf 'n' turf."

"Sounds good to me," he said. "Say, you know, it looks like they might get Nixon after all."

"Yeah, well, they're takin' their sweet time about it, ain't they?" I replied. "Don't misunderstand me—there's very few things I'd like to see more than I'd like to see that son of a bitch in a striped suit luggin' a ball and chain around. But you're kidding yourself if you think it's going to make any *real* difference. This country's been fucked up for a long, long time, and it ain't gonna change much just because they get rid of one creep."

"I know," said Mike. "I understand that."

"I mean, look at the fuckin' war, man. We've been through four fucking presidents since it started, and it's *still* goin' on. The only reason Nixon stands any chance at all of gettin' canned is because the rest of the power broker club is scared shitless. He's got his ass hangin' out so far, he'll take 'em all down with him if they don't get rid of him soon. Cut your losses and close ranks, you know? So they shit-can Nixon. So what then? Whadda we get? Gerald R. Ford. Who the hell is Gerald R. Ford?"

"Well, he's better than Spiro Agnew," Mike replied.

"Yeah, well, maybe. But when you need open-heart surgery, and somebody cuts into you with a butter knife instead of a hacksaw—what the hell, man? What are you supposed to do, say 'Thank you'?"

"Are you ready to order?" asked the waitress.

"I'll have the surf 'n' turf," I said. "Make that medium rare, baked potato with sour cream, and blue cheese dressing on the salad."

"The same for me," said Mike, "but give me the house dressing."

"No wonder Archie Davison went off the deep end," I continued after the waitress had gone. "God knows where I'd have ended up by now if I hadn't gotten a ship when I did. You hear anything from him at all?"

"Nope," said Mike. "Haven't tried to, either. I guess he's still living over in that Labor Committee loony bin in Oakland, but I don't know."

"He was a good man, you know?"

"I know."

"Fuckin' country just chews 'em up and spits 'em out by the thousands," I said. "By the millions."

"What ever happened to that guy you told me about?" Mike asked. "The Gainesville Eight guy?"

"He was acquitted. They all were. Last September—thirteen months after the original indictments—the judge threw the whole case out of court. Chewed the government prosecutor up and down for daring to bring it to trial in the first place. They didn't have a thing on 'em. How could they? They didn't *do* anything!"

"Well, that's good news, at least," said Mike.

"If you can call thirteen months of unemployment and anxiety and humiliation and wasted time good news. And he'll carry the stigma of it for the rest of his life. You ask any of these people sittin' around here if they know how the trial finally ended up. The indictments were front-page news. You know where they put the story about the verdict? Like page eighteen or something. Little two-paragraph blurb. There's your fucking free press for you. That's what you get for exercising your right to free speech in this country. That's what you get for tryin' to hold your own government accountable for anything. Christ almighty! Nixon, Ford, what the hell's the difference? The system's got a life of its own, man. You can't kill it, you can't beat it, and you can't change it."

"We could change it if enough people tried," said Mike.

"Fat chance. You think that's ever gonna happen? Look what happened to the antiwar movement the minute American GIs stopped comin' home in boxes, for Chrissake. Vanished. Just like that—all but the hard core, at least, and that's mostly the vets themselves anymore. The fucking American people—shit, man, as long as they got their McDonald's cheeseburgers wrapped in four layers of plastic, they don't know the difference. Feminine hygiene deodorant, man! You seen that stuff? Spray it up your cunt so you smell like a perfume factory. It ain't right to smell *human*, you know? And they got people out there buyin' it up like crazy. Millions of 'em! You think *they're* gonna change anything?'' Mike looked at me without replying. "Well?" I asked.

"I don't know, Bill. I just wish—ah, you've heard it all before," he said, shrugging his shoulders.

"Yeah, I have, Mike. Wishes, lies, and dreams. That's all there is. Come on, dig in. You ain't gonna eat like this in graduate school.''

Chapter 59

Mike dropped me off at the dock the next morning, and by early afternoon we were through the Golden Gate and heading out to deep water, bound for Anacortes, Bellingham, and Seattle. Roger and I were standing up on the bow.

"Listen," I said. "Can you hear them?"

"Hear who?"

"The mermaids, Roger, the mermaids. Listen." I cocked my head and cupped one hand behind my ear. " 'Come hither. Come hither, till we marry thee.' "

"Didn't you say you had your ears messed up in Vietnam?" he asked.

"Yeah."

"I thought so."

"You got no imagination, Roger," I laughed. "You're like those historians who say the ancient mariners were really hearing seals or sea lions. But they're wrong, you know? It was mermaids they heard. They're out here. They're out here somewhere. And they're beautiful.''

The wind whipped at our hair and clothes, and already the *Endeavor* was pitching heavily. There must be a storm out there to the west somewhere, I thought.

"You almost believe it, don't you?" asked Roger.

"Almost," I said. "I love heading out to deep water. There's not a feeling like it in the world, you know? Not even the open highway. It's like another world out here. It *is* another world. Fabulous, primeval, utterly free from time and sorrow and memory. The sea has a soul, Roger, and every seaman belongs to it.''

"You're in a rare mood today."

"You feel it, too, Roger. You sense it. Otherwise, you'd be back on the beach with some shore job."

"Well, I do like it out here," he said.

"So do I. Look at it back there, man." I turned around, facing the stern and gesturing toward the Golden Gate Bridge and the harbor beyond. "There's three thousand miles of continent back there. And it's nothing but a wasteland. I can't figure out why anybody would wanna bother with it when they could be out here instead. You know what—''

"Look!" Roger shouted. He was pointing at something off the starboard bow.

"Whales!"

"Thar she blows!" Roger shouted into the vast expanse of the sky.

They were about three hundred yards out, running north to south just below the surface. First you'd see a puff of steam and water suddenly appearing above the waves as each whale exhaled. Then the great black back would arch slowly and gracefully out of the water, just high enough for the whale to get another breath of air before descending again. And then it would be gone, and another would appear nearby. Sometimes a fluke would break the surface as a whale submerged. We watched them in silence for ten or fifteen minutes until they were almost out of sight.

"Geez, there must be fifteen of 'em."

"Magnificent creatures, aren't they?" I said. "Where can you see anything like that on the beach? In Miami, they've got a whale in a tank. They make it do tricks and stuff—jump through a hoop, stuff like that—like some kind of trained dog. You know they hunt whales with high-speed boats now?"

"Yeah, I know," said Roger.

"They use cannons with exploding harpoons. At least back in Herman Melville's day, the whales had a chance. Some species are extinct already. Gone forever. We'll never see them again. And a bunch more are on the endangered list. What incredible stupidity, Roger. We take what we want wherever we find it, and to hell with the consequences. Great auks—gone. Passenger pigeons—gone. Christ, we're even going to extinct ourselves before much longer."

"You don't really believe that," said Roger.

"Oh, yeah. It's just a matter of time. Next week, next year, fifty years. Sooner or later. You can't keep all that nuclear garbage around forever and *never* use it. Never is a long time. Think of it, man. Millions and millions of years it's taken to create this world—and once somebody pushes the button—well, that'll be that. I wouldn't even mind, you know? It's exactly what we deserve, really. What bothers me is that we're gonna take everything else out with us. Whales, elephants, hummingbirds, everything. That's what bothers me most."

"Come on, man. Your ass goes up in smoke, whadda you gonna care about the rest of it?" he said.

"It matters, Roger. It matters. You know, if God woulda had any brains, she'd have loaded all the rest of the animals on the ark, and left Noah standing on the dock."

"She?" said Roger.

"Sure, why not?"

"I don't know. Sounds funny, that's all."

"No funnier than giving God a pecker and a beard, is it?"

Roger shook his head and laughed. "Where the hell do you come up with stuff like that, Ehrhart? I wonder about you sometimes, boy."

"I'll bet you do," I laughed. "What time is it?"

"One-fifteen."

"I'm late for work. Come on over to my cabin tonight when you get off watch."

"Oh, goodness, look at this, pal," I said later that night. I stacked an ace on a nine, a two on an eight, a four on a six, and picked up the whole pile with the ten of diamonds.

"You bastard!" Roger shouted. "This is ridiculous! *Nobody* can win this game all the time. It's *impossible.*"

"Not when you're the world's greatest casino player."

"Up yours."

"Come on, it's your turn."

"There's nothin' *left,*" he replied.

"Well, then, I guess you just have to discard one, don't you?"

"Yeah, so you can pick it up."

"You wanted to play."

"Yeah, yeah," he said, throwing down a card. "Listen, I told the chief that I wanna take vacation when we get back to Long Beach this trip."

"Oh," I said. Damn, I thought. I'd been wondering when it was going to come. I knew he'd take vacation eventually, but as the months had piled on, I'd almost lulled myself into believing that we could go on sailing together forever. I really liked Roger. It was hard to imagine sailing without him.

"That's all you're gonna say?" he asked.

"What else *can* I say? You got a wife and kid. I knew you'd be taking vacation sooner or later." I studied the cards for a few months. "I'll miss you."

"Well, I'll miss you too, you old fart." He glanced away, looking down at his feet, and then studying his cards. "I never sailed with anybody like you before. Listen, before I leave, can you make up a list of books for me?"

"What kind of books?" I asked.

"Like the ones you been lending me. Books you think I oughta read. You got me interested in stuff I never even thought about before, but I wouldn't know what books to look for."

"Sure," I smiled. "Be glad to. Roger, you think there's any way you could work it so you ended up back on the *Endeavor* when your vacation's up?"

"Not likely, Bill. I got a one-in-seven chance, that's all. You know how it works. They'll stick me on whatever ship needs a third engineer by then, and there's not much I can do about it. Besides, I got nearly four months comin' to me. You won't be here when I get back, anyway."

"Oh, yeah?" I said. "What makes you think that? You know something I don't know?"

"Oh, you think you fit in around here, but you don't. You're just resting up. Sort of collecting your reserves, that's all. But you ain't gonna be content to sit out here much longer."

"Says who?"

"Says me. I got it all figured out."

"Oh, yeah? And just how did you figure all this out, may I ask?"

"Because you care too much, that's how," he replied. "All I hadda do was think about it for a while. Sailing's a great place to do some thinkin', ain't it?"

"Oh, brother," I said, rolling my eyes, "I hate to tell you this, but you're about as far off the mark as you can get."

"Like hell I am. You care more than anybody else I've ever met—"

"You're daft, man, I'm through—"

"Oh, bullshit," he said. "You don't care? So how come you're always readin' another book when I come in here? How come you can rattle off stuff like a goddamned encyclopedia? Why you bother to learn all that stuff? Every time we hit port, you come back with another armload of books."

"I like to read, that's all."

"Are you kidding me? The stuff you read ain't exactly pass-the-time reading. And how come you wrote that letter to your congressman? How come every time you talk about stuff like Vietnam and Watergate—nuclear bombs, whales, for Chris-sake!—your blood pressure goes up about fifty points? You're gonna try to tell me you don't care? Come off it. You can tell yourself that, if you want—but you can't get *me* to buy it."

"Well, hell," I said. I wondered if he was right. I felt suddenly confused and tongue-tied.

"Well, what?" he said, staring at me intently.

"What are you, some kind of shrink?"

"Well, how do you explain all that?" he asked.

"Hell, I don't know," I said slowly. "Maybe I do care—but I sure as hell don't wanna deal with it anymore."

"You're just tired. You've needed a little rest, that's all. I've run into a lot of losers out here—a lot of people who were really burned out—and you ain't one of 'em."

"You don't understand, Roger. Back there on the beach—Christ, how the hell do I explain it? It ain't my country anymore. Maybe it never was."

"The hell it ain't," he responded. "It's as much yours—and mine—as anybody else's. You've got more of a right to it than most of 'em."

"Rights? Rights? What the hell does that have to do with anything? You sound like Mike Morris. Don't you guys understand? That's comic-book stuff, man? That ain't the way it works."

"Well, it *ought* to," he said.

"Well, it doesn't! And it never has."

"Then do something about it."

"I'm *tired* of it, Roger! And it's only gonna get worse. You ain't seen nothin' yet! You watch, by the time your kid's in school, they'll be sayin' the war in Vietnam was some kind of noble crusade after all. And they'll be out there stickin' their fingers in somebody else's pie. And somebody else's after that. And they'll go on building their goddamned missiles, and they'll go on blowing up whales with their goddamned exploding harpoons, and they'll go on screwing people like you and me right to the wall. And there ain't a goddamned thing we can do about it!"

"Sure there is." Roger smiled broadly.

"Yeah? Like what?"

"Oh, I don't know—but you'll think of something. I got confidence in you, boy. You'll think of something."

"Well, thank you very much!" I said. "Just dump it all in *my* lap, why don't you?"

"There's lots of stuff you can do," he said. "You could run for Congress—"

"What? With my ideas? I couldn't get elected dogcatcher."

"You could be a teacher. Christ, I wish *my* kid could have a teacher like you. I wish *I* could have had a teacher like you—I mighta learned something."

"I wouldn't last three days in a public school. We weren't even allowed to read *Catcher in the Rye*, for Chrissake."

"There's other kinds of schools, aren't there?" he replied. "Or you could be a writer. Write all this stuff down, why don't you? *Tell* people about it."

"They don't wanna *listen,* Roger! I spent four *years* tryin' to tell people about it. They don't wanna *hear* it, man."

"So what? Tell 'em anyway. Make 'em listen."

"Jesus Christ, Roger, you're crazier than I am."

"What choice do you have, Bill?" he asked.

"What *choice* do I have? I've made my choice! I'm *here,* ain't I? And that's the last choice I'll ever have to make."

"We'll see," he grinned.

"Well, don't hold your breath, pal. *There!*" I shouted, picking up my cards and slapping down an ace. "Building aces!"

Roger's grin vanished. "Aces? How many more you got?"

"More than you have," I said.

"You got all the rest of 'em?"

"Yep."

"Goddamn it, that's the game."

"Yep."

He grabbed a fistful of cards and bolted for the porthole. I made no attempt to stop him. He threw open the porthole and hurled the cards into the waiting sea. I studied his back as he stood looking after them. He did sound a lot like Mikc. Were they right?

They couldn't be. What did I want or need or care about back there on the beach? Out here, I had wonders in the deep, and the thousand mermaids, and the hearts of infinite Pacifics, the moon's wide river, gulls soaring low between the waves, and the gliding schools of porpoises. They could have their crazy world full of dreams and wars and broken promises. Out here, I had a world unto myself. What else did I need? I could go on sailing forever. I could sail forever. Or at least till the mermaids married me. And that would be long enough.

Roger turned around, walked over to the desk, and sat down. He pulled a fresh deck of cards out of his shirt pocket and tossed it down between us.

"Deal," he said.

About the Author

W. D. Ehrhart was born in 1948 and grew up in Perkasie, Pennsylvania. He holds a B.A. from Swarthmore College and an M.A. from the University of Illinois at Chicago. He currently lives in Philadelphia, Pennsylvania, with his wife, Anne.

Ehrhart enlisted in the U.S. Marines in 1966, serving in Vietnam with 1st Battalion, 1st Marines from February 1967 to February 1968. He achieved the rank of Sergeant (E-5) while on active duty, earned the Purple Heart Medal, the Navy Combat Action Ribbon, and two Presidential Unit Citations, and was honorably discharged with the rank of Staff Sergeant (E-6).

Ehrhart's prose and poetry have appeared in numerous periodicals and anthologies, including *The Virginia Quarterly Review, New Letters, TriQuarterly, The Chronicle of Higher Education*, and *Vietnam Voices: Perspectives on the War Years, 1941–1982*. He is the recipient of grants and awards from the Academy of American Poets, the Mary Roberts Rinehart Foundation, and the Pennsylvania Council on the Arts.

In addition to his books *Vietnam-Perkasie, To Those Who Have Gone Home Tired*, and *Carrying the Darkness*, Ehrhart is the author of *The Outer Banks & Other Poems*, co-editor of *Demilitarized Zones*, and contributing editor to *Those Who Were There*.